Effective Supervisory Practices

**BETTER
RESULTS
THROUGH
TEAMWORK**

THIRD EDITION

Edited by Mary L. Walsh

Published for the ICMA University
by the International
City/County
Management Association

Originally developed in cooperation
with the Carl Vinson Institute
of Government
University of Georgia

International
City/County
ICMA
Management
Association

ICMA UNIVERSITY

Municipal Management Series

Effective Supervisory Practices
Advanced Supervisory Practices
Effective Communication
The Effective Local Government Manager
Emergency Management
Housing and Local Government
Local Government Police Management
Management of Local Planning
Management of Local Public works
Management Policies in Local
 Government Finance
Managing Fire Services
Managing Human Services
Managing Local Government: Cases in
 Decision Making
Managing Municipal Leisure Services
Managing Small Cities and Counties
The Practice of Local Government Planning
The Practice of State and Regional Planning
Service Contracting

Library of Congress Cataloging-in-Publication Data

Effective Supervisory practices—3rd ed. / edited by
 Mary L. Walsh.
       p. cm. — (Municipal management series)
    "Originally developed in cooperation with
 Carl Vinson Institute of Government, University
 of Georgia."
    Includes bibliographical references and index.
    ISBN 0-87326-074-0
    1. Local government—Personnel management.
 2. Local officials and employees. 3. Supervision of
 employees. I. Walsh, Mary L. II. ICMA
 Professional Development Institute.
 III. International City/County Management
 Association. IV. Series.
 JS155.E47   1994
 352'.0051—dc20   94-44681
                                              CIP

Printed in the United States of America
4/95

9 9 9 8

5 4

Contents

INTRODUCTION

Where this book is going

This book has been written for experienced supervisors who want to become more effective managers, as well as for those who have been recently appointed to supervisory positions in local government.

Local governments exist for many purposes, but the overriding one is to provide quality public services. These services range from highly visible ones such as police patrol or street maintenance to less obvious but still important ones such as employment counseling and building code enforcement. As a local government employee, you are involved in delivering these services to the public.

Your work is done in the context of a public organization. This means that the public—through elected officials, boards and commissions, and many types of governmental processes—helps determine what your organization will do. Often, this public organization concept is what actually sets your goals and priorities.

Good local government does not just happen. It happens because an informed citizenry, elected officials, conscientious public managers, and dedicated employees work together to make it happen.

You can take pride in being a part of this effort to provide such vital traditional services as police, fire, tax assessment, sanitation, public health, water supply, and street construction and maintenance, as well as many newer services such as programs for youth and the elderly, consumer education, housing relocation, drug and alcohol counseling, and special education. These services are provided through local government organizations: city and county departments, divisions, offices, units, shifts, stations, and crews that keep government operating twenty-four hours a day.

Effective Supervisory Practices takes the larger framework of your local government and relates it to your job and the way you work with your employees. The emphasis on teamwork underscores one of the most important aspects of current management strategies—empowering people to work together toward common goals and objectives. Much of this book addresses planning, leadership, motivation, and other aspects of working with people, so that you, as a supervisor, can do a better job of getting work done with and through others.

This book serves as the basic text for the training program *Effective Supervisory Skill Building*, which is designed to help you and your local government provide better services to people. The book and training materials bring together basic principles of supervision, up-to-date findings from behavioral studies and other appropriate research, and practical, how-to guidelines for improving your supervisory skills and applying effective supervisory practices on the job.

The training approach

Though much of the material in this book is presented in the form of simple models, step-by-step guidelines, or checklists, effective supervision goes beyond that. It is a dynamic process—in part an art. But the art of supervision must be practiced on a solid foundation of knowledge with mastery of a wide variety of skills. This art of supervision also requires that you have the ability to adapt to the ever changing requirements of modern management practices.

This book is intended to help you by serving as a blueprint for fashioning a personal approach to supervision—an approach that will fit your personality, background, and work experiences, the unique nature of your supervisory position, and the special requirements of the local government organization you serve. It will help you bring together the processes of the job and the people who do the work so that services can be delivered more efficiently and effectively to the citizens in your community.

A standard format is used in the book to facilitate reading, note taking, and group discussion. Each chapter begins with a few questions to set the pace and guide later discussion. Primary and secondary heads are used to organize the text, and each chapter includes a checklist to summarize major points in the text. Illustrations and captions are also used to highlight major points in the text.

We hope that many supervisors will find a number of chapters sufficiently stimulating to make them want to explore these subjects further. Many of the topics covered in this book are the sole subject matter of other works. You are urged to consult the brief bibliography at the end of this book to delve more deeply into those areas that are most important to you.

International City/County Management Association

Training programs are provided by hundreds of organizations in the United States and Canada, including the continuing education provided by university extension agencies, the correspondence and on-site short courses sponsored by professional and trade associations, and the almost countless offerings of both commercial and nonprofit schools.

Since its founding in 1914, the International City/County Management Association (ICMA) has set its sights on two major objectives: improving the professional competence of local government administrators and improving the management of local government in general.

Since 1934, the Institute for Training in Municipal Administration (ITMA), sponsored by ICMA, has provided correspondence courses for on-the-job training of local government managers and supervisors. Many of the courses are based on the textbooks in ICMA's Municipal Management Series. In 1978, the ITMA was redesignated the ICMA Training Institute with a broader, two-fold mission: (1) to strengthen the capacity of local governments to develop their own, self-run training programs, and (2) to provide directly a much wider range of courses, training materials, and services for local government training and employee development.

In 1994 ICMA members identified eight groups of practices essential to effective local government management. ICMA established the ICMA University (a nontraditional university without walls) as a comprehensive delivery system to identify and provide professional development tools and activities related to these groups of practices. This book addresses several of the groups, including staff effectiveness, service delivery management, strategic leadership, and communication.

In 1965 the first version of this book was published as a series of fifteen bulletins. In 1978 a completely revised version of *Effective Supervisory Practices* was prepared by the University of Georgia's Institute of Government and Center for Continuing Education. The book's second edition, published in 1984, was prepared by the same organization, now designated the Governmental Training Division of the University of Georgia's Carl Vinson Institute of Government and Georgia Center for Continuing Education.

This book, the third edition, retains almost all the material from the second edition. Minor revisions have been made to the material to update it, and some new material has been added to address the trends, concerns, and issues that affect local government supervisors today. At the request of many users of the second edition, examples of supervisory situations have been added to the end of each chapter for discussion.

Those who worked on this book

All who have contributed to the writing of *Effective Supervisory Practices* are broadly experienced in local government. They have had many years of management or consulting experience in a variety of local governments across the country, ranging from large cities to small rural counties. They have emphasized the practical dimensions—the practices that work and the skills that are necessary for effective supervision.

Primary responsibility for the second edition was undertaken by Harold F. Holtz, administrator of the Governmental Training Division of the University of Georgia's Carl Vinson Institute of Government and Georgia Center for Continuing Education. Others in the Governmental Training Division who revised or wrote selected chapters were John F. Azzaretto, assistant administrator; Kitty Williams Clarke, management development consultant; Kenneth K. Henning, director of the Certified Manager Program; Janine Hall, management development associate; and Howard N. Smith, Jr., management development associate.

Mary L. Walsh, chief administrative officer, Missoula, Montana, revised the text of the second edition and contributed new material and supervisory situations for this edition.

We are grateful to three individuals who thoroughly reviewed all of the chapter drafts for the second edition. They were (with 1984 affiliation): Walter Barry, city administrator, North Kansas City, Missouri; Clifford R. Vermilya, town manager, Bloomfield, Connecticut; and Mac White, personnel director, Plano, Texas.

We are also grateful to James N. Holgersson, city manager of Waco, Texas, and the ICMA Member Committee on Workplace Diversity for their help in revising the second edition.

The Municipal Management Series is the responsibility of ICMA's director of publications, Barbara H. Moore. ICMA staff members who worked on the 1984 edition of this book were David S. Arnold, who had primary editorial responsibility and worked closely with the Governmental Training Division faculty and staff in planning and developing the text and illustrations; Christine S. Becker, who was active in the early planning of the book and reviewed all of the manuscript; and Christine Ulrich, who handled final editing and assisted in the final checking of manuscript and illustrations.

Several ICMA staff members worked on this edition: Verity Weston-Truby, who had primary editorial responsibility and substantively edited the manuscript; Eileen Hughes, who served as copy editor and production editor; Phyllis Brown, who input the manuscript; Dawn M. Leland, who coordinated production; and Jane Pellicciotto, who revised the book's design and oversaw its layout and production.

Several freelancers contributed to the project. Herbert Slobin handled the graphic design of the second edition; Jeanne Berger created the layout for this edition. Illustrations were prepared by David Povilaitis and Herbert Slobin.

We thank all the persons mentioned above for their enthusiasm for this project, for the many hours they have devoted to it, and for the great interest they have shown in making management a more effective part of local government.

William H. Hansell, Jr.
Executive Director

International City/County
Management Association

THE SUPERVISOR'S JOB

The ancient Greek definition of happiness was the full use of your powers along lines of excellence.

John F. Kennedy

1

CHAPTER 1

THE SUPERVISOR'S JOB

Twenty years ago, as a local government employee you were likely to be part of a growing organization. But today you are more likely to be part of an organization that is struggling to provide even essential public services as your local government attempts to balance its budget with revenue that is barely growing or perhaps even declining in real terms. Why has this change taken place?

For almost thirty years after the end of World War II, our country experienced rapid growth. Our population grew rapidly and also became highly mobile. Existing businesses expanded steadily and whole new industries came into being to meet the rising, changing demand for goods and services of our growing, shifting, younger population.

Year after year most people were better off financially than ever before. And since they expected the next year to be even better, they were willing to buy expensive items and to buy on credit. An increasing number of families had two incomes, as one worker took a second job or both husband and wife worked. Two workers in a family often required two cars. Because they could afford to do so, many families moved from rented housing in established neighborhoods into houses of their own in new subdivisions. Then, as their family size and income increased, they moved to larger houses in newer, often suburban neighborhoods. Many families relocated from the Northeast and Midwest to the South and Southwest to take advantage of new and expanding economic opportunities in these rapidly developing parts of our nation. Life styles began to change.

In these new communities, which required water service, sewer lines, sidewalks, and paved streets, the citizens expected and got new schools, more police and fire protection, and more parks, playgrounds, and swimming pools as well. During this time of growth and expansion, the federal and state governments provided a great deal of financial aid to local governments.

But then, beginning in the late 1970s, all levels of government began to realize that the money to pay for these new and expanded services, which were getting more expensive every year, was not increasing at the same pace as demand. Property and other taxes started to rise sharply. As federal, state, and local taxes went up, more taxpayers found it harder to pay them, because the costs of food, clothing, medical services, and other necessities were soaring also. Citizens began to object to the rising costs of government.

Today, as a result of this demand for a ceiling on costs many local governments have had to refocus their efforts. The great need in government today is to manage well the delivery of public services. Cutting back is not the entire answer to today's challenge. Through excellent management of our local governments, we can do more with less—now and in the future.

For reasons that will be explained in Chapter 2, we can be certain that just as supervising in local government today is much different from what it was only a few years ago, the years ahead will provide new challenges and opportunities for our cities and counties and, therefore, for supervisors in local government. Tomorrow will be different from today, for we are living in a time of great and rapid change.

How do you provide necessary local government services, which cost more each year, without raising taxes—especially property taxes—every year? It takes a well-organized, properly managed local government to do the job. And that kind of organization requires well-organized, highly effective supervisors in every department of local government. It depends on you, working at your best. To help you shoulder this very important responsibility, this chapter explains what your job is, where it begins and ends, and how you can do the kind of job you want to do.

Responsibilities of a supervisor

As a supervisor you deserve congratulations! You are extremely important to your organization's effectiveness and efficiency because you are on the front lines, helping your work unit do its job well. You help your team keep on schedule, decide what tools are needed, and assign the work to be done. You have a great deal of responsibility, and you deserve a great deal of credit. You are the person who provides the supervision to get the job done, and done right.

Supervisors' job descriptions may vary, but five major responsibilities are common to all supervisory jobs:

- Getting the job done
- Keeping the work area safe and healthy
- Encouraging teamwork and cooperation
- Developing employee skills
- Keeping records and making reports.

Let us take a closer look at each of these responsibilities.

Getting the job done

First and foremost, you are paid to get the work done properly and on time. To accomplish this you have to

- Plan carefully to get the most and the best work done with the least effort and confusion. You need to schedule work so that employees know what they are supposed to do and what results you expect.

- Organize workers so they cooperate and work together as a team.

- Delegate as much work-related authority as you can, so that employees can develop pride in themselves and in their jobs. They will do a better job if they have responsibility for the work. (But remember that you are still responsible for the results.)

- Measure and evaluate the work that you are responsible for. Then you can tell whether it is going according to plan and whether every member of the work team is doing his or her fair share. You can also catch little mistakes before they grow into big disasters.

Keeping the work area safe and healthy

Accidents are bad news—tragic news if someone is hurt or killed. They not only affect the worker but can cause suffering and loss for the worker's family as well. And when someone is off the job, that job may not get done. Accidents also mean that insurance rates go up and add to the cost of running local government. Nobody wins; everybody loses.

That is why it is so important to

- Set a personal example by obeying all safety rules yourself and by using safety equipment. By doing so, you also protect yourself and your family.

- Plan each job with safety in mind.

- Teach safety whenever you teach a worker a new job.

- Enforce safety rules at all times—with no exceptions.

Good supervision helps develop teamwork.

Encouraging teamwork

You are responsible not only for the work of those you supervise but also for their attitudes toward work. In fact, you cannot separate the two.

Employees who do good work almost always enjoy their work. They have high morale, and each person feels he or she is making a contribution to the team. They have common goals and are willing to cooperate to reach those goals. These employees are satisfying their own needs while working toward the goals of the department and the local government. It is up to you to see that your employees work together.

But getting cooperation in your own unit is not enough. Remember, too, that there are other work groups in your organization: there should be cooperation between your work group and the rest of the management team, as well as between your work group and other work groups in the organization.

Developing employee skills

Start out by believing that most people will surprise you with what they can do if only you will give them a chance. This could mean teaching them a new skill or encouraging them to take on more responsibility. It usually means helping them correct errors, praising their efforts, and recognizing their accomplishments. You are doing some of your best work when you help your employees grow on the job.

Keeping records and making reports

There is no way to keep track of your operation without records and reports. It is important to keep your records neatly and accurately and to get your reports in on time. In that way you keep yourself and management in the know and out of trouble.

Duties of a supervisor

A good way to look at your major responsibilities as a supervisor is to focus on what you need to do to get your work accomplished. It is helpful to identify what your main tasks are and then figure out the best way to perform them. Imagine that your job is like a pie, and each slice is a duty that you perform to accomplish your job. If you see your supervisory job as a large pie and break up the duties into pieces of the whole, you will be better able to see those areas that are causing you difficulty and make changes where necessary. Your responsibilities as a supervisor entail, broadly, the following four major duties:

▪ Planning what needs to be done, and by when

▪ Organizing your employees for the job

▪ Developing and maintaining a motivating climate so that employees will be productive

▪ Evaluating how well the job is being done.

The following list will give you a better idea of the specific duties that most local govern-

ment supervisors have. (They are listed at random, not in order of importance.)

▪ Developing and explaining policies, procedures, and rules

▪ Planning and scheduling work

▪ Training employees for the job and developing in them a desire to serve the public faithfully and well

▪ Training employees in safety practices

▪ Ensuring that tools and equipment are inspected and properly cared for

▪ Ensuring that materials and equipment are used economically

▪ Getting tools, equipment, and materials to the job site on time

▪ Making work assignments

▪ Getting the right employee on the job at the right time

▪ Controlling accident hazards

▪ Maintaining good housekeeping on the job

▪ Building and maintaining morale

▪ Encouraging teamwork

▪ Settling differences among employees

▪ Improving discipline

▪ Handling complaints

▪ Checking and inspecting work

▪ Improving quality and quantity of work

▪ Controlling attendance (absence and tardiness)

▪ Keeping records and making reports

▪ Working cooperatively with other local government departments or offices

▪ Building and maintaining good relations with the public.

Solving problems: The supervisor's place in the organization

Supervisors are vital members of the local government management team. They oversee the individual employee's work and represent the work group on the management team. Indeed, one management expert claims that the supervisor—the point of contact between employees and managers—is at the most vital spot in management.

Because a supervisor is at the same time a member of the local government management team *and* a member of the work team, supervisors often feel conflicting pressures when they try to identify both with management and with their work team. Don't be concerned if sometimes you feel caught between the need to satisfy management and your responsibility to represent the needs of your work group. All supervisors sometimes feel this kind of stress. It's just a part of being a supervisor. Truly effective supervisors enjoy the opportunity they have to link their work team into a real, ongoing partnership with the other managers and work units of the local government team.

Your effectiveness as a supervisor is especially important because you meet face to face with your employees every day. Your dealings with them will affect how they feel about management, how willing they are to work, what they think is important to management, how they behave on the job, and how much they grow and develop as persons and as skilled employees.

As a supervisor you have the opportunity to do two things that are vitally important both to your local government and to the other members of your work team. You have the opportunity to be a model for your employees—a leader they can look up to with respect and affection, someone whose behavior they will want to emulate. You can be someone who will carry out in action what you say in words. You also have the opportunity to be the coach of your work team, helping its members become more skilled and productive as employees and helping the team become a closely knit, highly effective, and efficient part of your local government.

Remember that you have the power to directly affect the quality of work life for your team members. Others in your organization to whom you report may or may not be good managers. You have little or no impact on their behavior. But you do have control over how you behave and how you treat your team.

Supervisors play a vital role through their face-to-face contacts with the work team and management.

Problems of the new supervisor

Most of us like the idea of advancing to supervisor. We like the prestige, the authority, the feeling of moving ahead, the recognition of our own good work, and of course the higher pay.

New responsibilities

Before you were part of the management team you may have seen your supervisor riding around in a government car while you were working in the rain, or talking on the phone in a private office while you were in a cubicle, entering data into a computer.

It does not take long, though, to realize that it is not as easy as it looks. From the first day, you are faced with situations that require knowledge, skill, understanding, good judgment, and immediate action. Problems seldom arrive one at a time, and one wrong decision or careless remark can take weeks or months to straighten out. No wonder you sometimes long for the good old days when you did not have to worry about schedules or deadlines, or about workers who were absent or late.

Perhaps it will relieve you to know that the effective supervisors that you see today were themselves originally new and inexperienced. After a period of adjustment they came to enjoy their work and to find it satisfying.

Common mistakes

Before they reach that point, however, many new supervisors seem to encounter similar problems and to make similar mistakes. Perhaps reading about them here will help you avoid them.

Before you had supervisory responsibilities, you had only your own work to think about. Now you are responsible for seeing that others do their work. It is important to remember that your job is now to supervise this work, not to do it yourself. But many new supervisors find it hard to shift from *doing* the work to *supervising* it. They know as much about the work as the employees do—or perhaps more—but they are not sure what a supervisor is supposed to do, especially if they have not received any training. Thus, they spend most of their day doing what the employees should be doing, or looking over the employees' shoulders.

Another mistake of some new supervisors is to let authority go to their heads—to act as though they are better than the employees and to pull rank, order people around, and let everyone know they are "the boss." Most employees will either laugh at such supervisors (behind their backs, of course) or will become resentful and stay out of their way. These supervisors thereby lose touch with their employees.

Other supervisors may swing too far in the opposite direction. They may try to keep up the "buddy" kind of friendship they may have had with their fellow workers before they were promoted. The new supervisor should realize that he or she must strike a balance between being one of the gang and being the one in charge.

Leading employees includes handling their complaints properly and promptly while maintaining the right kind of discipline in the work group. Both you and your workers must understand at the outset that you are not just another worker. You are the supervisor, with all the authority and responsibility that go with the job. At the same time, though, it is important to show by your actions that you are concerned about your employees and that you are working together with them toward agreed-upon goals.

Toward better supervision

As a manager, the supervisor should be able to get work done through others. This means that you, as supervisor, should organize work and motivate employees so that they will do what they are required to do voluntarily and with high performance standards.

If you want to test your ability to do this, find out whether your employees work as hard when you are away as when you are there. Willing, well-supervised employees work hard when the supervisor is away. Your job will be more rewarding—and you will become more valuable to your organization—if you use management skills to make work easier and more effective.

Getting work done through others

Getting work done through the efforts of others is not as easy today as it used to be. In the so-called "good old days" an employee either worked hard or was fired. In most jobs the supervisor was a man and often the type who could "lick every other man on his crew"—and did, if the worker did not do as he was told. Although time has added a legendary gloss to those railroad, steel mill, and packinghouse foremen, there remains a substantial element of truth to their awesome powers of hiring, disciplining, and firing workers.

But times have changed. Today's workers, particularly younger ones, require a different type of supervising. Employees today have a sense of their rights and of their worth as individual men and women. The work-pusher type of supervisor cannot survive when workers are protected by civil service provisions, union contracts, grievance procedures, antidiscrimination laws, and the willingness of workers to go to court to protect their rights.

Today's employees respond willingly to leaders whom they respect and admire. A good beginning is to try asking your workers for advice or help. Ask them to help you plan what needs to be done and how best to do it. Let them have a voice in deciding how to organize to get the job done.

Individuals and small groups can be remarkably effective at planning, organizing, and carrying through on specific assignments. The gains in productivity and work quality can be impressive, and the employees will take great pride in *their* achievements.

Get to know your workers. Find out each person's strengths and weaknesses. Try to learn what each person wants and needs to get from his or her job. By your actions let your employees know that you have confidence in their ability and trust them to do things the right way.

Treating employees fairly

Treat everyone fairly. It is important to avoid playing favorites and to be consistent in your behavior. You lose credibility if you are standoffish one day and everyone's pal the next.

Above all, do not let your personal beliefs interfere with your decisions as a supervisor. Let us take a closer look at this point. As a citizen, you have a perfect right to your views about what is right and wrong, good and bad. Under the law, however, we cannot practice those beliefs that limit the rights of others. As a supervisor,then, you cannot treat employees differently because of their race, religion, nationality, sex, age, life style, or physical ability.

Regardless of your own opinions, your employees are guaranteed equal opportunity by law. If you violate their rights as citizens or violate the equal opportunity laws, you can be sued and made to pay damages out of your own pocket; in addition, such a violation could cause serious problems for your local government.

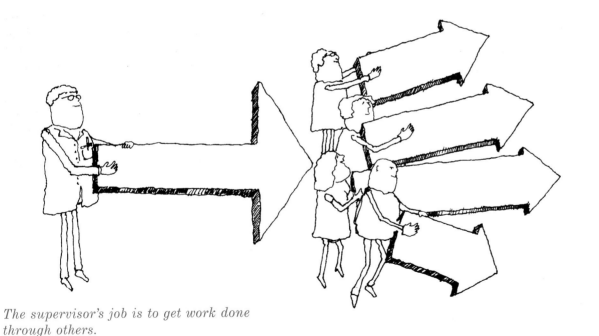

The supervisor's job is to get work done through others.

It is important to be fair with your workers in still another way: Remember that you have authority over them *only* during working hours; you *do not* have authority over their private lives or what they do on their own time.

If your local government has rules about appropriate dress, your employees should dress accordingly. But you may not add your personal requirements to those regulations. If the requirement is for neatly groomed hair, you cannot add to that your own preference for short hair. If an employee drinks off the job but has a good attendance record and is always sober at work, then that drinking has nothing to do with his or her job or with your job as supervisor.

Remember, too, that giving workers advice about their personal problems—even if they ask for it—can be a mistake. You should concern yourself with an employee's private life *only* when it affects job performance. This does not mean that you should not be willing to *listen* to employees with personal problems. Listening to your employees when they want to talk about their problems helps you to understand them better. It also improves relationships and communication between you and your employees. It is important to know, however, when and how to advise an employee to get professional help, instead of trying to solve a problem yourself.

In any situation in which you suspect that your personal preferences or an employee's personal life may be involved, it is important to ask yourself, "Does this have anything to do with the employee's job performance?" before you do or say anything. You can get into serious trouble if you use your supervisory authority to regulate or influence an employee's behavior outside of working hours.

Taking care of yourself

Your job is a difficult one and can at times be stressful. In order to take care of yourself, both mentally and physically, it is important to follow a regular self-care program. Minimizing stress and maintaining an overall sense of well-being will contribute to your effectiveness as a supervisor. There are several steps you can take to safeguard your positive attitude toward your job and work unit:

- Balance your home and work life. Know your priorities.

- Practice effective time management.

- Maintain a healthy diet and regular exercise program.

- Be assertive. Voice your ideas and opinions.

- Treat yourself. Do something you really enjoy during a time of day you regularly set aside just for yourself.

- Recognize the importance of humor in the work place.

- Practice relaxation techniques such as deep-breathing exercises when the going gets rough.

- Attend training sessions to build your skills and keep yourself aware of the latest supervisory techniques.

It is important to remember that feeling in control of your job and other aspects of your work and personal life helps reduce the feelings of stress that can be a result of the fast-paced, changing world we live in. How highly you regard yourself is also an important part of your sense of contentedness on and off the job. Do you like yourself? If you genuinely like and feel good about yourself, you will be better able to withstand the pressures of your job, and you will be a far more effective supervisor.

If you do not feel good about yourself it is going to be difficult for you to be confident enough to lead your work unit. If you suspect that you do not have high self-esteem (often measured by how easily you take criticism or laugh at yourself), then you may want to seek assistance. There are many workshops and courses on the topic, self-help books are available in most bookstores, and trained therapists can offer professional help. In any event, the old adage "know thyself" can be very useful advice in your ongoing efforts to be an effective supervisor.

Summary

You're a front-line supervisor and you have a great deal of responsibility. In order to do a good job, you need to be aware of how vital your role is in your organization's operations, and you need to learn some practical techniques to help you fulfill your responsibilities. As you read through this book you will be given an overview of some of the factors that influence how you manage, including emerging trends in management, changes in culture and economic patterns, and advances in technology. You will also review fundamental skills that every supervisor needs to practice in order to be effective in your work.

You should look carefully at your duties and responsibilities because effective supervision depends on handling every part of the job well.

Some supervisors are so intent on production that they overlook safety or training. Some supervisors neglect records and reports, while others give too much time to paperwork. Some supervisors become so concerned with people that they neglect work. All of us have parts of our jobs that we like much better than others. The trouble starts when we pay too much attention to some parts of our job and neglect others.

We should strive for balanced supervision. This means that the effective supervisor will put proper emphasis on each responsibility and duty.

And we should always remember that an effective supervisor is not a person with special personality traits and unusual skills. Research tells us that all a supervisor has to do to become highly effective at supervision is to learn how to behave like an effective supervisor.

These behaviors can be learned, and they will be discussed in the chapters that follow.

Checklist

Be a leader, not a boss.

Ask your workers to help you plan what to do and how to do it.

Ask your workers for advice and help in getting the job done.

Let your workers help decide how to organize their work.

Show confidence in your employees' judgment by letting them make some of the decisions, but remember you are still responsible for the work they do.

Be sure that everyone knows the what, how, and when of every major task.

Get to know your workers; learn what they need and what they can contribute.

Build teamwork among all the persons in your organization.

Teach and enforce health and safety rules, and set a good personal example.

Keep your records and reports accurately and neatly, and get them in on time.

Try to be a teacher, a helper, and a leader—not a tough boss or a lenient buddy.

Treat everyone fairly. Since everyone is different, however, remember that treating everyone in exactly the same way may be unfair to some.

Do not allow your personal beliefs to interfere with your treatment of employees or your job decisions.

Do not interfere in the private lives of your employees.

Remember that your job is to get work done through others.

Take care of yourself in order to minimize stress and maintain a sense of well-being.

Supervisory situation 1/1

Mary is a newly appointed supervisor in the refuse collection department. She is an excellent equipment operator and a safe worker. Mary had worked as a refuse collection truck operator for five years before her new assignment. She felt confident in her abilities and really enjoyed her work. Previously, she got along well with her co-workers, but in her new role as the boss of a twelve-member crew she is filled with self-doubts. Mary is concerned about whether she can handle her all-male crew and constantly wonders what they think of her. Since she is new at supervisory tasks she feels far less confident than she did in her previous position.

Mary has received some introductory training in basic supervisory skills but has not had much time to practice any of them except in real-life situations. "When I'm not sure what to do, or I make a mistake, I just know everyone thinks I'm not a good supervisor," she has said.

Mary's worries have contributed to her obvious lack of concentration at meetings and her seeming inability to give clear and concise directions to her crew. Last week she ordered her crew to make an emergency stop to pick up medical wastes at a local hospital. Unfortunately, Mary directed the crews to the wrong hospital, which resulted in a three-hour delay. Mary was sure the crew members were talking about her as they punched out that afternoon.

1. *What do you think is the basis of Mary's problems in taking on an active leadership role?*

2. *What are some methods you would suggest for Mary to overcome her anxieties?*

Supervisory situation 1/2

As the supervisor of the road maintenance division, Ron prides himself on getting assignments completed ahead of schedule. He has been known to push his employees to increasing levels of productivity—but no harder than he pushes himself, as he is proud to say. Lately, however, there have been a number of serious accidents involving Ron's crew, and absenteeism is higher than usual. Ron is at a loss to determine the cause when questioned by his department head.

Aware that he is under increased scrutiny, Ron is pushing his crew more than ever. He's convinced that by working harder and faster he is fulfilling his responsibilities as supervisor. Just last week, Ron had his crew work overtime to finish overlaying a highly traveled main street through the central business district. It was the third night in a row that Ron had his crew working several hours overtime. His crew had complained all day about the extreme heat, but Ron had shortened their break times so they could finish the job that day. Because they were shorthanded (two of the asphalt rakers had called in sick), Ron had assigned his flagperson to help with the raking. Ron had set up traffic cones to slow down the rush-hour traffic, and would occasionally direct traffic himself.

About a half-hour before Ron thought they would finish, a compact car tried to squeeze between the cones and the crew's paving machine. The fender of the car hooked onto the paver, and the sudden jolt knocked the operator out of the cab. Ron was the first on the scene and was shocked to find his operator unconscious. "Now we're really behind," Ron exclaimed.

1. *What are some key elements about the responsibilities of a supervisor that Ron needs to consider?*

2. *What are some possible causes of the safety and absenteeism problems that Ron is overlooking?*

THE SUPERVISOR AND THE CHANGING ENVIRONMENT

Life is either a daring adventure or nothing. To keep our faces toward change and behave like free spirits in the presence of fate is strength undefeatable.

Helen Keller

THE SUPERVISOR AND THE CHANGING ENVIRONMENT

What is happening in our country and in the world around us that is changing your job as supervisor?

Why and in what ways are today's employees different from employees of the previous generation?

Can a supervisor be made to pay damages personally for wrongful actions that are job-connected?

How should today's employees be supervised?

If you had left your job in 1950 and returned in 1960, things probably would have been much the same as when you left. But if you left your job today and came back ten years from now, you would probably be startled by how much had changed.

Exactly the same is true of our communities, our country, and the world in general. A number of powerful forces are rapidly changing the world around us and the attitudes of many of us toward life and work. These forces affect the values and behavior of today's workers and have caused the supervisor's job—your job—to change as well.

These forces include the following:

▪ The tremendous growth in world population

▪ Major changes in the economy of our country and of the world

▪ A major shifting of our population—from central cities to suburbs and previously rural areas and to the Southwest and Northwest

▪ A more diverse work force; the high percentages of older people and young adults in the work force, and the impact of a new "baby boom"

▪ New laws and court decisions about basic rights of citizens

▪ New attitudes toward life and work

▪ The impact of telecommunications and the development of the "information highway."

Changes in our world and our country

Let us look first at the big changes that are taking place in the world around us and in our country—then at how they are affecting the way employees think and behave. Then we can look at how the supervisor's job has changed, and what the supervisor must do to continue to supervise effectively.

Increased population since 1850

In 1850, there were approximately a billion people on the earth. Today, it is estimated that there are more than 5.6 billion. By the turn of the century, there probably will be about 6.5 billion, and less than a hundred years from now, some 12 billion.

You can see very clearly how rapidly the world's population is growing if you look at the number of years it has taken to add each billion people to the population of the earth. It took many centuries for that population to reach one billion, but only 80 years to add a second billion, 31 years to reach three billion, and then only 14 years to add a fourth billion.

What does this rapid growth in the world's population mean for local government? Some experts think it means continued inflation for our country and, therefore, rising costs for local government. Remember that there is only so much gas and oil, iron ore, coal, and other natural resources in our planet. Two or three or four times as many people as before demanding to use resources means that prices are likely to rise. Food prices also are likely to rise as a growing world population requires two or three or four times as much food as was needed before.

The population of the United States is approximately 250 million. By the year 2000 we probably will have added another 20 million, to make a total of almost 270 million Americans—nearly twice as many as there were in 1945.

This population growth is one reason why local governments expanded so rapidly during the 1950s, 1960s, and the early 1970s. And since our population is still growing, though less rapidly than before, the demand for essential local government services will continue to grow. Population growth also means that many people will be living and working under more crowded conditions, while others will be moving as far away from the crowding as they are able.

What does this have to do with you, the supervisor? It means that you will have to deal with some of the problems that grow out of greater crowding on and off the job. Some of you who supervise in areas of continued population growth probably work in larger departments and larger local governments. Many of you whose departments and local governments are not growing may experience some of the problems associated with crowding on the job as your cost-conscious local governments strive to be more efficient and economical in using space. Research tells us that crowding tends to lead to behavior problems—problems may arise from crowding on the job or workers may bring stress-related problems with them to the job.

In a larger organization workers often feel like small cogs on a large wheel and they need large doses of recognition and responsibility to help them feel important. Today's younger workers sometimes feel that their names are not as important as their social security numbers (and they may be right). They may feel that larger organizations do not see them as human beings or as individuals but only as "hands" or "personnel" or "employees."

Many have grown up in crowded cities or in suburbs where the population was highly mobile and where they did not get to know their neighbors and their neighbors did not get to know them. Many have no deep roots in a community as their parents and grandparents probably did, because their families moved from place to place while they were growing up.

Today's workers also differ from their counterparts of a generation ago in that they are likely to be better educated, more independent, more assertive, and more inquisitive—and to expect more of their society. They want to participate, be important, and be involved. All of this means that supervisors need to give employees both the opportunity to be distinctive and a sense of belonging at work. It is important for supervisors to make sure that each employee is part of his or her work team and that the morale of the team is high.

The growth of metropolitan America

In 1800 only 6 percent of the people in the United States lived in cities (as defined by the Census Bureau). The rest of the population lived in rural areas and was mostly engaged in farming. By 1990 the Census Bureau reported that 75 percent of our population was living in cities, towns, and other "urban" areas. Of the 25 percent classified as rural in 1990, less than 2.0 percent lived on farms. Most of the workers in the rural population commute to cities, towns, and other population centers for non-farm employment.

It is expected that by the year 2000 an even smaller percentage of the population will live in rural areas. By that time about 30 million more people probably will have moved to, or be surrounded by, subdivisions and suburbs built on what is rural land today.

You can see why local government will be growing in some areas, declining in some areas, and changing the kinds of public services provided in other areas.

Major economic changes

In 1950, 65 percent of U.S. workers were employed as laborers in industry. Today, that percentage has dropped to about 20 percent as our economy has undergone a restructuring. Our nation has made a major transition—from a manufacturing society that produces automobiles, steel, appliances, textiles, clothing, and shoes to an "information society," manufacturing and servicing computers, designing computer software, and developing and operating chains of financial services "supermarkets." More than 57 percent of American workers today are employed in creating, processing, and transmitting information. This trend is highly likely to continue, with "knowledge workers" (i.e., non-industrial workers) composing the majority of the work force.

In 1800 almost everyone—94 percent of the population—lived in rural areas. By 1990, 75 percent were living in cities, towns, and other urban areas.

Along with the restructuring of our national economy has come yet another major shifting of our population in addition to the shifts of population from farms, rural areas, and central cities to suburban areas. Manufacturing plants must be located near adequate supplies of labor, water, and raw materials such as coal, and near transportation centers. Information companies can locate almost anywhere, and what they tend to look for in deciding where to locate is the quality of life in a community—climate, education systems, cultural attractiveness, availability of recreational areas. Local governments must keep these factors in mind as they attempt to attract and retain information companies as part of their economic development efforts.

These factors are equally important in the international arena. Through telecommunications and the rise of multinational companies, countries around the world are becoming increasingly interconnected. This "global village" means that local governments too are able to share with each other more information, technology, and methods for delivering services. But it also means that governments are part of the worldwide competition to attract business and new development.

In other words, your local government will need to provide superior service and a high quality of life to attract and retain economic enterprises that are able to consider locating just about anywhere in the world where conditions are favorable. Local governments, then, will need to be aware of how the cities of Madrid or Marrakesh, for example, provide services. As a supervisor, you will increasingly become part of your municipal and county government efforts to provide quality service that at least equals that of other high-quality localities around the globe.

A more diverse work force

Population shifts and the growth in the world population have been coupled with changes in work force composition. White males, who once constituted the majority of workers in the U.S. work force, now account for less than half. Work teams are now composed of far larger numbers of women, people of color, Asians, Hispanics, and Native Americans. Some sources estimate that in the next decade as many as 90 percent of new workers will be immigrants, Americans from a wide variety of racial and ethnic backgrounds, and women—many of whom will be employed in nontraditional jobs as, for example, heavy equipment operators, firefighters, and police officers. Many people with disabilities will also be included.

In 1990, fewer than 1 in 54 U.S. workers were on farms. Most workers commuted to a city or town for employment an average of 40 minutes per day round trip.

In addition, labor force trends indicate that during the next decade we will have a labor force with larger numbers of older and younger workers. Baby boomers will be in the 45 to 54 age group by the year 2005, increasing the number of workers in this age group by 75 percent since 1975. However, in this same period there will be a marked decrease in the number of workers between the ages of 25 to 34, the result of a decline in the birth rate in the late 1960s. The children of the baby boom generation, on the other hand, are now beginning to enter the labor force. The numbers of 16- to 24-year-olds will markedly increase in the mid-1990s through 2005.

The result of all these changes is that additional responsibilities are placed on the supervisor—to understand the ideas and attitudes of both older and younger workers, and to blend different values and attitudes into a working whole.

You will be called upon to manage this diverse work force and to create a team of people with very different backgrounds, ways of communicating, and work ethics. Learning to appreciate their differences and to discover what motivates them is a real challenge for today's effective supervisor.

Population Trends by Percent of Race, 1980 and 2080

"Immigration and birth-rate trends of the 1980s are pointing toward dramatic changes in the U.S. population mix over the next century. If current patterns hold, slightly more than half of all Americans will be Hispanics, Asians, and Blacks by the year 2080."

	1980	2080
Whites	79.9	49.9
Hispanics	6.4	23.4
Blacks	11.7	14.7
Asians, others	2.0	12.0

Source: "Profile of Tomorrow's New U.S.," *U.S. News and World Report* 101, No. 21, November 24, 1986, p. 32. Primary source: U.S. News and World Report—Basic data: Population Reference Bureau, Inc.

Laws and court decisions

Since the mid-1960s Congress has passed numerous laws covering civil rights and discrimination, consumer protection, the environment, worker safety and health, and privacy of citizens. In addition, citizen rights under the U.S.

We live with a tidal wave of information. Your ability to navigate will determine your ability to succeed.

Constitution are being more vigorously enforced than was the case a decade ago. For example, while in 1960 there were only 247 civil rights suits in federal courts against government officials, by 1979 there were nearly 25,000 such lawsuits. From the point of view of the supervisor the most important of these laws and decisions are those pertaining to citizen rights, particularly in these areas:

- Freedom of speech

- The right to assemble peaceably and to petition the government for correction of grievances

- The rights of African Americans, Hispanics, and other minority citizens

- The rights of those with disabilities

- Protection against unlawful searches of people or property and unlawful seizure of personal belongings

- The right to due process of law

- The right to equal treatment regardless of sex

- The right to equal employment treatment for those forty to seventy years of age.

These laws mean that all people have specific rights as citizens. Most of these rights are spelled out in the Bill of Rights to the U.S. Constitution. All citizens have these rights whether they are white, African American, Hispanic, Eskimo, American Indian, or belong to any other race or ethnic group.

These basic rights belong to men and women; individuals with religious beliefs and atheists; citizens born in this country and abroad. They apply regardless of whether your family came from England, Poland, Italy, Mexico, or New Jersey.

It is important that supervisors be aware of the rights people have under the law. A local government can be sued and made to pay damages if found guilty of violating federal law. A supervisor, too, can be sued and made to pay damages if found guilty of depriving another person of his or her legal rights. *You, personally, can be sued* in these cases—even if you, the supervisor, were acting according to state law, local ordinance, or departmental rule.

One of the most recent laws of which supervisors should be aware is the Americans with Disabilities Act (ADA). This civil rights law was passed by Congress in 1990. It prohibits discrimination against qualified applicants or employees who are disabled or become disabled during their course of employment. Organizations must make every effort to accommodate an employee or prospective employee so that he or she is able to perform the job. With the support of this law, many persons with disabilities are holding jobs that formerly may not have been open to them.

As a supervisor you may have an employee who suffers from Acquired Immune Deficiency Syndrome (AIDS), which is a communicable disease that may be disabling. However, as with any other illness or disability, a person suffering from AIDS may not be discriminated

against in hiring, assignment, promotion, transfer, and provision of benefits, and is accorded work place accommodations in the same manner as persons considered disabled.

As a supervisor, you might get into trouble with the law for various types of discrimination. For example, let us suppose you are a lieutenant in the fire department and a woman is sent to you to be interviewed for a job. You decided long ago that a woman can never meet the demands of firefighter jobs, so you reject her application without talking to her or giving her a chance to show what she can do.

If you reject this application only because she is a woman, you could be in trouble. The law says you may not discriminate against any applicant just because that person is older, is a woman, is a person of color, or has a disability. You may turn down only applicants who do not have the qualifications for the job. Of course, if you *do* hire the applicant *only* because the applicant is a woman, you may be in trouble, too, unless that person is a qualified applicant.

Let us take another example of a way in which you as a supervisor could get into trouble with the law. Assume that you give an order to a worker on the job. The worker does what he is told to do, but he also tells you a few unflattering things you do not like to hear. You fire him on the spot.

You may be in trouble again—this time for violating the employee's rights to free speech and due process of law. If an employee refuses to obey your proper instructions, you may discipline the employee for disobeying. You may as a supervisor have cause to discipline an employee for sounding off, but you could get into trouble for firing someone for exercising free speech or for firing someone without properly informing that person of the reason and giving that person a chance to tell his or her side.

The way to handle such a situation is to take the case through the proper disciplinary channels, described in Chapter 13. Both you and the employee are allowed to state your case. You have to prove that what the employee said seriously interfered with proper discipline, and the employee is able to present his or her side.

In short, as a supervisor you should respect the constitutional and statutory rights of everyone you work with; following good supervisory practices will help you to do that.

Know and carefully follow your personnel policies and procedures. If in doubt, contact your personnel officer and/or Equal Employment Opportunity (EEO) Compliance Officer, your organization's legal department, or your manager.

New attitudes toward life and work

For many years most Americans believed in and lived by what is called the Protestant ethic. Many still do. This is a set of values and beliefs that emphasizes hard work, standing on your own feet, thrift, saving for a rainy day, knowing your place, and obeying anyone who is older or has higher rank. Rest, vacations, and leisure are earned—they are the rewards of hard work.

Today many Americans—especially many of those under thirty-five—live by a different set of values. It is sometimes called the "psychology of entitlement" because its adherents believe that all people are entitled to certain basic necessities, such as a decent job and dignified retirement, decent housing, comprehensive medical care, a clean environment, and safe consumer products.

Leisure is also considered by many to be a right rather than a privilege earned by work. One way of seeing how our values and attitudes are changing, for example, is to compare some typical attitudes and values from our past with those that many people are embracing and expressing today.

Yesterday's employees lived to work. They wanted to get and keep good jobs because they remembered the Great Depression. A good job was any job that offered job security and a pension for their old age. The possibility of another depression was always in the back of their minds. They saved faithfully for "a rainy day" and they paid off their mortgages as quickly as possible.

But many workers today are not preoccupied with financial security. They are more likely to work to live. The Great Depression, with its widespread bankruptcies and enduring bread lines, has little or no meaning for them. Of course, the deep recession of the early 1980s may have had an impact on the values of some of these workers. But approximately 90 percent of workers were not personally unemployed and many of those who were may feel even more strongly that they are "entitled" to a decent job. Besides, today's employees have social security for their families if they die or become disabled and for themselves in their old age (although many younger workers now question whether social security benefits will be available to them when they retire). Almost anywhere today's employees work they will have a pension plan plus medical and life insurance. If they lose their jobs they can expect unemployment compensation. Therefore, you do not hear as much talk as in the past about rainy days or nest eggs.

But you probably do hear quite a lot about people doing their own thing, because many of today's younger workers believe in it—in the chance to be themselves, to develop their own special set of talents. They also want their lives, including their work, to be interesting and meaningful.

Today's employees realize that while they are decision makers in their homes, their churches, their clubs, and their voting booths, this is often not true at work where they spend about a quarter of their lives. Many of them speak openly of their resentment and anger at having very little say about how they should do their jobs. And when employers deny today's workers what they need and want from their jobs, many will not hesitate to fight back through grievances or even law suits.

Finally, today's younger, better educated, and more assertive worker is less likely to say to supervisors or upper management, "O.K., if you say so." Instead, many may reply to a direction or suggestion, "Why?" or "Why not?"

The impact of technology

What sort of impact has the influx of computers had on supervisory practices? In today's office you will find computers at almost every work station. Supervisors as well as clerical staff are expected to be computer literate. While the specific uses for computers vary widely, there are certain applications that are found almost universally.

Word processing is perhaps most common. Programs like MicroSoft Word, WordPerfect, and others have made the creation and writing of memos, reports, and other word-based documents faster and more efficient. Through the use of *spreadsheet* software such as Lotus 1-2-3, it's possible to automate budgeting and other number-crunching procedures that require extensive mathematical calculations. Like a huge, extensively cross-referenced Rolodex, *database management* programs track and classify thousands of related items. This can be invaluable for organizing, tracking, and quickly accessing large collections of data, such as inventories, mailing lists, and personnel records.

One of the most popular uses for computers is to facilitate *communications*, both internally and externally. Electronic mail (e-mail) systems allow staff to "post" electronic messages to others within their organization, as well as download and read messages sent by other staff. Other kinds of networks (e.g., wide area networks) allow communication with persons located off-site.

Some organizations use communications software and modems to tap into vast information databases available from on-line vendors. These databases allow users to search huge reference collections consisting of thousands of trade journals, national newspapers, news-wires, government documents, and more. The latest and fastest growing form of electronic communication and data gathering is via the Internet system.

The Internet

The Internet is a vast web of about 20,000 computer networks, found in over 60 countries throughout the world. There are estimated to be about 20 million people on the Internet—and that number is increasing by more than 100,000 every month! Until around 1993, few people had even heard of the Internet, but by 1994, almost no one had *not* heard of it. What significance does this phenomenal growth have for supervisors?

The Internet should be understood and utilized where appropriate. Its resources include not just mountains of documents and reports, but

the expertise of user group members, who may be dealing with (or have already resolved) issues that your organization is presently confronting. The Internet can also be used to facilitate communication—for example, to pursue joint projects with other governments or to stay in touch with consultants or contractors located off premises.

Telecommuting

In fact, the "information highway" of the 1990s has created new opportunities for work to be performed away from the work site. "Telecommuting," working at home or at another site away from the office for one or more days a week, is now an option. Information can be shared and accessed through computers and other telecommunications devices so that many workers no longer have to be in a specific location to accomplish their tasks.

What are the advantages of telecommuting? It is estimated that new telecommuting programs will recover the costs to establish them in one year or less. Studies show that this cost benefit is based on a number of factors, including a decrease in the reliance on the automobile and subsequent reduced environmental pollution, lessened impact on office space requirements, and increased productivity.

Besides reducing potential overcrowding at the worksite, telecommuting can improve employee morale. For example, telecommuting can reduce the stress on an employee who might care for a chronically ill family member.

It might also be an option for an injured employee who can perform light-duty assignments while at home recuperating.

Supervising someone who telecommutes can be a challenge for both worker and supervisor. If your organization has a telecommunications program, or even if you are supervising only one or two employees in your work unit who telecommute, you will want to follow certain supervisory practices to ensure that the worker performs efficiently when working out of the office.

■ *Establish trust.* As a supervisor of someone who works at home at least part of the time, you will need to be sure that you build a strong sense of trust that the worker is performing his or her duties while out of your direct observation. The worker in turn must feel that you will accept him or her as a "regular" employee and recognize the telecommuter's work as important to the work unit.

■ *Schedule work.* It's essential to make sure that the employee has a specific schedule of assignments due.

■ *Establish performance standards.* It is critical in a decentralized work environment for you and the telecommuting worker to agree on what is expected in terms of job performance. One technique is to develop a written work plan so that roles and duties are clearly laid out.

■ *Keep in touch.* Regular communication with telecommuters is very important in order to ensure that work is being performed in a timely fashion and that the telecommuter is kept apprised of office news. Scheduling regular face-to-face meetings will help keep lines of communication open.

■ *Provide training.* Successful telecommuting doesn't just happen. You need to make sure that all the members of your work unit, including the telecommuter(s), know the basics of telecommuting, including effective techniques for scheduling work at home, setting up a home office, conducting effective teleconferencing meetings, and relating to co-workers.

■ *Select your telecommuters wisely.* Not everyone is cut out to work independently away from a more structured office environment. You need to know the capabilities of the worker before you approve telecommuting as a work option.

■ *Provide an adequate telecommunications network.* Make sure that the technology is in place so that you and telecommuting staff have the type of reliable hardware and software to perform the job away from the main office location.

Some disadvantages of new technologies

While technology may often lead to welcome increases in productivity and efficiency, there are also pitfalls. One is the potential for physical injury to workers who spend much of their day working at a computer. Some of the most common ailments reported are back and neck pains and injury to the wrist muscles, a condition known as carpal tunnel syndrome. Supervisors can help prevent these problems by ensuring that workers have appropriate furniture and a correctly designed ("ergonomic") workspace and by encouraging computer users to take regular stretch and walk-around work breaks to avoid eye fatigue and muscle aches.

Another tricky technology issue relates to privacy. Some supervisors might be tempted to read their employees' e-mail or monitor data inputting through electronic keystroke monitoring. Either of these actions raises ethical and possibly even legal questions. Although electronic monitoring of employees is not normally illegal, many feel that it is unethical and an invasion of the worker's privacy. In 1994, a variety of organizations worked to get Congress to hold hearings on a bill that would strictly limit and control instances in which an employer could electronically monitor workers.

Both you and your employees, then, must be ready for change and for progress. It is important that you encourage employees to learn more about the work they do, that you train them in new ideas and new methods, and that you help them to keep up with new developments and to understand that new developments can change the nature of a job or do away with a job entirely. Beyond that, it is important for you and for them to understand that change is normal—especially today—and may be a very good thing.

Above all, it is important that you as supervisor keep up-to-date yourself. You can learn from your younger workers or from other associates who may have been in school more recently. You can also learn from those who have had special training that you have not had. Take time to read, to think, and to question.

What does the future hold? There's no question that the use of computers and related electronic technology will continue to expand in the work place. While much of this technology will serve an organization's need for greater efficiency and productivity, it will not necessarily also further workers' level of motivation, feeling of job satisfaction, or ultimate performance. Ensuring those vital matters will remain the responsibility of the people managing the organization, and in particular, the ongoing job of the effective supervisor.

Changes in management practices

The cultural, scientific, and technological changes that are occurring at such a rapid pace mean that local governments must keep pace with an ever-changing environment. In order to respond to the needs and demands of the communities they serve, government organizations must constantly adapt their current ways of delivering services and develop policies and procedures to meet the demands future change will bring.

While change is inevitable, local governments do have control over how they meet the challenges that change creates, as well as help shape the direction of that change. Supervisors as well can control how change affects their work teams and quality of work life in three primary ways: by keeping track of the major cultural and economic trends that have been discussed, building skills in information technology, and learning the latest and most effective changes in management practices.

Quality management

The role of this country in the world economy has changed dramatically in the last twenty years. Global competition from Japan, Western Europe, and more recently the Pacific Rim, has forced U.S. companies and government at all levels to examine just how they do business. New management styles (quality management, quality circles, self-managed teams), rightsizing (reorganizations, lay-offs, early-retirement programs), quality customer service (focus groups, customer surveys, niche markets), and information networking (local area network, Internet) are phrases that form the lexicon of new business terms.

Quality management, often referred to as total quality management or TQM, is a management methodology that focuses on improving the processes by which a product is manufactured or a service is delivered, seeking input from both management and workers as a team and striving to provide the highest quality of goods or services, as defined by the customer. This type of management was shaped in large part by theorists W. Edwards Deming and Joseph Duran and varies considerably from the bureaucratic model first formulated by Max Weber in the 1920s. According to Weber's theory, the most effective way for large organizations to operate was to have decisions made at the upper levels of management and relayed downward through mid-management levels to front-line supervisors and finally to the workers forming the base of the bureaucracy's pyramid.

In the 1960s the Japanese adopted Dr. Deming's practice of total quality management, and Japan soon became a leader in the world market for many products, including automobiles and consumer electronics such as televisions, computers, and stereo equipment. U.S. corporations and government agencies on the federal, state, and local levels are now changing management processes and adopting quality management principles.

In their book *Reinventing Government*, David Osborne and Ted Gaebler have put quality management concepts into a workable context for governments. According to the authors, governments that are responding successfully to the changing environment

promote *competition* between service providers. They *empower* citizens by pushing control out of the bureaucracy, into the community. They measure the performance of their agencies, focusing not on inputs but on *outcomes*. They are driven by their goals—their *missions*—not by their rules and regulations. They redefine their clients as *customers* and offer them choices—between schools, between training programs, between housing options. They *prevent* problems before they emerge, rather than simply offering services afterward. They put their energies into *earning* money, not simply spending it. They *decentralize* authority, embracing participatory management. They prefer *market* mechanisms to bureaucratic mechanisms. And they focus not simply on providing public services, but on *catalyzing* all sectors—public, private, and voluntary—into action to solve their community's problems.

What does this mean for you as a supervisor? Quality management means that as a supervisor you will involve your work team in decision making and that you will seek the input of your customers as well. That means you will need to be skilled in team building, group problem solving and decision making, consensus building, and customer service.

Effective supervisors need to be flexible in light of the new models of management and governance that are evolving. It is an exciting time, because you are involved in helping to provide a higher quality of life for the citizens you serve and the employees you supervise each day.

Reengineering

The reengineering movement is the direct result of a book by Michael Hammer and James Champy called *Reengineering the Corporation*. The premise of reengineering, like that of TQM, is that organizations must reexamine their work flow to ensure that their organization is fully meeting its customers' needs. Unlike TQM, though, the reengineering process doesn't try just to improve current work pro-

cedures, but questions the purpose of each process and requires a rethinking of the prevailing wisdom behind each step. The reengineering process has been likened to a disassembly procedure, where a product is disassembled, studied, then reassembled.

The authors explain their view of the reengineering process as "the fundamental rethinking and redesign of...processes to achieve dramatic improvements in critical contemporary measures of performance such as cost, quality, service, and speed...a process is anything that delivers value to the customer." Ultimately, the fully reengineered government doesn't just satisfy its customers' needs, but anticipates them, and it is nimble enough to be capable of quickly making adjustments to meet those needs.

Some of the steps of the planning process for reengineering are the same as those for instituting TQM. The key steps are the need for the total backing of top level management; the creation of clear objectives and goals; worker participation; and a process audit, which may include the creation of a process map. But because reengineering's effects are so much more dramatic, making sure those steps are well planned out and executed is even more critical.

What is expected of today's supervisor?

Today's effective supervisor recognizes the new realities and tries to find ways of effec-

tively dealing with them and with *all* employees. This means building good relations with employees and strengthening their willingness to work harder and better. Remember that those employees who embrace the newer attitudes toward life and work are *not* less motivated than workers who believe in the work ethic. It is just that they have higher expectations from their work, and for them work has to compete more directly with other values in their lives.

To build good relations with employees and strengthen their willingness to work harder and better, today's supervisor must have a greater appreciation of how complex human beings are and a better understanding of what motivates them and how they relate to the changing world around them. The supervisor must be able to sense and adapt to the changes in employee needs—from time to time and from situation to situation. And today's supervisor must be both patient and reasonable. If you push today's younger employees, many are likely to push back, aware of their rights under the law.

Following are techniques that should serve as useful rules to follow in supervising today's employees.

■ *Anticipate and plan.* Today's supervisor spends more time thinking about tomorrow's problems and planning for them. Changes are easier and smoother for the work team if the supervisor has anticipated what is coming and has planned for it. Since changes are happening at a faster pace in the world, changes can be expected to happen faster on the job, too.

■ *Help employees set goals.* Today's supervisor helps workers identify their goals. Supervisors need to help workers find ways of satisfying their own needs and meeting the goals of the organization at the same time.

■ *Make employees part of the work team.* Today's supervisor finds ways of making each employee a part of his or her work team, of giving each employee a sense of belonging, while valuing the diversity among members of the team.

■ *Keep employees up-to-date.* Today's supervisor gives the growth and development of employees top priority, keeping them from being narrow specialists by enriching their jobs, providing them with the broadest possible range of skills, and seeing that they are kept up-to-date.

■ *Give employees responsibility and the authority to carry out that responsibility.* Today's supervisor gives greater work-related responsibility and delegates more authority. By bringing employees into the planning process and by putting more trust in them, supervisors can challenge employees to do their very best.

■ *Show respect for employees.* Today's supervisor shows that he or she respects employees and values their diversity. For example, the supervisor addresses an employee by name, not by "hey, you."

■ *Encourage employees to speak up.* Today's supervisor encourages employees to provide information and suggestions, or to pose questions or problems. The supervisor encourages employees to express resentment, complaints, or differences of opinion. If a worker tells off a supervisor, the effective supervisor remains calm, knowing the worker may be right and that supervisors can learn, as well.

■ *Listen to employees.* Today's supervisor listens carefully to employees and tries to understand, giving employees the same attention the supervisor would expect from his or her own superior. Suggestions or questions are followed up with a report. "I'll check on that and let you know by Friday." And the effective supervisor does report back, by Friday.

The United States still has a mobile society. We are moving minds to information centers. You are hiring minds (not arms and backs) that are attracted to the quality of life you can offer.

Checklist

Be aware of those changes in our society that have had or are likely to have an impact on your organization.

Be aware of the technological advances that are now affecting your local government and its employees.

Be sensitive to employee needs for a sense of responsibility, of individuality, of belonging.

Keep up-to-date on the advances in technology and other fields of knowledge affecting your work.

Be fully aware of all your employees' rights as citizens, and workers.

Maintain an understanding of the values and attitudes of a diverse work force that may include younger workers, and workers from other cultures.

Supervisory situation 2/1

Stanley Cramer is a supervisor in the accounting division of the water department. Stanley has worked for the county for many years, first as an accounting clerk, then as an accountant, and finally as a supervisory accountant. He is about forty years old, dresses conventionally, and has lived a quiet life with his wife, two cats, and a cocker spaniel.

Under the personnel system, applicants for certain jobs could be certified on the basis of completing a college degree program. This was true in accounting. In fact, the county got many of its young accountants from the university.

One morning Stanley received a call from the division head saying that a vacancy in Stanley's office had been filled and that the newly appointed accountant would report for work the next day. First thing the next morning the sound of a motorcycle with a broken muffler announced the arrival of Tom Jones, the new accountant.

In Stanley's eyes, Tom, dressed in faded blue jeans and a red-and-black flannel shirt, was a sight to behold. And if the clothes were not enough, the picture was completed by sandals, a beard, long hair in dreadlocks, and an earring.

"Hello," said Tom, "I'm the new accountant. Are you Stanley?"

To say that Stanley was startled was an understatement. The county had a dress code but it simply stated that dress would be "appropriate for the occasion." Actually, the code had been written primarily to cover secretaries and was a direct result of the mayor's objection after having seen a young secretary with silver fingernails and a very low-cut blouse.

"Yes, Mr. Jones," said Stanley, "I'm Mr. Cramer, your supervisor. We might as well get one thing straight at the beginning. This is a public office and people expect public employees to dress properly. That means no blue jeans, no long hair, and no earrings. If you and I are going to work together, we might as well understand that."

"Stanley," said Tom, "those kinds of ideas are old-fashioned. Let's just say that I'll do my job and you do yours. You don't worry about my clothes and my hair, and I won't worry about yours, OK?"

1. What should Stanley do?

Supervisory situation 2/2

Robin is a new supervisor in the personnel department. She had worked for the past five years as a personnel analyst in the department. For the most part, she enjoyed her job but found some of the data entry work to be routine and often tedious.

Robin used to have lunch on a regular basis with two of the five workers she now supervises. During the lunch breaks, Pam and Lee used to complain about how repetitious and boring their work could be. Entering changes in employee pay classifications, addresses, and insurance coverage was just one of the routine assignments they performed.

As a result, Pam would often call in sick as a way to break up the routine. Lee would sometimes leave early for doctor or dentist appointments or use any reasonable excuse she could think of to get out of work. Robin, however, was a hard worker and had the highest production rate of anyone in her office.

All of Robin's employees spend most of their workday entering and receiving data on their computers. As a newly appointed supervisor, Robin wants to make sure that her staff is as highly motivated and productive as she is. She has called her work unit together to discuss her expectations and those of her unit.

1. *Given the type of work they perform, what are some ways in which Robin can help ensure that all of her staff are as productive as possible?*

2. *How could Robin approach Pam and Lee about their attitudes?*

BASIC
SUPERVISORY
SKILLS

We believe that civilized society cannot function effectively without effective government.

David Osborne and Ted Gaebler

BASIC SUPERVISORY SKILLS

To do an effective job, supervisors must develop some fundamental skills or competencies. Later chapters will give you more specific guidelines for putting these basic skills to work. Now, however, we should talk about these essential skills, which are

- Stopping problems before they get out of hand
- Setting goals and reaching them
- Building a team and keeping it going
- Giving workers a say about their jobs
- Being a leader
- Making jobs more interesting and rewarding
- Coaching workers to improve their skills.

Understanding the meaning of and reasons for these essentials of good management gives the supervisor a firm foundation on which to build more specific skills and a good work organization.

Stopping problems before they get out of hand

Effective supervisors watch for small signs of trouble in order to deal with them before they grow into serious problems.

To catch a problem while it is still small, you will have to develop empathy as a kind of sixth sense that can alert you to trouble ahead. Many of us use empathy in personal situations. It tells you that the friend you are with is feeling a lot worse than she admits; that your son is embarrassed even though he is acting rudely; that your wife or husband is thinking about something else while you are talking; or that the other poker player has a very good hand.

In all these cases we are observing small clues in a person's face or voice or posture that tell us to be on guard. In the same way we can learn to be observant at work. Supervisors who genuinely care about the members of their work team and are sensitive to their feelings will probably be able to sense when a problem is beginning to develop. (Empathy is discussed in more detail in Chapter 10.)

Keeping one step ahead of trouble also means being able to see trends or patterns in the clues that you notice. For example, if a usually cooperative worker suddenly becomes difficult to work with, that is a clue telling you that there may be trouble ahead. But if other workers who are usually friendly begin looking away when you pass by, a *pattern* of trouble may be developing. You can assume that the problem involves more than one worker and that it is a lot more serious than it may have looked at first.

Your early warning signals can come from your employees or from other people in your organization, as well as from people outside of local government. Supervisors who are approachable, whose supervisory style makes people tend to confide in them and talk frankly with them, who maintain good relations with everyone inside and outside the organization—these supervisors have the best chance of getting help in anticipating problems.

For example, one of your employees may tell you that repair work on your vehicles is not being done properly. You would then be able to take action before a breakdown or a serious accident occurs. Or a neighbor who knows and respects you might alert you to the fact that one of your employees is offering items for sale that might be local government property. You could then check the facts and take corrective action if necessary.

Anticipating problems means more than simply being the kind of supervisor that people find it easy to talk to. It also means being a supervisor who has budgeted the time to gather information, to think, and to plan.

Setting goals and reaching them

The second basic skill a supervisor must have is the ability to pinpoint *what* must be done, *when*, and *by whom*. In other words,

Setting a goal means deciding what…when… by whom; it also means setting priorities.

supervisors must be able to guide the work unit in setting goals and stating them clearly.

Before you and your work team formulate goals and objectives, it is helpful to determine your unit's mission, or the reason you exist as a unit; to create a vision of what you want your work unit to be in the future; and to identify the underlying principles or values that guide activities. These initial steps in your planning process will help you set long- and short-range goals that are both meaningful and useful.

Determining your mission, creating a vision, and identifying values

Your work unit's mission statement answers the questions "What is our purpose" and "Why do we do what we do?" By answering these questions your team is setting the framework for your goals, which provide the methods for accomplishing your mission. Your work team's vision is a picture of what it would like to be in the future. It is a statement that focuses on the ideal, but it does not specify how to reach that ideal. Rather, it is a short statement of what your work team could be if it fulfilled all of its potential. It is a picture that all the members of your team can feel proud of and want to strive to achieve.

Guiding principles are the values that your work team considers worthwhile. They are the standards that your work team believes in and that reflect their integrity. These principles should be reflected in the goals that you set. Your mission statement, vision, and guiding principles could look something like this

example from a public works department vehicle maintenance team:

Our mission is to provide for the maintenance and repair of the city's fleet in order to ensure that city departments have properly operating and safe vehicles and equipment to deliver their services effectively and efficiently.

Our vision is of a team of well trained, energetic, professional people with the facilities and resources to provide a fleet of equipment and vehicles that efficiently enhance the efforts of all the departments and divisions within our city government.

These are the principles that guide our actions:

We believe honesty and sound work ethics are valuable assets.

We believe every member of our team has valuable skills that contribute to our combined success.

We believe in respecting those who work with us and in turn ask for their respect and acknowledgment.

Setting clear goals

A goal is a target. It is an exact statement of what must be done and when it must be completed. Here, for instance, is an example of a goal statement: Crew 1 is to complete properly all curb and gutter work on the north side of the 1400 block of Oak Street no later than 4:30 p.m. on Friday, 15 November.

This statement gives the supervisor and the workers the specific goal that must be reached. It also gives everyone an exact deadline for getting the job done. This is much more effective than simply urging employees to work harder and faster, as some supervisors do. The clearer the idea that workers have of what they are supposed to do, the greater the possibility of its getting done.

There is another good reason for stating goals clearly. Goals are needed because progress can be measured only if we know exactly what the team is moving toward. In other words, the players cannot tell when they have scored if there is no goal line. For example, if the curb and gutter work is not completed on time, the supervisor and workers should get together to figure out why. Was the deadline too short? Did the workers let the supervisor down? Was equipment late in arriving? Once the reason is found, it will be easier to do a better job of planning the next time.

Setting goals does not mean simply stating what the next work order on the pile requires the work crew to do. Before a goal is stated, supervisors should think through which job *should* be next in line. Priorities must be set so that work is done in order of importance, with the most important job placed at the top of the list.

In addition, tasks can often be grouped so that similar tasks are done together or consecutively. Time and materials can often be saved by grouping work elements in this way, and the work crew is thus working more efficiently.

While the most effective organizations involve their supervisors in setting work goals, the goals of a work team sometimes are determined by management other than the team's direct supervisor. When this happens, effective supervisors strive to influence management to set realistic and appropriate goals that involve work team input. They try to help the higher levels of the organization understand the realities of the work situation by providing timely and accurate information.

Building personal goals into organizational goals

The supervisor who recognizes that workers have goals of their own, and who tries to help workers reach these goals, has gone a long way toward getting employees to work willingly and well.

At work, personal goals might be to get promoted or earn more pay. But many personal goals have to do with an employee's interests outside the job, such as going hunting, doing holiday shopping, or painting a room in the house.

In the past, sanitation workers often were required to return to the public works department after garbage and trash were collected, to sit idly around until the workday was over. Now, in many local governments, supervisors are authorized to allow the workers to go home when the collection routes have been satisfactorily completed. The workers have properly accomplished the goals of their local government and are free to go about accomplishing their personal goals, whatever those might be. Under such an arrangement workers are strongly motivated to work both quickly and well. As a supervisor, perhaps you don't have this kind of authority delegated to you. But when you *are* able to bring the organization's goals and the employees' personal goals together, the result is motivation. This result is most easily obtained by supervisors who encourage employees to help in planning and setting goals for their work team.

Building a team and keeping it going

Some supervisors give orders only to their *subordinates*; others head work *groups*. But the most effective supervisors are leaders of closely knit work *teams*. A group is simply a collection of individuals, but a team is something more. It is a group of people who trust one another and count on each and every member to help with the work. They share the same goals, attitudes, and values; they have team spirit.

Team spirit grows out of the same feeling of pride and belonging that people get from being members of a championship athletic team. We usually give more of ourselves to organizations that have team spirit than we do to others.

When a group of workers becomes a true team, two important things take place. First, the workers gain the sense of belonging mentioned above. Second, the whole becomes greater than the sum of its parts. This means that a team of people working together can get more done than the members of the team can accomplish working individually.

But teams must be built; and once built they must be maintained. Like a fine piece of machinery, unless they are handled carefully and given preventive maintenance they will break down.

Giving workers a say about their jobs

The supervisor should recognize that an employee who is doing a job eight hours a day, five days a week, twelve months a year, knows more about that job than the supervisor does. The supervisor may have been an expert at the same work some time ago, but since he or she became a supervisor he or she has probably not actually patrolled a beat or posted entries in the account books.

Your workers, then, may be the best sources for ideas on how to perform their jobs—and how to perform them most effectively, efficiently, and economically. And employees whose supervisors seek their advice on these jobs will generally perform well because they have a sense of "ownership" in their work and they feel that their knowledge of the job is valued.

Delegating is managing through others

When you delegate authority for work and accept the decisions workers make about how best to do their jobs you are truly managing through the efforts of others. Such a relationship helps the supervisor become the leader of the team rather than the boss of the work group.

Delegating helps employees feel valued. They feel their work competencies and skills are respected when they are given the opportunity to directly participate in how their work is carried out.

Delegating authority to employees also makes their jobs more interesting and helps them to grow and develop. Finally, delegating authority gives the supervisor the most effective control he or she can have: self-control on the part of the workers themselves. When self-control is operating, then employees are doing what needs to be done even when the supervisor is not present.

Delegation is not loss of authority

Many supervisors find it hard to delegate authority because they are afraid of losing control. If they understood the true meaning of delegation they would see that this does not, in fact, happen.

A supervisor does not delegate his or her authority as a supervisor. Supervisors always retain the authority delegated to them by the organization—the authority to decide what work must be done, in what order of importance, when, at what level of quality, and by whom.

True delegation involves giving workers *only authority related to work*—authority to decide *how* the work should be done. Besides, this authority is delegated only to employees or work teams who have demonstrated that they are experts at their jobs.

If employees do not have the knowledge or skills to make proper decisions about how their jobs should be done, the supervisor should first train them and then work with them to improve their skills and abilities. Work authority can then be delegated increasingly to these workers as the supervisor becomes satisfied that they can make proper decisions on their own, without further guidance.

Involving workers in decision making

Today local governments are empowering their employees by giving them a much greater say in organizational decision making. Effective supervisors allow the members of their work team to directly participate in many decisions, including planning, goal setting, scheduling, and allocating resources. This democratization of the work place is a real change from the old top-down hierarchical form of management.

You cannot assume that members of your work team will be immediately able to switch to this new method of including everyone in deciding how work is accomplished. Perceptions will need to changed, trust in the new system will need to be established, and training in assertiveness, group problem solving, and decision making will need to be provided.

Some organizations even have self-managed work units that have a great deal of autonomy in carrying out their functions. The supervisor's role then becomes one of facilitator and coach, guiding the unit rather than imposing controls.

Being a leader as well as a supervisor

As a supervisor you have what is called the formal authority that goes with your position—the authority that is assigned to you by your organization.

You probably also have the authority which is based on your knowledge of what is done in your work unit—the authority of an expert. When something technical has to be decided, people tend to accept the judgment of the person they believe knows more about the matter than they do. Chances are, then, that workers in your unit look to you when difficult technical questions come up.

It is not necessary, of course, for a supervisor to have authority as the expert in every situation. If, for example, a complicated piece of equipment breaks down you might consult one of your workers who is an expert mechanic. You are likely to accept this worker's judgment about whether the machine should be repaired or replaced because you respect his or her superior knowledge.

It may surprise you to know that it is not enough to be a supervisor and to be expert in your line of work. It is not enough to have formal authority and the authority of the expert.

An effective work group has team spirit and a sense of belonging, so that the whole is greater than the sum of its parts.

If you are going to be an effective supervisor you must also have leadership authority.

If formal authority comes from management, we can say that leadership authority comes from the workers. Workers have to accept the fact that you are the supervisor. However, they do not have to accept you as their leader as well. You must *earn* their acceptance as their leader.

Workers select their own leader, who may or may not be the supervisor of their work unit. Once they have selected the leader they follow this person willingly, not because management has told them to do so. A supervisor who has not earned leadership authority will find that workers have assigned leadership to someone else. In many instances they will then follow the instructions of this leader rather than those of their supervisor. This can be a source of problems for the supervisor and for the local government in union and management relations when the employees are unionized.

It is difficult to get early warning signals of trouble from workers unless you have earned their acceptance and respect. There is no way of building a true work team if you have not earned the position of leader. (The art of leadership is discussed in the next chapter.)

Making jobs more interesting and rewarding

One of the more important skills a supervisor needs is the ability to redesign jobs in order to make them more interesting and challenging for workers. Many of us make the mistake of assuming that more money is what workers want most from their jobs. Yet time and again research has shown that this is simply not so.

A study in the early 1970s—one of the largest of its kind ever made—found that workers rank interesting work as the most important among twenty-five factors associated with work.

Over the past forty years more than a hundred other studies have shown that workers also want to have more control over their work. Employees today—especially younger ones—rebel against work that is monotonous or meaningless. They want to feel that they are important and that the work they do is important. They resent being supervised too closely, or being pushed and threatened.

In short, employees want more authority to tackle their jobs on their own, more information to enable them to do their work better, and greater opportunities for developing new skills or special abilities.

The time and effort a supervisor puts into enriching or redesigning his or her employees' jobs is likely to become visible in better employee attitude and morale, higher production, better work quality, lower turnover, and less absenteeism. Here are two examples of what job enrichment can accomplish.

Maintenance workers in one organization were not getting the buildings clean. In addition, the employee turnover rate was 100 percent every three months. In other words, four people had to be hired each year to keep one job filled!

Management learned from the workers that the problems were that the work was boring and that the workers had no say about how the work should be done. The solution was to enrich the workers' jobs by giving them more authority, more responsibility, and less supervision. Each worker was given a voice in planning work, setting goals, scheduling work, and figuring out how best to get the job done.

The result? The turnover rate dropped from 100 percent every three months to 10 percent. Building cleanliness increased by 20 percent. Sixty percent of the original workers were able to do the entire job, so that fewer workers had to be hired to replace those who left. And, finally, the organization saved $103,000 a year.

In another organization clerical staff were copying form letters day after day in routine answers to letters received. These form letters were then proofed and signed by the supervisor. Turnover and absenteeism were high because the work was boring, offering neither challenge nor satisfaction. Management decided to allow clerical staff to compose their own answers to the letters and also to proof and sign them. After this change was made, turnover was practically eliminated and absenteeism decreased by 30 percent.

One excellent way to make jobs more interesting is to *cross-train* your work team members. Let them learn how to do each other's jobs. As the supervisor, you can train them in the new skills that are required. Or, better yet, you can make the work of your team members even more interesting by having them cross-train each other. That way each has the chance to be a trainer as well as to learn a new skill. Cross-training also provides backup for your work team. If a team member is sick or absent, other team members can do that worker's job. One or another can fill in until the absent member returns to the team.

Coaching workers to improve their skills

In sports, a great team often is made up of players of average ability who become outstanding because of excellent coaching. Similarly, supervisors must coach workers of average ability to do above average work. If supervisors challenge their workers and help them gain the skills they need, most workers will surprise themselves with how well they can do the job.

Good coaching requires that workers have an agreed-upon work plan and positive, continuous feedback from supervisors. Positive feedback means that supervisors should praise both good work and improved work, in addition to helping correct mistakes. Instead of giving negative criticism, supervisors should show employees how to avoid and correct errors and how to learn from these errors.

Providing continuous feedback means giving workers frequent readings on how well they are doing individually and how well the team as a whole is progressing.

Giving each employee a performance evaluation at the end of the year by just filling out the required form is not very useful or constructive. This approach is like sitting in judgment on the worker—a report card rather than a joint learning process involving both the worker and the supervisor, or a way of developing the potential of the employee.

Checklist

Anticipate problems: try to identify problems that are just developing so that you can solve them early on.

Set clear goals for your work group: better yet, encourage your workers to help you set clear goals for the group. Try to ensure that organizational goals and employees' personal goals are combined and blended.

Build and maintain a work team.

Delegate work-related authority while retaining your supervisory authority.

Be a leader, not a boss.

Accept your responsibility as a supervisor for making jobs more interesting and challenging.

Be a developer, not a judge, of employees.

Supervisory situation 3/1

Roy was forty-two years old, had a high school education, and had worked for the city as the foreman of the sanitation division for fifteen years. Roy was trained under a system in which the city hired "garbage men" who rode the backs of trucks, who sometimes missed work on Mondays, and who usually quit after a relatively short time.

For many years the sanitation crews had not done an effective job of picking up the city's refuse. There had long been a steady stream of citizen complaints about garbage scattered over driveways and on the streets, and about missed collections.

However, with the election of a new mayor and the appointment of a professionally trained public works director, efforts were begun to improve the situation.

Experienced in the old system, Roy was unprepared for the new techniques brought in by the new public works director. At a meeting with Roy the new director startled him with a list of suggested changes that ranged from new titles for sanitation workers, to curbside pickup trucks with special lifts, to new training programs for all sanitation employees.

The director closed the meeting by saying: "We can't afford the turnover in personnel. We can't afford the reckless use of equipment. We can't afford the dead-end nature of these collectors' jobs. We must make them feel that they have an important role to play in our city. I can do some things to help, but there are a number of things you must do."

1. *What should Roy do to improve the management of the division?*

Supervisory situation 3/2

Al is a supervisor in the vehicle maintenance division. He has always developed his unit's annual work plan. Recently, however, the city manager has directed that work plans be developed by all members of work units as a team project.

Al is a self-starter and puts a great deal of energy into his work. In the past he has performed all the planning and scheduling for his work unit. He feels that if you want a job well done you have to do it yourself.

Al's supervisory style tends to favor one-to-one encounters with members of his unit. He reluctantly holds crew meetings once or twice every two or three months. He does not want to waste everyone's time talking and strongly feels that if he wants something done he should just give directions to an employee who can perform the task.

No one seems to interact much in his shop. Employees punch their time clock each morning, go right to their work stations, and begin to do their work. Al encourages his crew members to work quietly by themselves because they can concentrate without being distracted by unnecessary talk. Even at break time his crew does not get together as Al has scheduled everyone for different break times.

Al is not at all sure his work unit will be able to work well together on developing a work plan. He has always assigned the work and usually gives the same assignments to the same people. "That way, everybody gets good at one job," he maintains.

1. *What advice would you give Al about how to help his work unit begin the planning process?*

2. *How would a written vision, guiding principles, and mission statement help Al's work unit work more effectively as a team?*

LEADERSHIP

*When the best leader's work
is done, the people say,
"We did it ourselves!"*

Lao-tzu

LEADERSHIP

In the preceding chapter it was recommended that a supervisor try to become the leader of a team rather than merely being the person in charge of a group of workers. The point was also made that the authority a leader possesses comes from the workers themselves. When they become willing followers, the workers individually give their consent for a particular person to lead them. They might consent to follow the leadership of their supervisor—or they might select someone else. This person could be another member of the work group or someone who frequently relates to the membership of the group. When the workers follow the lead of someone other than their own supervisor, it works against that supervisor's authority and effectiveness.

This chapter discusses the art of leadership, describing how effective leaders behave, what skills they possess, and what a supervisor needs to learn and practice to become a more effective leader.

What is leadership?

One definition is that a leader is a person who shares a vision with a group of people, articulates the vision so that everyone understands it, and shows the group how to make that vision come true. For example, Franklin Roosevelt was a leader who articulated for his followers the fear that they were feeling and showed them specific ways to overcome that fear in order to prevail during World War II. During the late 1950s and 1960s, Martin Luther King, Jr., articulated the thoughts and feelings of people of color and showed them constructive, nonviolent ways to overcome discrimination and segregation.

Front-line supervisors are called upon to be leaders of their teams. While supervisory work is less dramatic than the work of either Roosevelt or King, the effective supervisor can lead his or her team in ways that can have profound impact on the quality of the team's work life and productivity. The supervisor practices leadership in a variety of ways. He or she

- Forms a team from a group of individual workers

- Articulates the vision and goals of the team

- Provides ample opportunity for the team members to develop the skills necessary to achieve their vision and goals

- Provides opportunity for the team members to exert power and influence over the way their work is performed.

Some management experts believe a person is born with certain personality traits and abilities that make him or her a "natural" leader—the kind of individual that people admire, trust, and want to follow. Others believe that leadership depends on the situation. Such experts believe that while Franklin Roosevelt could lead the country out of a deep economic depression and successfully through most of a world war, he probably would not have been as effective on the battlefield. And while George Patton was an effective leader in battle, he probably would not have been as effective as the nation's president. Still other experts believe that both personality and situation are important factors in leadership.

Many managers wish that the experts could agree on what effective leadership is and which leadership style is "best." Unfortunately, leadership is not that simple. Because humans are so complex and so different from one another, even the experts have a hard time deciding what style of leadership works best in a particular situation.

The fact is that a supervisor may lead well under certain conditions and not so well under others. Factors beyond differences in the supervisory situation itself can influence how effectively a supervisor is able to lead. One influencing factor is the maturity of the work group. Some work groups are more capable than others in setting challenging yet attainable goals. Some are more willing than others to assume responsibility for their own actions.

In addition, work groups obviously vary in the level of member skill and experience.

Another influencing factor is the intensity of pressure or stress under which a work group is operating. In a situation involving high stress the work group may need and expect the leader to provide quick relief. Quite another leadership style may be the most appropriate when stress is not a critical element in the situation.

But while it may not be possible to outline one formula for how to be an effective leader in each and every supervisory situation, certain fundamentals about leadership are well established. A leader *leads*. A leader leads *willing* followers. And a leader leads in a *situation*—at work, on the battlefield, etc. Let us look at these elements as they relate to the supervisor's responsibilities.

Leaders and teams

A leader can lead only by being "out in front" of the followers. This does not mean that a leader is always on the scene and is always more active personally than any of the followers. But a leader has a vision of what is needed, of what is possible, and of how to go about it.

A supervisor can be out in front of his or her work team in terms of ideas, as well as through the employment of proper supervisory practices, for example:

■ By seeing opportunities that others do not see

■ By identifying problems that are just developing and that team members do not realize are taking form

■ By carrying out good planning so that there will be few, if any, crises or unpleasant surprises for team members and many rewarding and unexpected accomplishments for them.

The familiar saying "You can lead a horse to water, but you can't make it drink" is an excellent illustration here. A supervisor leads his or her work team by helping members to work willingly and cooperatively toward agreed-upon goals. The important point is that the team is willing. Tough, driving, self-serving, and inconsiderate supervisors can get their employees to work—but only up to a point. Workers may do what they are told to do when the supervisor is around, but when he or she is not around they will ease off. When, temporarily, they have had enough of their supervisor's pushing and driving, they may not come to work for a day or two. And when, finally, they have had their fill of not being treated as human beings they may file a grievance through their organization's grievance procedure or even through their state's human rights commission. Or they may quit their jobs altogether.

A leader is able to gain and hold the loyalty of the workers so that they become willing followers. Loyalty is *earned* by a supervisor's actions. It cannot be demanded by a supervisor's rank or commanded by supervisory authority. It should be borne in mind that even when workers are unionized, a supervisor who is respected and trusted as a leader will be able to work effectively and cooperatively with the employees and their union representatives.

The supervisor who recognizes that each employee is a distinctive individual with his or her own needs, personal likes and dislikes, strengths and weaknesses, and hopes and dreams has already taken the first large step toward earning the loyalty of those employees. And the supervisor should be able to maintain leadership if he or she, out of a genuine interest in employees as individuals and through the use of correct supervisory practices, leads employees toward satisfaction of their needs and helps them to become what they can and want to become.

Situations and decisions

The situation surrounding each decision a supervisor must make is unique. Each situation has three elements that require sensitive consideration. These three elements are (1) the nature of the problem requiring a supervisory decision, (2) the nature and mood of the employees in the work group at the time, and (3) the way decisions are made.

The nature of the problem

When considering a problem that requires a decision, a supervisor should carefully examine three aspects of that problem that are directly related to gaining and maintaining leadership. The first aspect is the amount of information the supervisor possesses. Here you should ask yourself: Do I have the technical knowledge and all the facts required to make a sound decision, or do I need to obtain additional information or consult with others? If I need additional information, who has the knowledge or facts I require?

A second aspect concerns the efficient use of time. Here the question a supervisor should ask himself or herself is: How quickly do I need to act? In emergencies when time is very important, you probably will want to decide quickly. But when time is not a critical factor, you may wish to make the decision using a different approach in order to gain long-term leadership benefits.

The third aspect to be examined is the importance of the decision to the workers. You will want to ask yourself: Will the solution to the problem have important consequences for the members of the work group? If you believe it will, you should consult with your work team members before deciding.

Understanding the nature of the problem needing a supervisory decision is very important in making *correct* decisions. Poor understanding leads to wrong decisions; and supervisors who make many wrong decisions will have trouble convincing others to follow them.

The nature and mood of the employees

A second important element in the making of supervisory decisions is an understanding of and sensitivity to the work group and its individual members, especially an accurate sensing of the mood of the group at the time for decision. Understanding your employees is an ongoing process. It involves knowing their individual needs and abilities and keeping track of their skills development and the degree of teamwork shown. Sensing involves accurately gauging the group's current attitude, morale, and level of motivation, fatigue, and stress. If, for example, your team members are skilled and experienced, are functioning well as a team, have not been under any unusual pressures, and have trust in you and confidence in your decision making, involving them in every decision is unnecessary and can be inefficient. However, if your workers are not overly skilled or experienced, have not been functioning as a team, have been under some pressure recently, or perhaps do not trust management entirely, involving them in decision making to a substantial degree might be a desirable way of improving relations and increasing productivity.

The way decisions are made

When you have considered the nature of the problem and have carefully read the mood and current organizational needs of your workers and of the work group, you are in a position to choose the way you should proceed:

The *tell/sell/test/consult/join* model is a very helpful tool for a supervisor at this point. If you, the supervisor, have the necessary skill and information to make the decision and your sensing of the mood of your work team sug-

A leader visualizes opportunities, identifies problems, plans for the situation, and leads willing team members.

gests this is a proper way to decide, then *tell* your group what should be done and perhaps even how it should be done as well. This is an efficient way to use your supervisory time. It is also an especially appropriate way to make decisions in emergency situations or when your workers are operating under high stress.

If you have the necessary skill and information to make the required decision yourself but believe that your work group members might not understand your decision and might not fully support it, then you may need to *sell* your decision to your work team. Explain why you decided as you did and strive to convince them that it was the proper decision to make under the circumstances. When they understand all the facts, they probably will support your decision. Sometimes you may want to sell to your work team a decision you plan to make, so that the members will understand your decision and support it when it is made.

If you feel the need to *test* some or all of your alternatives before making a decision, you may wish to use some members or all of your work team as a sounding board to get suggestions and reactions to the choices you are considering. You may actually undertake a trial run of a new way of doing the job or a new technique to see how well it works.

When you don't have all the technical knowledge or facts necessary to make a correct decision, then you will want to *consult* with some or all members of your work team or with your supervisor or others who have the knowledge or information you need and who can advise you on the best way to proceed.

And there are many, many situations in which the best way to decide is to *join* with your work team members, allowing them to participate fully with you in making the decision.

Knowing when to decide by yourself and when and to what degree to share decision making with your employees is very important in the earning and holding of leadership. A good rule to follow is to involve them in the decision-making process if you possibly can if the decision is going to affect the workers directly—for example, by adding to the work they do, by changing the work they do or the way they do it, by making them feel less secure, by requiring them to stretch their skills and abilities, or by affecting their pay, benefits, or free time. Giving the workers a voice in deciding those things that affect them directly and personally will help win their willingness to cooperate with you in the decision that is made. It is important not only to make correct decisions, but also to make them in the proper way.

Characteristics of the leader–supervisor

Supervisors who are truly leaders differ from other supervisors in four important ways. First, supervisors who are leaders have a personal and active attitude toward goals. They have a strong vision of what could be and should be and are able to pass this on to others.

Supervisors who are not leaders tend to have a passive attitude toward goals. They may see goals as necessary because the organization requires goals. They do not see them as a means toward a *desired* end.

Second, leaders are willing to take some risks—carefully considered risks—in order to reach a desired end. Ordinary supervisors tend to do things by the book.

Third, leaders inspire others and enable others to identify with them, to become "committed to the cause," whereas ordinary supervisors merely *work with* people in a decision-making process.

Fourth, leaders try to change or improve those things that need to be changed or improved, while ordinary supervisors see themselves as regulators of the status quo.

Leadership attitudes

The style of leadership that a supervisor uses is the product of that supervisor's attitudes and assumptions about people, about their competence, and about how to get work done. Some supervisors believe that being interested in getting work done and being interested in people are contradictory concepts.

Therefore, some supervisors focus their attention and effort on production alone. These supervisors tend to view workers as mere tools for getting the job done. They tend to believe that if they had "better" people they could get

Employees should not be involved in every supervisory decision.

more and better work done. They are the tough, driving "bosses."

Then there are other supervisors (and these also believe that concern with work and concern with people are in conflict) who assume that *all* people are dedicated and hardworking and that the supervisor's task is to take care of employees and to try to keep them happy. They focus their supervisory attention and effort on creating and maintaining a "happy family" relationship among their subordinates. This type is the "sweetheart" supervisor.

Still other supervisors (who also believe concern for work and concern for people are contradictory) personally have a low level of motivation, or do not think of themselves as supervisors at all, but rather as more experienced police officers, or firefighters, or accountants, perhaps. This type tends not to focus attention and effort either on production or on people. This person is the "indifferent" supervisor.

Still other supervisors, while believing that concern for work and concern for people are in conflict, try to balance the two. They try to find a compromise between the organization's needs and those of the workers. These "balancer" supervisors may attempt to spend half their time on work and the other half on people. Some supervisors of this type manage "by crisis." They focus on production when the work is behind schedule or when there are no obvious serious problems involving people. But as soon as they believe that significant problems are developing with people, they tend to forget about work responsibilities and to concentrate on people. While they are doing this the work may again fall behind, thereby producing another crisis.

The effective *leader–supervisor* does not see a conflict between work and people. He or she does not believe that workers are lazy and must therefore be pushed and driven. Nor does this type of supervisor believe that everyone will work hard if the supervisor leaves them alone, or makes them happy. Effective leader–supervisors think that it is possible to blend concern for work and concern for people. They feel that if work is made more interesting and meaningful, and if workers can satisfy their own personal needs through work, then a lot of high-quality work will be done because the workers *want* to do it and gain satisfaction from doing it.

Leadership behaviors

A supervisor's attitudes and assumptions about people and how best to get work done influence how that supervisor will behave when planning or attempting to get work done. These same attitudes and assumptions influence the way in which a supervisor evaluates how well a job is done or how well a worker is performing.

Planning the work

Tough, driving "bosses" do the planning themselves and typically do not involve their workers. They tend to use personal standards in making planning decisions, such as, "That's the way *I* want it," or, "You'll do it that way because that's the way *I* like it done."

"Sweetheart" supervisors usually do not plan unless the work group wants to, and then only because it will make the workers happy.

"Indifferent" supervisors tend to use "how we've always done it" or the organization manual as the basis of planning. In that way they avoid investing much of themselves in this supervisory function.

"Balancer" supervisors tend to do the planning themselves until it is *time* to be concerned with people. Then they may share the planning with their workers.

Effective leader–supervisors strive to involve their team members in planning—especially in those areas where the members' personal interests and concerns are strong. They encourage participation, to gain a higher level of commitment from the team members and because they truly believe that "many heads are better than one."

Getting the work done

As with the planning function, a supervisor's attitudes and assumptions about the nature and competence of people influence how that supervisor will behave in attempting to get tasks accomplished.

Your leadership style says a great deal about your perceptions of people.

Tough, driving "bosses," since they believe that workers are lazy and are attempting to avoid work, will try to be at the work scene as much as possible, personally providing step-by-step direction to the workers. The underlying supervisory attitude here is perhaps best expressed in the following two statements: "As soon as you turn your head, they'll goof off on you," and, "If you're not right on top of things every minute, they'll goof up and do it all wrong."

"Sweetheart" supervisors frequently provide no direction to the workers. They concern themselves more with supporting their workers—maintaining their morale and answering their technical questions. A "sweetheart" supervisor might be concerned primarily with making sure a street-paving crew has cold drinking water at the work site or with breaking off work early if the day has been exceptionally hot.

The "indifferent" supervisor tends to tell the workers what needs to be done and how, and then to avoid further contact with the work and workers unless a problem arises.

"Balancer" supervisors tend to tell the workers what needs to be done and how. They usually then advise them that if any problems develop they should let the supervisor know immediately. If work is running behind schedule such a supervisor may spend more time on the scene and may behave more like the tough, driving "boss." When things are going well

again this supervisor may spend some time "mending fences" with workers.

The effective leader–supervisor tries to function as a member of the team while the work is being done. He or she does this not by doing work along with the others but rather by providing such special skills and knowledge as he or she may have and by promoting teamwork.

One skill quite useful to the leader–supervisor in getting more work done willingly and well is the *art of delegation*. Less effective supervisors either do not delegate at all or go to the other extreme and give up their supervisory authority, allowing the workers to take charge. The supervisor who does not or cannot delegate ends up trying to do everything personally—planning, deciding how things should be done, directing and controlling employees as they do the work, checking up on the quality of performance, and so on.

We all have limits as to how far we can push ourselves. There are, after all, only so many hours in a day. And a supervisor cannot be in more than one place at a time. Therefore, the supervisor who does not delegate places severe limits on how much can be done. And the supervisor who cannot tell the difference between delegation and abandonment of supervisory authority will lose control of the situation and the work group.

True delegation by a supervisor involves giving the "how to do it" authority to the work team as a whole or to those team members who

have the necessary job skills and experience and whose attitude toward the organization is positive. If a member does not have sufficient skill or experience to be entrusted with the authority to decide how—that is, by what methods—the work should be done, then the supervisor needs to work with that person to increase his or her skills and experience. And when there is a team member whose attitude may be less than that desired, the supervisor should relate to and work with that employee to help him or her develop a more positive attitude.

All team members need to receive adequate training and coaching to increase the entire team's ability to decide how work should be done.

What a supervisor *should not* delegate is the authority he or she has in relation to the whole team. And, of course, a supervisor *can never delegate* the responsibility for the team that has been assigned by the organization and accountability for the team's attitude, morale, performance, and work behavior.

A helpful rule to follow with regard to proper delegation is "Keep your hands *on* the work situation, not *in* it."

Evaluating individual and group effort and performance

Again, what a supervisor believes about employees and how best to handle work and people will influence how that supervisor evaluates performance.

Tough, driving "bosses" tend to fix their attention on mistakes. They look for things that are wrong, often overlooking those things that are done well. When they find a mistake they criticize the person who made it. Often they suggest a penalty that will be forthcoming if the mistake is repeated. Some genuinely believe they are developing competence and maturity in their workers, although their usual attitude is "The tool is not working properly; therefore, fix it so that it won't break down again." This type of supervisor usually provides only negative feedback.

"Sweetheart" supervisors tend to say nothing if they cannot pay a compliment. They have the following attitude: "We're all human and make mistakes, so let's forget it and get on with the work." This style of supervisor tends to provide only positive feedback to employees.

"Indifferent" supervisors usually provide no feedback at all unless they are required to do so by the organization. Then, typically, they merely fill out the required performance evaluation form. Usually, when filling out such a form, they rate employees in the middle of the range. They feel that in this way they will not get in trouble with upper management by scoring too high or with their workers by scoring too low.

"Balancer" supervisors focus on both successes and mistakes, trying to offset a criticism with a compliment. Preceding criticism with a compliment, however, causes a worker to question the sincerity of the compliment. Frequently, such supervisors practice the technique of criticizing in private and complimenting in the group setting.

Effective leader–supervisors provide feedback continually. When things are going well the supervisor and the team members together discuss how and why this is so. When things are not going well they discuss how to set them right. When an individual is not doing things properly, the supervisor and the employee get together to plan what needs to be done to correct matters. The leader–supervisor wants to develop people as a means of improving the work and to assist individuals in improving themselves. This type of approach enables the supervisor to increase the skills and abilities of the team members and to develop the capabilities of the team as a whole.

The leader thinks beyond the current ways of doing things. A creative supervisor wants not only to ensure that tasks are accomplished according to the current prescribed rules but to try to "think outside the boxes" to devise other methods of delivering services in order to achieve the highest standard of quality.

One of the ways you can enhance your creativity and that of your team is to benchmark your activities. Benchmarking is a method for identifying the best practices for a particular activity that can lead to changes and improvements in the way you deliver your service. By discovering how outstanding organizations perform their operations or deliver specific services, you can establish new or revised standards for achieving excellence.

The benchmarking process involves these key steps:

■ Identifying organizations that are known to have outstanding practices in the area you are interested in analyzing

■ Collecting data on the exact practices and procedures to be used as benchmarks

■ Noting the differences between how your work is performed and the best practices you have identified

■ Developing improvement goals with your work team

■ Implementing changes in your work processes

■ Monitoring and evaluating the results with your team

■ Continuing to benchmark.

Together, the attitudes and assumptions about people and the behaviors a supervisor demonstrates on the job add up to a supervisor's leadership style.

The most successful and respected supervisors follow rules that say, in effect, "Treat people like adults," "Respect employees as the unique individuals they are," "Develop your team members into truly outstanding individuals and workers," "Coach your people into becoming a winning team and winners as individuals."

Remember that the key elements in achieving excellence in a work team are *trusting, respecting, developing*, and *coaching*.

And if you, the supervisor, behave like a highly effective leader–supervisor, you

- Show that you value your people just as highly as you value your production goals

- Are honest in your relations with people

- Are open and truly listen

- Encourage input and participation

- Are sensitive to the needs and feelings of your team members.

If you do these things, then the work team will have pride, will be highly productive, and will do excellent work.

Checklist

Evaluate your leadership style regularly. Try to judge whether your workers would "elect" you as their supervisor if they had the chance. If you think they might not, ask yourself why.

Help your work unit draw a mental picture of what it would like to do and become in the future.

Avoid always using the same decision-making approach—for example, making most of the decisions yourself. Let the situation determine which approach is best.

Develop an accurate understanding of your workers' needs, desires, and concerns, and an accurate sense of your work group's current mood and why it is such.

Remember not to prejudge your workers. Ask yourself what assumptions you tend to make about your workers. Are they correct assumptions?

Learn how leader–supervisors typically plan, work with team members to get work done, and evaluate how work is going, and then try to practice these approaches and techniques.

Become a facilitator. Keep your hands on the work and the work situation, but avoid getting into everything.

Learn to build trust and rapport among your work unit.

Show respect to each of your workers as unique individuals.

Supervisory situation 4/1

The wastewater treatment division of Shady Grove has traditionally had a high number of employee grievances. Morale is low, and the accident and absentee rates are high. Bill Johnson has been the division supervisor for over nineteen years. He has always maintained that his crew is lazy and that certain members of the crew should have been fired years ago. Bill's favorite saying is "If you want a job done well, do it yourself." He has been known on several occasions to jump into a trench, relieve the crew leader, and take over the project.

At 2:00 p.m. one recent afternoon, Bill instructed Chuck, a backhoe operator, to drive across town to backfill a small 3' x 5' trench that had been dug that morning for a sewer main repair. Chuck resisted the assignment unless Bill approved overtime for the work, since Chuck's workday ended at 3:00 p.m. Bill refused to consider any overtime since he felt that the assignment should not take more than 45 minutes to complete, including travel time.

Chuck finally went to the assignment and returned to the shop at 3:45 p.m. Bill angrily confronted Chuck when he arrived, accused him of taking much longer than necessary, and refused to pay any overtime. Chuck stomped out after telling Bill he would file a grievance.

When questioned about this incident, Bill's response was, "What do you expect? They'll do anything to start trouble."

1. *What type of a supervisor is Bill?*

2. *If you were to take over Bill Johnson's supervisory role, would you handle the crew differently from Bill? If so, how?*

3. *What are specific leadership skills that Bill could practice to help his unit function as a team?*

Supervisory situation 4/2

Barb has worked for the town of Baybury for eight years. After mastering a variety of jobs in the accounting department, she was promoted to a supervisory position six months ago. In her new position, Barb supervises six employees, all of whom used to be her peers. At first, she was awkward about her promotion and anxious that the employees would resent her for it. She downplayed her supervisory role by maintaining a friendly rapport and chipping in whenever help was needed. She emphasized team spirit and included her employees in the decision-making process—deciding priorities, delegating responsibilities, and establishing work rules.

The jobs she supervises require a lot of routine data entry and filing. Barb constantly looked for new ways to enhance the jobs and break up the monotony. She delegated some of her tasks that involved interacting with citizens, which she believed was the best part of working for the city. She made sure that the employees received training in customer relations so that they were readily able to handle their new responsibilities and so that they would be eligible for promotion or job enhancement. In time she got used to being the boss and used her new authority to correct problems that had frustrated her before her promotion.

She fought hard to get them the best equipment, the best job assignments, and the best benefits possible. She also allowed them to take longer breaks than was allowed by the department's rules.

The town of Baybury requires all new supervisors to have a performance review after six months. In preparing for this review, Barb noticed that her records indicated a steady decline in her work unit's productivity. In addition, there was a higher rate of absenteeism than ever before.

Last week, Barb overheard two of her employees discussing her behind her back. They complained that she was shifting her work and responsibilities onto them. She clearly wasn't ready for a promotion, they said; after all, she couldn't make a decision without their help. She was hurt. She had done everything that she could do for them, hadn't she?

1. *What type of leadership style was Barb employing?*

2. *What did Barb do right when assuming her new leadership position? What mistakes did she make?*

3. *Should Barb use her performance review to get assistance or advice from her supervisor? What help should she ask for?*

PLANNING
WORK AND TIME

*There is nothing so useless
as doing efficiently that which
should not be done at all.*

Peter F. Drucker

CHAPTER 5

PLANNING WORK AND TIME

You probably know a few supervisors who always look as though they had a tough day at work. Their employees either do the wrong things or do the right things the wrong way. These are often supervisors who will have everyone on overtime one day, and on the next day have almost nothing for their employees to do. The work in their units is all right sometimes and not good enough at other times. And it is often late. You can almost see them going home and arguing with their families, or spending half the evening trying to unwind.

And yet these supervisors may in fact have the same basic abilities as their more successful counterparts. Have you ever wondered why their days are so complicated and unproductive? Much of their problem may be not lack of basic ability but lack of planning—planning of both work and time.

Before you became a supervisor, you were responsible only for your own work. But now you are responsible for seeing to it that all the work assigned to your team is done on time and properly. A multiplier effect is working on you. Since you are now responsible for much more work, planning is more important than before. If you don't do a good job of planning for and with your work team a lot more can go wrong. Also, as supervisors, some of you are probably finding that because of interruptions and the demands made on you by other people, you often have less time than you need to do your job and do it well. And this may be causing you stress.

Good planning can help you stay on top of things, have more time to do those things you must and want to do, and reduce stress.

What is planning?

For supervisors, planning means deciding *what* must be done, *when*, and *by whom*. It also means scheduling your time and the time of your employees, as well as scheduling the use of equipment, materials, and everything else needed to get a job done well and on time. And it may involve changing the way work is done. Some supervisors plan in their heads and tell their employees about the plans in group meetings or by talking to individual workers. This may work well for some situations, especially if the planning is simple and the job is small.

In most cases, however, written plans work better. They cannot be forgotten, everyone can look at them from time to time, and everyone can see whether the work is moving along as it should.

Whether a supervisor develops written plans or not, good planning is a "state of mind." It is

Planning: what must be done...when...by whom...how.

based on a supervisor's recognition and acceptance of the fact that the clearer the idea one has of what one is trying to do, the greater the likelihood that it will get done. And good planning helps to clarify for everyone involved what needs to be done, in what order, by when, with what support, and by whom.

A good plan should have the following major parts:

▪ A clear statement of the specific goals to be accomplished and the order in which they are to be reached

▪ A step-by-step description of the tasks that must be done to reach these goals

▪ A schedule for the people, supplies, equipment, materials, and space needed to reach the goals

▪ A description of ways in which progress and results will be measured.

Studies have shown that good planning gets good results. Supervisors of teams that produce a great deal of work spend much more time on planning than do those whose work groups have low production rates. These same studies show that work teams with high production rates think of their supervisors as very good planners.

How is a plan made?

The main steps in making a plan are described in this section. They are stating goals, streamlining the work, listing tasks, scheduling resources, and checking on the progress of the work.

Step 1: Stating goals

Stating goals helps focus the attention of both the supervisor and the work team members on the specific projects and tasks they must accomplish together. Goal statements should answer these questions: What must be done? Where must it be done? By when must it be done?

To illustrate, think back to the goal statement used in Chapter 3: "Complete properly all curb and gutter work [*what* must be done] on the north side of the 1400 block of Oak Street [*where*] no later than 4:30 p.m. on Friday, 15 November [*when*]."

You also have to decide which goals are the most important, or which have to be reached before work can begin on others. Stating goals clearly, while setting their sequence or priority, is the first step in any effective work plan.

Good planning also means breaking a goal down into tasks, subtasks, and activities that must be performed in order to reach that goal. Supervisors and work team members should work together deciding how to schedule these steps and listing the order in which they should be done.

Step 2: Streamlining the work

Fast cars and planes are streamlined in design so that they can move forward using the least amount of energy possible. Perhaps your work can use streamlining, too. Is there anything that is done in your work unit that could be done more easily? With fewer steps? In less time? With less effort or fewer people or materials? How might the work be simplified? How might it be done more easily, cheaply, or efficiently?

Ask yourself—and ask your employees—the following questions at this stage:

▪ Which jobs or parts of jobs could we eliminate or simplify without harming the quality of the work?

▪ Which activities could be combined to save time, effort, materials, or space?

▪ How could we change the way work is done in order to improve efficiency? Could we change to a new or better machine? To more useful forms?

Step 3: Listing tasks, subtasks, and activities

Let us assume that you are supervisor of Fire Station No. 1 in Hometown, Ohio. You have been assigned the following goal: Reduce fire losses by $25,000 in the area served by your station during the next fiscal year. What *tasks* would be involved in accomplishing this goal?

Begin by writing them down. Many local governments have printed forms that supervisors may or must use to plan their work. If yours does not, you will probably invent your own after a while. In the meantime, a blank sheet of paper will do.

Your list of tasks might read like this:

▪ Increase inspection of homes in the neighborhood for fire hazards.

▪ Increase inspection of business properties in the neighborhood for fire risks and compliance with fire safety ordinances.

▪ Teach citizens in the neighborhood how to spot fire hazards, prevent fires, and report fires promptly and properly.

▪ Get more citizens involved in fire prevention and protection.

Most of the tasks you list will have to be broken down into a series of *subtasks*. For example, under the first task you might have the following subtasks:

▪ Assign station firefighters to inspect 10 percent more homes in the neighborhood.

▪ Provide an updated fire safety checklist for building and housing inspectors to use when they are inspecting.

▪ Give the police department a short list of home fire hazards. Arrange with police patrol officers to report any fire hazards they see in or around homes in the neighborhood in the course of their regular patrols.

▪ Prepare short lists of home fire hazards for garbage and trash collection crews to use to report any fire hazards they see while they are working.

▪ Ask school officials for permission to enroll interested students in a junior firefighting company. These students can report fire hazards they see in the neighborhood.

After listing these subtasks under the first task, do the same for the remaining tasks.

In carrying out the subtasks you have listed, you will probably need to break these down further into specific *activities*. Under the first subtask, for example, you might list the following activities:

■ Brief fire prevention personnel, coordinate the additional inspections, and get information and forms with which to make reports.

■ Identify neighborhood areas that are high fire risks.

■ Survey these high-risk areas.

■ Identify additional houses to be inspected.

■ Determine how many more personnel hours will be needed to conduct the additional inspections.

■ Check the effect of these extra inspections on the station's readiness to respond to fire alarms.

■ Schedule the dates and times of the additional inspections.

■ Check with the building inspector's office to make sure the extra inspections do not interfere with other inspections scheduled.

■ Schedule the station personnel who will do the inspections, making sure that the schedule fits in with duty hours, training time, and vacations.

■ Arrange to get any equipment that is needed.

■ Conduct the additional inspections as planned.

■ Follow up on inspections to see that hazards have been eliminated.

■ Report the results of inspections to the fire prevention bureau or to the officer in charge.

The same kind of activity list should be made for each subtask. Next, you should work out and assign beginning and completion dates for each activity and indicate who is responsible for carrying out each activity. When all this information is in place, the result is a plan of action.

Step 4: Scheduling resources

Now that your work plan is finished, you will need to schedule the time in which you plan to use the equipment and materials and even the

space to carry out that plan. But, most important, you must schedule the time of the people who will be doing the work. You must make sure that your employees are not expected to be in more than one place at a time, and that the work load is evenly divided.

While you cannot always avoid conflicts with employees' personal plans, it is a good idea to talk to each employee before scheduling his or her time so that such conflicts come as infrequently as possible. Make every effort to resolve conflicts, but keep in mind (and remind your employees) that your first responsibility is to get the work done.

The staffing schedule is a key item in your scheduling of resources. Like a work plan, a staffing schedule needs no special form, although some governments provide them or

M	T	W	Th	F
Task A				
Subtask 1		Subtask 2		
Activity 1a	Activity 1b	Activity 2a	Activity 2b	

M	T	W	Th	F
Task B				
Subtask 1		Subtask 2		
Activity 1a	Activity 1b	Activity 2a	Activity 2b	

Float Time ▨

Work planning starts with a goal that is broken down into tasks, subtasks, and activities that are scheduled by working days. Do not forget to allow for float time.

insist on them. First, list workers' names alphabetically down the left side of a sheet of paper. List the working days, for one week or more, across the top of the page. Be sure you include the month and date along with the day of the week.

When you schedule a worker for an activity that week, draw a dotted line opposite his or her name across those days on which the work will be done. (You can write the name of the activity on top of the dotted line to help you remember who is doing what.)

As the work gets done, show the progress of each job by making the dotted line solid. If the worker has worked two days and accomplished only what was planned for one day, mark only one day solid and extend your dotted line to allow more time.

This kind of chart (shown on this page) tells what each worker is assigned to do, how well the work is progressing, and when each worker will be available for new assignments. It also keeps you from assigning one person to do two jobs at the same time.

An equipment and materials schedule can be done exactly like the staffing schedule, by listing equipment and materials needed on the left side of the page. Show under the heading of days and dates when the equipment will be used and when the materials will arrive.

No matter how carefully work is planned, it is impossible to know when the unexpected will happen. Blizzards, flu epidemics, equipment breakdowns, and energy shortages are usually unpleasant surprises. But you can learn to expect the unexpected and to plan for it.

Experienced supervisors set aside a contingency day or two in the overall schedule to take care of unforeseen delays and complications. You should have enough float time to take care of the unexpected but not so much that your unit becomes inefficient.

Of course, emergencies such as fires, accidents, and tornadoes may need more than extra time on your schedule. You should know in advance what you and everyone else in your unit must do if such emergencies arise (especially those that are most likely to occur in your area) and train your workers always to be ready. Indeed, they should be able to handle all emergencies whether or not you are there. This is one sign of effective supervision.

Elected officials often allocate a larger share of a local government's limited monies to those units in which careful planning is reflected in goals, tasks, subtasks, and activities that have taken schedules and dollars into account. While supervisors will not make major decisions about the department's budget, they can make a worthwhile contribution to it. If the supervisor involves them in planning, workers can also contribute.

	Jan. 2 Mon.	Jan. 3 Tues.	Jan. 4 Wed.	Jan. 5 Thurs.	Jan. 6 Fri.	Jan. 7 Sat.
Brinkman					inspection follow-up	
Carozo		inspection				
Fine	in-service training—chemical fires					
McCann	vacation					
Phillips		inspection				
				writing reports		

This simple activity chart can show work progress as well as worker availability.

Step 5: Checking on the progress of work

An effective supervisor knows exactly where the work he or she is responsible for stands at any time. The secret of this lies in having a definite plan for checking *regularly* on the progress of work (Are we on schedule?), the accuracy and quality of work (Is the work being done right and done well?), and the need for training workers (Could any part of the operation be improved by teaching new skills?).

You have your work plan. People, materials, and equipment are scheduled, and you have helped your department head set up a realistic budget. Everything is moving along as it should. Or is it?

To find out, you should ask yourself the following questions at the end of each day. Make a chart, if you like, or simply list these points on a piece of paper as a reminder to yourself:

▪ Has all work scheduled for today been completed?

▪ What has to be carried over?

▪ Why does work have to be carried over?

▪ Will it be necessary to make changes in tomorrow's work schedule (or the whole week's schedule) to get today's unfinished work done?

▪ What changes should be made to avoid this delay in the future?

▪ Is all equipment operating properly?

▪ Did all the supplies come in as scheduled?

▪ Will there be any absences from work this week that were not in the plan?

▪ Has everything been done that I committed myself to do or check on today?

▪ What should I give special attention to tomorrow?

▪ Were there any tasks, subtasks, or activities completed today earlier than scheduled? How will this affect tomorrow's work?

With practice you will find that you can zip through this list at the end of the day in a few minutes, checking *every* item as a way of getting ready for the next day.

When you have finished your checklist you will know whether the work is on schedule and you are ready for tomorrow. And even if work is not on schedule you know what is wrong and what must be done to get back on track.

One thing to bear in mind is that effective supervisors check on the progress and quality of the *work*. They do not check on the workers themselves. Employees should feel that you trust them if you are going to earn their respect as a team leader.

Developing a procedures manual

Having a manual that outlines in detail the standard operating procedures for the major activities of your work teams can be a helpful planning tool.

A work procedures manual outlines the steps that are necessary to perform a given job productively and safely. A good manual identifies the standards and goals that have been established for specific jobs within an organizational unit or function. It then breaks down those jobs into major tasks and presents those tasks in the order in which they are to be performed.

The manual can provide a basis for goal setting, planning and scheduling jobs, and monitoring and evaluating work performance. By explicitly laying out job standards, as well as the methods to be used to achieve them, a work procedures manual can also be a valuable tool for re-evaluating existing procedures and standards.

Creating or updating a manual can be an excellent team project for your work unit. Select a lead person who has good writing and organizational skills and a good eye for detail. The rest of the work team can participate by providing information about how tasks are performed and by reviewing written drafts for accuracy and completeness. The work team can also help decide on the format and layout of the manual since members will be the primary users.

Finally, the work team can review the current work procedures to help determine which tasks can be changed or altered to meet certain criteria, such as making work processes more efficient, customer oriented, and safe.

Managing your time

The demand for more services and lower taxes is perennial for cities, towns, counties, and other local governments. You may feel there is never enough time or money to get any job done right—that you are always pushing harder and harder to meet deadlines, while more and more work is pouring in. And you may be right.

Although little can be done about the demand for services or the lack of funds, there is something you can do to lighten the load on yourself. You can learn to use your time more wisely and more effectively.

It may surprise you to know the results of some studies of the work that supervisors do. These studies show that most supervisors spend only about 20 percent of their time on the activities that produce 80 percent of the results. The rest of their time—80 percent of it—is spent on work that has little payoff. Think of how much could be accomplished, and how much wear and tear you could save yourself, if that 80 percent were used more productively.

To start, you might do the kind of work planning described earlier. State your goals clearly, and then put your time where your priorities are. Concentrate on doing those things that help your team get results and reach goals.

Identify your number-one priority and tackle that first. If you are procrastinating and putting off working on projects, it may be because a job looks too big to handle. If it's a large project, then break it into smaller parts. This will make it seem manageable and not quite so overwhelming.

Next, keep a log for one week to see exactly how you are using your time. Every hour write down what you did during that hour. After five days review your log carefully and ask yourself: Did I use my time in a way that helped my team to reach its goals? What kinds of time traps do I often fall into?

You might notice that you spend a lot of time talking on the phone. Or maybe a lot of your time is taken up by people who just drop by to chat.

Once you have pinpointed how your time is being used, you can take steps to save time. For example, if too many phone calls are too long, try jotting down the main points you want to discuss before you make a call. Be friendly on the phone, but businesslike. End the conversation when you have finished discussing what you planned to talk about. Do not go into social chitchat on the phone unless you believe that socializing will help your team achieve its goals. Avoid playing "telephone tag" by making phone appointments and marking them on your calendar just as you would for any meeting.

If you find that a lot of your time is taken up by people who drop by, then control this situation by *scheduling* your appointments. And when you cannot control the drop-in visitors, do not be afraid to tell some of them that you are sorry but you are very busy at the moment—that you can see them another time. Then *schedule* an appointment with them.

If the people who drop by are members of your own work team with questions or problems, it may mean that you are not using your supervisory time wisely. You may be spending too much time in your office or doing paperwork.

You might plan to visit more frequently where your team members are working. This technique of "management by walking around" may enable you to accomplish a number of things: You will be available to your team members if they have any questions or problems, so they won't find it as necessary to drop by your office with their inquiries or concerns. Perhaps you can do a little coaching or skills development, showing members of your team how and where to work "smarter" to produce better results with less effort. And very important, you may catch your people doing well so that you will be able to praise them and thus encourage them to do even better. If you can see how things are going; answer questions; help solve problems; and do some coaching, developing, and motivating—all in the same short period of time—you really are managing your time well.

Plan into your daily schedule some time for unexpected interruptions. Then, even if some of your time is taken up unexpectedly, you will still be able to accomplish the things you planned to do. It is also a good idea to schedule some time for "housecleaning" and getting yourself organized—time, that is, for cleaning your desk top, putting papers back in files, and organizing your own paperwork. If you allow for time to get things in place so that you can find them easily, you will save time whenever you need information.

A very popular time management tool is the notebook planner, which usually has daily, monthly, and yearly calendars, as well as to-do and appointment lists with specific time slots, and a telephone and address section. These booklets help keep all your important information and reminders in one place.

Increasingly, supervisors are relying on their desktop computer for scheduling and organizing their work day. Several computer software scheduling programs are available at a reasonable cost. One advantage of the computer scheduler is that it can be accessed both by yourself and, if you are on a computer network, by anyone else in the organization you choose—without anyone having to leave his or her desk. One rule of thumb when using a computer scheduler: keep it regularly updated and always have a hard copy back-up until the program is de-bugged to your satisfaction.

Finally, practice the art of delegating "how to do it" authority to your employees. Chapter 4, on leadership, discussed this in detail. Remember that you must invest time in training and developing workers so that they will be able to answer their own questions or the questions of others. If you find yourself spending a lot of time telling workers how and where to make the next move, you may want to reread Chapter 4 carefully.

If you are confident that you and your team have planned the work carefully and have made provisions for the unexpected; that the work is progressing in accordance with the plans; that your work team is developing steadily in competence and self-control; and that your team members are well motivated, you may find your supervisory responsibilities less stressful.

Checklist

Make your plan before work begins.

Remember that the purpose of planning is to get the results you want.

Remember that effective supervisors spend much more time planning than less effective supervisors do.

Be sure to start with a clear statement of goals.

Identify your top priority and accomplish that first.

Decide with your team what must be done, where, and when.

Try to simplify the work and avoid unnecessary steps.

Develop written work procedures that clarify your tasks, subtasks, and activities.

Schedule the basic elements needed to achieve your goals: people, equipment, materials, money, and space.

Plan for emergencies, and expect the unexpected.

Check regularly on the progress and quality of the work that is being done.

Manage your time by putting more of it into activities that will get multiple results.

Break up large projects into smaller, more easily managed parts.

Don't procrastinate.

Supervisory situation 5/1

Joan is known for her team-building skills as a supervisor in the personnel office. She has a facility for helping her employees cooperate with each other. They all work closely together under Joan's leadership. "We're family," they say. "We support each other and care about each other as if we were related."

Joan has four people in her work unit. Kathy, a twenty-four-year-old personnel analyst, has worked in the unit for the past two years. She assists administrative support departments, such as the legal and budget departments, with their personnel issues. Tim, thirty-three, is also an analyst. He is assigned to the fire, police, public works, building inspection, and parks and recreation departments. Tim has been a member of the team for six years. Greg, forty-two, is a senior personnel analyst who has been with the unit for six years. He assists Tim and Kathy with their work loads and is also responsible for assessing long-range personnel needs, updating the city's personnel manual, and coordinating labor negotiations with the labor relations and budget offices.

Joan has just informed her work team that they will be developing a strategic plan for the first time. "This is just one more project where we'll all have to put our heads together and work toward a common goal," Joan told her work team. "The city manager has instructed all departments and divisions to come up with a road map for their work units. Our responsibility, then, is to go through a strategic planning process and develop a three-year plan for our unit."

1. *What are the steps Joan's team is likely to follow in developing their strategic plan?*

2. *What role would you see Joan taking with her team during the planning process?*

Supervisory situation 5/2

As the supervisor of the data processing division, Donna has been struggling to increase the accuracy and productivity of her work unit. She has noticed a marked increase in errors whenever temporary or seasonal employees are hired to cover the vacation and sick leave of her regular employees.

Donna has decided not to hire outside help again, but to cover for absences herself or increase the workload of regular staff when vacations occur.

1. *What other problems may occur if Donna follows through with her proposed solution?*

2. *What are some ways Donna might alleviate her problem, without overburdening her staff?*

ORGANIZING
A TEAM

*It has been demonstrated
throughout human history that
most individuals can achieve more
of their goals or achieve them faster,
easier, more completely, or more
efficiently through organizations.*

Herbert G. Hicks

ORGANIZING A TEAM

Good organization is what it takes to make things work. It means that all parts or pieces have been put together so that the finished product functions smoothly and makes sense. This is true whether you are assembling a bicycle, a jigsaw puzzle, or a group of people in a work situation. That is why you need to know how to organize people in order to have the work done as effectively as possible.

First, you need to understand the different ways in which systems such as local governments are organized. This will show you what the alternatives are and will give you the advantages and disadvantages of each. Then you will have a better picture of how your work unit fits into the organization of your department, and how your department fits into the organization of the entire local government.

Second, you need to know something about the ways by which you can organize people in your unit into a team and how you can keep that team going. This information will help you become the kind of supervisor who can turn a group of individuals into a *team* of productive workers.

Formal vs. informal

As you know, any organizational chart shows how the people in an organization are supposed to work together—who is responsible for what, who reports to whom, and how each person is expected to relate to everyone else. It also shows how one unit is supposed to work with all the other units in the government or business.

This is called the *formal* organization. It tells us on paper what the chain of command is and what the areas of responsibility are. For example, your government may be formally organized into departments, which operate under a city or county manager. Each department may be run by a department head, and, according to this formal plan, you are shown as the supervisor of your work group.

While it is important for you to know and understand the formal organization of your unit, department, and government, it is equally important for you to know that another kind of organization also exists. This is called the *informal* organization, and it may be quite different from that shown on the organizational chart.

The problem, of course, is that you cannot really make people work together in a certain way by putting their names in boxes on a chart. People respond to other people for their own reasons: because they like or dislike them personally; because they go to the same church or bowl on the same team after work; or because they come from the same small town in Arizona.

You have probably seen this sort of thing happen many times. A local government, for example, hires as chief of police a person who was previously chief in another local government. The new chief brings into the department several officers from the other local government's police department. Because these newly hired officers have known and worked with the chief and each other earlier, they probably will be closer to and therefore more influential with their chief than will other officers of the same rank in the current department.

Thus the informal organization may have nothing to do with the worker's rank or the department he or she works in. And the grapevine, which is the communications system of the informal organization, may not be transmitting the same information as the formal newsletters and memos do.

How can a work unit function when these two very different organizations operate at the same time? The answer is given in the second part of this chapter, which talks about teamwork. In a well-managed local government, in which people work as a team, there will be very little difference between the formal and informal organizations—between the way things are and the way they are supposed to be. People work well together in their assigned roles in spite of their personal feelings and friendships.

We will return to that subject, but first let us consider some of the models of formal organizations and explore their advantages and drawbacks.

Types of organization

The major models of formal organization are

▪ Line organization, or chain of command, which is the simplest type

▪ Line and staff organization, which is similar but uses experts to advise line officials

▪ Functional organization, in which each of the organization's specialized functions has its own department headed up by an expert or specialist in that function

▪ Program or project organization, which calls for a different arrangement of personnel for each project that the organization works on

▪ Quality improvement organization, in which the organizational structure is a series of interlocking teams that follow a process to continually improve services.

Most local governments are organized using the functional model, with separate departments for fire, police, public works, personnel, finance, and so forth.

While a local government might be organized functionally, particular departments of that government might be organized using other models, for example, line and staff or quality improvement teams.

Line organization

Authority flows directly from the top in this military type of organization. People get their orders from those above them through a chain of command. Everyone at the same level of authority does approximately the same kind of work and has about the same amount of responsibility.

Because this organization plan is simple and direct it is often used by small police and fire departments. The person at the top has complete authority, and everyone else's authority and responsibility is spelled out clearly. A police sergeant has more authority and responsibility than a corporal and less than a lieutenant, for example. All lines of responsibility are clear-cut; therefore, discipline is relatively easy to maintain, there is little confusion about who does what, and orders can be carried out quickly.

But there are disadvantages. While the top person has the benefit of complete authority, this can be a tremendous burden because it means being an expert in all phases of the work—from personnel to purchasing. This means that key people are hard to find and are hard to replace when they leave. Also, communication between people and between departments is often difficult in line organizations because everyone is expected to go through formal channels.

People will not stay put on the organizational chart—the formal chart, that is. The real challenge is to bring the formal and informal organizations together.

For example, if you are at the lower level of one division and you want to pass along an idea to someone who is at the lower level of another division, officially the message is supposed to go up your chain, over to the other chain, and then down that chain of command, even if the person is sitting across the room from you.

So you must make the suggestion to your supervisor, who passes it up the line to the head of your division. The head of your division passes the idea on to the head of the other person's division, and it then goes down the chain of command until it reaches the person across the room. (The same process would be involved in coordinating the work of different units.) Of course, in actual operation informal or "unofficial" communication is frequently used to facilitate the passage of information through the organization.

Line and staff organization

This form of organization is different from line organization in only one respect: staff experts advise the person at the top. These advisers—whether they are personnel specialists or financial experts—have no line authority except in their own offices.

An advantage of this system is that it gives top management the help of experts in making difficult decisions. It is also more flexible, because the experts often communicate with people in the organization without going through the formal chain of command.

A disadvantage is that conflicts often arise between the advisers and the line officials. The personnel adviser may, for example, favor one policy while line officers favor another.

Functional organization

Specialized departments are set up in this type of organization, each headed by a specialist. In government, for example, these specialized departments might be fire, police, building and housing inspection, public works, finance, and personnel.

This form of organization works more efficiently than the line and staff method because the experts are not merely advisers, they are in the chain of command dealing directly with problems. But an important disadvantage is each department's tendency to think of itself as more important than the others, or to forget that it is part of the government as a whole.

Program or project organization

In this type of organization people are assigned to a project because of the particular skills they have, regardless of the department or unit of local government they happen to work in. Once the project is completed an entirely different set of people may be assembled to work on the next project.

Each project is headed by a different project director. While people are working on a particular project they report to that project director instead of to the director of their regular department.

This type of organization is usually used along with the line, line and staff, or functional types. It is particularly useful for special projects, such as construction projects not put out to bid, which may not fit under one particular department's responsibility but may require the services of several departments.

Quality improvement organization

As Chapter 2 mentions, the impact of the quality management movement has meant that organizations are increasingly looking to flatten their hierarchical structures. Increasingly, the newer team concept is replacing the traditional chain of command model. This shift in emphasis from experts at the top and workers at the bottom means that building and maintaining an effective team is more important than ever.

The quality improvement organizational structure is a series of interlocking teams. A quality improvement process is followed by all teams in which specific steps are taken to plan and implement program improvements. Improvement in production or service delivery made in one part of the organization becomes linked to other parts of the organization.

Quality improvement organizations focus on the customers (both internal and external) and how to satisfy them. Local government customers are in a unique position. They not only receive services through their tax dollars, but they are also often members of the team that delivers those services. By serving on city councils, citizen task forces, and boards and commissions, citizens can be an important part of the local government organization.

Of course, there is no hard and fast line between any of these different methods of organization. All of them can be useful in certain situations and most governments use some combination of them all. For instance, the local government itself might be functionally organized into specialized departments, while the fire and police departments might be organized on a line basis. The line and staff method might be used, for example, in the case of the city attorney advising the mayor.

Quality improvement teams may be used in certain program areas. For example, a city's safety program can be organized to include members of departmental safety teams, of work unit teams, and of a city-wide team having interlocking representation. It could work like this: A work unit safety team selects one or two of its members to serve on the departmental team, and the departmental safety team selects a representative to serve on the city-wide team. The city-wide safety program then reflects the ideas and innovations from the broadest spectrum of the organization.

Organizing for supervision

Many years ago a management expert tried an experiment in supervision. He realized that supervisors had a great many duties to perform—too many, perhaps—so he decided to make each supervisor a specialist in only *one* of the duties normally expected of a supervisor. One supervisor was in charge of seeing that the proper amount of work was done, another checked on the quality of the work, a third handled only record-keeping chores, and so on.

Needless to say it didn't work. After Supervisor A told a worker to speed up production, Supervisor B told her to slow down so that she could do a better job.

The management expert found that no person can serve two masters. It is a basic concept of life and of organization also. It means that each worker should have only one supervisor and that all supervisors should know which employees they are responsible for.

Of course, supervisors can do an effective job only if the number of employees they supervise is neither too large nor too small. Supervisors who are responsible for very large numbers of people can do little more than oversee—like the captain on the bridge watching the deckhands below.

On the other hand, supervisors who are responsible for only one or two people are likely to watch them too closely and not give them the freedom and responsibility they need. What, then, is the ideal number of workers for a supervisor? A number of management experts believe five to seven workers is about the right number for effective leadership, although this number may vary somewhat depending on the nature of the work being done, the physical separation of workers, and various other factors.

Many studies suggest that five to seven people is the natural size of a social group. Apparently that number of people can relate to each other often enough and closely enough to form meaningful relationships. Since natural social groups form the basis for a working team, this seems like a good size for a work group.

Supervisors who must manage more than about seven employees should consider appointing subleaders to help them, since, when more than seven people try to work together, subgroups and cliques begin to form anyway. If they are not formally organized, they may make it harder to keep the group together as a team.

Building a team

In most work situations you do not start out with a team. You start out with a group of individuals who are *supposed* to work with each other. That is what the formal organization chart says.

But the informal organization is there, too. What actually happens is that people spend most of their time with employees they like and avoid those persons they do not have much in common with. They form groups and personal friendships on the basis of age, sex, race, background, or interests. All the old-timers may be in one group, all the employees from a minority group in another, for example.

Your task in building a team will be to reduce the differences between the formal and informal organization as much as possible. Your job is to close the gap between what is and what should be, so that workers begin to talk about "us" or "our shop" instead of "my friend and I" or "we" and "the others."

People are more highly motivated to work toward common goals and objectives when they feel part of a team effort. The support that comes from team members is invaluable in helping individual members sustain interest in a project and in persevering through difficult times. Team members give each other a feeling of being valued for their participation. A genuine trust in each other and a feeling of not wanting to let each other down contribute to a team's effectiveness and productivity.

Groups, on the other hand, are a collection of individuals with no strong sense of responsibility to each other. There is little or no concern for the successful outcome of a project since there is no collaborative effort to accomplish common goals. In fact workers in the beginning stages of forming a group often do not necessarily feel they have much in common. A lack of unified effort and camaraderie marks a group as opposed to a team.

A group generally passes through four main stages on its way to becoming a team. This theory of group development was first advanced by B.W. Tuckman. Many groups do not proceed precisely through four stages in the exact sequence outlined by Tuckman and some groups may be in two stages at once. However, this theory does provide a good roadmap for the supervisor as to what to expect when work groups are formed:

■ *Forming* is the first stage, when members come together and are uncertain about the nature and role of the group. The completion of this stage is marked by members seeing themselves as part of the group.

■ *Storming* is the second stage of group formation and is marked by conflict, mainly over who will lead the group.

■ *Norming* is the third stage, characterized by cohesiveness and closeness among group members. The group has built its own value structure to govern behavior and members accept the norms or values of the group.

■ *Performing* is the fourth stage, when the group moves forward to accomplish its objective. If this stage is sustained through continuous cooperative activity, the group can be considered a team. The supervisor's role then becomes one of maintaining the energy level of the team and continuing to build team rapport.

How, then, do you build a close-knit, highly motivated, productive work team? Seven steps are outlined below.

Step 1: *Show workers where they fit into the system.*

Many people do not know what goes on beyond their desk or work area. It is helpful for them to see how they fit into the whole department or governmental operation so that they understand why things are done the way they are, why certain things must be done or cannot be done, and what authority you, the supervisor, do and do not have. It is also helpful for them to understand how working in a complex organization, while it has benefits, puts certain limits on each worker.

Step 2: *Hold frequent planning meetings with employees.*

Try to set aside about fifteen minutes every day or two—or at least once a week—for a meeting at which you can plan ahead and also discuss how things are going. It is important, however, to see that these meetings do not turn into fifteen-minute lectures from you. Those fifteen minutes belong to all team members, you included.

Be careful to see that the meetings do not waste time. Have an outline in mind for each meeting. Plan to talk about items that team members have suggested as well as items you yourself think are important. Some examples might be the following questions:

■ How are we progressing in getting our job done?

■ What problems are we facing?

■ What can we do as a team to solve those problems?

■ Is there anything bothering any of us? If so, what can we do as a team to work it out?

The informal organization (on the left) is built on personal ties of friends, neighborhoods, age groups, and similar interests that are separate from the objectives of the work group. Team building (on the right) helps bring the informal and formal organizations and their objectives together.

■ Is there anything the team leader can do to make the work better or easier for our team? To make the work more interesting or satisfying? Or to make the work situation more pleasant?

If any action needs to be taken as a result of these meetings, or if information is needed to clear up a problem, start the next meeting by telling team members what was done or what the team needed to know. Remember, however, that you should not run the meetings—you should merely guide them.

Step 3: Set goals with your workers.

All the employees in your unit should have some say about these questions: Where are we going? Why are we going there? What are the best ways for us to get there? It is your job to help your workers understand what specific goals must be reached by the team, and then to let *them* help *you* set other goals and find ways of reaching them.

Step 4: Encourage workers to suggest solutions to problems.

You are taking a big step toward gaining respect when you welcome suggestions, and an even bigger one when you welcome criticism and do not take it personally. Your employees will respond when you demonstrate that you want to make the work situation better and easier.

When an employee makes a suggestion, express your thanks even if the suggestion cannot be used. When an employee points out a problem, it is important not to be defensive and try to explain it away. Think about it. Investigate it. Above all, let the employee know you are checking it out and trying to change things for the better.

Then report back to the employee explaining what was done (or why nothing could be done) about the problem.

Step 5: Let workers tell you things you may not like to hear.

Just when the team seems to be coming together an employee may tell you something about you or the work situation that has been bottled up for some time. This may happen at a meeting or in a face-to-face conversation. If it happens, try to remember that in most cases it is better to get the facts out in the open than to have resentments and misunderstandings smoldering silently inside people.

Once the air has been cleared and members of the team have leveled with you and with each other, everyone can begin to deal with the situation and can arrive at a better understanding of it and of one another. And respect should grow from this understanding. They may not like one another any better, but respect and understanding are worth more than superficial friendship in a team.

Step 6: Let team members help set standards.

You cannot build or maintain a true team if some employees feel you play favorites or are unfair in any other way. If employees have a say in setting standards and in deciding how well workers are measuring up to those standards, complaints should be few and judgments should be fairer in your unit.

Allow team members to help you decide what the value of each member's contribution is or how good the performance of the team as a whole has been. And be sure that everyone has the team's goals in mind when these decisions are made.

Step 7: Be sensitive to diversity.

Supervising a diverse work team will require you to become familiar with different cultural backgrounds and to practice the motivation and communication techniques discussed in this book. You'll want to apply several approaches to managing diversity:

■ Communicate clearly. Avoid using slang common to your own culture.

■ Accept that people from different backgrounds also have valid perspectives.

■ Learn the nonverbal cues of the various cultures represented in your work unit.

■ Make sure that members of your work team also understand who you are and how your perspective may differ from that of members of your work team.

Value each of your employees as individuals who bring special talent and skills to your work team and the organization as a whole.

Empowering a team

A team is more likely to achieve its goals if team members feel that they have control over their work and the power to make decisions. Empowering team members to take responsible control of their work life requires the supervisor to recognize the importance of high self-esteem for each team member, relinquish a degree of decision-making power to the work team, and know what will motivate each individual member of the team.

One attribute that will determine the effectiveness of a work team is the self-esteem of its members. Self-esteem is the feeling one has about oneself. Someone who has high self-esteem feels good about himself or herself and is confident about his or her own abilities. A person with low self-esteem is not self-confident and is often self-consciously plagued with doubts and fears about his or her capabilities. A highly productive and effective work team has members who have by and large a positive regard for themselves as individuals. Teams with low productivity, besieged with performance problems, are likely to have a large portion of members who do not think well of themselves and consequently feel disempowered.

To build self-esteem among the work team requires that the supervisor know the personality characteristics of each team member and provide support for team member development through providing job growth, job enrichment, and mentoring.

Job growth. Providing for a career ladder within your work unit will enable those who have achieved success in their work to move forward to new challenges. The trick is to know when an employee is ready, willing, and able to try something new and then encourage him or her to do so.

Helping someone develop in order to take on additional responsibilities or new job tasks may not be something you can do all by yourself. Usually, the organization needs to provide a system (for example, through job classification, training, counseling, and education) that supports and encourages job growth. As a supervisor, however, you can have significant impact on your team's job growth by encouraging members to take advantage of the job development programs your organization has to offer, such as tuition reimbursement programs, and then giving them the opportunity to participate in these programs.

Job enrichment. Develop ways for members to fully participate in the way their jobs are structured and the decisions that are made on the job. Job enrichment means giving workers the opportunity to develop their skills and to use skills and talents that they may ordinarily use outside the job. For example, a worker skilled in photography may be called upon to take pictures of the work team for the annual team picture or to photograph specific steps in performing a task as illustrations for the work unit's procedures manual.

Mentoring. You can be of great help to your organization's work force by being a mentor to workers whom you believe to have real potential. You can also link up members of your team with other supervisors or managers in the organization who can serve as mentors. Mentors offer encouragement to members of the organization who can benefit from one-on-one support. Supervisors who serve as mentors can be good role models for those who have the motivation and capability of one day becoming supervisors themselves. Women and minorities can especially benefit from mentors since historically they have been excluded from the decision-making process.

An excellent tool for getting to know team members' personality characteristics and how they prefer to process information and make decisions is through self-evaluations such as the Myers-Briggs Type Indicator, the short form of which takes about a half-hour to administer. The results show individuals' personality type (for example, extrovert or introvert) and the communication style and social behaviors they prefer. This can be a great team-building exercise, since participants can better understand their own personality styles and how they may differ or be similar to their colleagues. This personality test builds employee self-awareness and also improves understanding among team members as to why other individuals think and act the way they do. Your local community college or a training consultant specializing in team building is likely to have someone knowledgeable who can administer the test.

Supervising a team

The right kind of supervision—that which involves a shared effort—encourages teamwork. One of your tasks as supervisor will be to take a long look at what you yourself are doing to create team spirit. What kind of supervisor are you? What kind of supervisor should you be? You might like to take another look at Chapter 4, which describes the different types of supervisors and the effects they can have on workers.

The good supervisor does not oversupervise, undersupervise, or treat workers like dependent children. Effective supervisors who are building a team are probably responding to workers in the following ways:

- Sharing decisions about planning and scheduling work with employees
- Encouraging workers to give their honest opinions and suggestions about the work
- Helping each member of the group to understand the work, to get personal satisfaction from doing it well, and to grow and develop on the job
- Recognizing and valuing diversity within their work team.

Under these circumstances, the group becomes a true team. More work is turned out. Members cooperate with each other and with other units of local government. They are capable, independent workers. They take responsibility for doing the work properly and for handling emergencies on their own.

Once you have reached this point you have successfully organized a working team. Your next job will be to keep this team together, to help it grow, and to help it turn out more and better work. This means leading your team—a very important function discussed in detail in Chapter 4.

Checklist

Understand the formal and the informal organizations in your department and in your work unit.

Check to see which of the major types of organization, or combinations of them (line, line-staff, functional, and project), are used in your local government and in your department and how they affect work in your unit.

Use the seven-step method for team building.

Show workers in your unit how all of you fit into the entire organization.

Work with your employees in planning, scheduling, and assigning work.

Always keep employees informed.

Encourage employees to give you their honest opinions and suggestions.

Work with individual employees to help them understand their work, gain satisfaction from doing it well, build self-esteem, and grow and develop on the job.

Practice a balanced style of supervision; do not oversupervise, undersupervise, or treat employees like dependent children.

Look for ways to make your work unit more democratic.

Become a mentor for someone in your organization who has potential and could benefit from one-on-one support.

Supervisory situation 6/1

Jack is a recent law school graduate and a newly hired attorney in a municipal law department. Brenda, the city attorney, has noticed that Jack keeps to himself and has not socialized with other members of the staff. Jack does not speak out at staff meetings and seems to be most comfortable working by himself.

Jack's work seems to be thoroughly researched and presented in a concise and detailed format; however, Brenda is uneasy with Jack's lack of sociability. She has overheard members of her staff talking about Jack as being unfriendly and stuck up. Brenda is now wondering whether she made a mistake in hiring Jack. She doesn't see him fitting into her team.

1. *What suggestions would you have for Brenda in dealing with Jack and the rest of her staff?*

2. *What specific management tools could Brenda use to help make Jack an accepted member of the work team?*

Supervisory situation 6/2

Traditionally, the parks department had had the poorest safety record in the county government and the highest incidence of citizen complaints on appearance, attitude, and performance. The new parks superintendent had called the first line supervisors together and had laid down the following challenge:

"We've got to do something about our department. I'll admit we don't pay our people enough, but it's difficult to justify salary increases with our record and reputation. I'll also admit their work is dirty and hard, but they knew that when they came to work. Now, I'll let you have first crack at coming up with recommended changes. If I don't think your recommendations will do the job, I'll be forced to take some further action."

Over the next several weeks the supervisors spent a lot of time on the problem and came up with the following recommendations:

New uniforms and safety equipment for the crews

Construction of a new washroom

Regular training in safety and public relations

Replacement of obsolete tools and vehicles

Painting of vehicles.

1. *How will the parks superintendent react to the proposed changes if she is familiar with good management practices?*

2. *What are some ways the superintendent could have encouraged the supervisors to include all the members of their department in resolving the problem?*

3. *What type of further action do you think the superintendent could take that would promote team building?*

SELECTING, ORIENTING, AND TRAINING EMPLOYEES

It is a fine thing to have ability, but to discover ability in others is the true test.

Elbert Hubbard

CHAPTER 7

SELECTING, ORIENTING, AND TRAINING EMPLOYEES

What is the supervisor's part in selecting an employee?

How do you conduct a successful employee interview?

What steps should be taken in orienting new employees?

What should you consider in setting up a helpful training program?

Three of your most important tasks as a supervisor are selecting, orienting, and training the people assigned to your job area. You are more likely to get the job done with and through other people if your employees are carefully selected, are told what is expected of them when they start working, and are kept up-to-date by on-the-job training.

Selecting the employee

Today, in many cities, towns, counties, and other local governments, personnel departments screen people who apply for jobs. If this is the way people are hired for your organization it is your job to provide correct, up-to-date information to your personnel department. Do you, for example, furnish a current, accurate description for the job you are trying to fill, especially if changes in the job have been made recently? Check your job descriptions to see whether they state clearly and accurately the duties and responsibilities of an employee as well as the skills the employee will need.

If, on the other hand, you work for an organization that gives you some of the responsibility for selecting employees you should know how to conduct a job interview and how to prepare for it.

Preparing for the interview

You want an interview to go well so that you can get the information you need to select the right person for the job. But there is another reason for conducting a good interview: you are not only interviewing, you are *being* interviewed. Your interview will be that person's first contact with his or her new supervisor, and you will want that first impression to be a good one.

Get ready for the interview in advance. You will need time to collect information, to read the application, and to get your thoughts together. With good preparation you can use the interview time wisely and well.

First, spend some time looking over the person's job application, so that you will not ask questions that the applicant has already answered on paper, and also so that you will know what questions or topics have *not* been covered and what questions do need to be asked during the interview.

Second, spend some time looking inside yourself to find out what your personal preferences are. Ask yourself, "What kind of person do I hope to hire for this job?" If your requirements are different from the qualifications listed on the job description, be sure you realize this.

Keep in mind that equal employment guidelines say specifically that you must not disqualify a person because of race, sex, age, religion, nationality, disability, or other personal characteristics that have nothing to do with the person's ability to handle the job.

For example, you may have stored at the back of your mind the notion that a good bookkeeper is a quiet person who wears conservative clothes. That means you will really be looking for a quiet, conservatively dressed person even though these requirements are never in the job description. (In fact, they have nothing to do with being a good bookkeeper.)

If you look for your personal prejudices in advance, you can stop yourself from making an unfair, perhaps illegal decision about a person. When the times comes to decide, you should be able to say to yourself, "I like John. He is more neatly dressed than any of the others. But he doesn't have the education the job calls for. Susan's hair is rather disorderly and I don't like the way she dresses, but she certainly has better qualifications. I think we should hire Susan."

After you have looked through the application and have evaluated your own expectations, you will want to gather information that answers the following questions:

■ What skills will the worker need right away?

■ What skills can the employee learn on the job?

■ What personal biases and expectations should I guard against?

■ What questions shall I ask?

■ What topics do I want to discuss? In what order?

■ How long will the interview take?

Your organization's personnel office, Equal Employment Opportunity officer, or legal department should be consulted for guidance about the criteria for screening and the questions to be asked during the job interview. Legal requirements protecting certain classes of employees (such as women, minorities, and disabled applicants) are quite specific and change over time. It's better to check with the experts who keep up with the legal aspects of personnel, than to take a chance and perhaps incur a lawsuit!

Interviewing the applicant

Your interview will be more successful if you can accomplish the following four objectives:

■ Put the applicant (and yourself) at ease.

■ Phrase questions so that they will give you the information you need.

■ Listen carefully.

■ Write down your observations promptly after the interview.

You and the applicant will learn more about each other if both of you are relaxed. Begin by introducing yourself. Use the other person's name right away, and continue to use it frequently throughout the conversation.

Try to create an informal atmosphere. When the interview begins, see that the applicant is comfortable. There should be no physical barriers, such as a desk or table, between you and the applicant.

A person's dress, hairstyle, and other personal characteristics have nothing to do with his or her ability to handle the job.

You might begin by briefly reviewing a description of the job. This can also serve to supplement information about the job.

Avoid questions that can be answered by a yes or no, such as "Have you ever done this kind of work before?" "Do you think you can do this job?" The chances are that you will get a quick yes in reply. Ask, instead, "What skills do you think you have that would make you the right person for this job?"

You should also avoid questions that lead to obvious answers, such as, "Do you like people?" The applicant can hardly say no to such a question! If you want to know how the applicant really feels about people, ask, instead, "How would you handle an agitated taxpayer who comes storming into your office about his garbage, which has not been collected for two consecutive weeks?"

It is no longer permissible under federal standards and guidelines to ask prospective employees questions regarding their marital status, children, national or ethnic origin, age, or religion. Employment interview questions can be considered discriminatory when they ask about areas that are not a true measure of a person's ability to perform a job. For example, such questions as "How long have you been married?," "Do you plan on having children?," or "Who will take care of your children while you are at work?" are questions that do not relate to an individual's job skills and could be used to discriminate against the person because of false assumptions we may draw

from the answers that are given. An effective supervisor exercises good judgment and is always fair and consistent when asking interview questions.

Most of us are so busy with our own thoughts while another person is talking that we often miss a great deal of what is said. But interviewing means hearing everything that is said as well as hearing *how* it is said. In other words, you should truly listen. To do this, you should see that there are no interruptions by people or the telephone.

When the applicant speaks, listen until he or she is finished. Do not begin to think about your answer until the applicant has stopped talking.

Do not worry about pauses in the conversation. It is not necessary to say something as soon as the other person stops talking. Give applicants time to gather their thoughts and continue with what they are saying. And give applicants a chance to ask questions about the job. They need a clear understanding of what is expected. Also, you can often tell a lot about a person by the kinds of questions he or she asks.

If you are interviewing someone from a cultural or ethnic background different from yours, you should be sensitive to possible differences in interviewing styles. For example, someone from an Asian culture may smile, not out of understanding of something you said, but rather, to avoid embarrassment or to "save

face." Or, he or she may be reluctant to respond to a question about his or her individual job skills and strengths. It is common among peoples of Asian cultures not to talk about their own accomplishments since it is considered impolite.

Misinterpretation of these actions on your part could lead to an unsuccessful interview. Your organization's EEO compliance officer can help you prepare for an interview with an applicant from a cultural or ethnic background different from your own.

Finally, write down your thoughts about the applicant *as soon as the interview is over*, while the ideas are still clear in your mind. Use a standard form to record your reactions. Such a form will help you look for information on the same characteristics in each applicant, so that you can make fair comparisons. It can also guide you in choosing your questions.

You may want to consider using a team approach to both screening and interviewing employees. Criteria for screening candidates are devised by a screening committee that develops a comprehensive list of the most important qualifications and characteristics a person should have for the position. The screening committee is usually composed of members of the work unit, along with representatives from personnel and other departments or divisions within the organization. A real effort should be made to reflect the diversity of the organization in the composition of the screening com-

When questioning an applicant, be sure that you and the applicant are talking about the same thing.

mittee, especially in achieving gender and racial balance.

The interviewing process can be done by this same screening committee or by other representatives of the work unit and the organization. The interview can be conducted by a panel of representatives asking questions specific to performance of the job. The candidate might also be asked to demonstrate how she or he might perform certain tasks. A performance demonstration can be an especially helpful assessment tool if the position requires operation of equipment or machines.

Orienting new employees

Job orientation is another of your supervisory responsibilities; it benefits the worker, you, and, in fact, the entire agency. An employee who is properly oriented is much more likely to become a productive worker.

The four main ingredients of a job orientation program are: making the new employee feel welcome, discussing expectations, explaining and informing, and setting up a check-back system.

Welcoming the new employee

As the supervisor of a new employee it is your responsibility to ensure that he or she gets off to a good start. The first day is critical to making a new employee feel welcome and at home. If your new employee is made to feel like an important addition to your work team right from the outset, he or she will feel motivated and delighted to be working with you. You will want to maintain the positive attitude and high energy that most new employees bring to a new job. If your new employee feels neglected, he or she can quickly become negative and demoralized.

Your role then is to welcome new employees and let them get to know you as their supervisor and the coach of their work team. You will want to provide a friendly atmosphere as well as introduce the essential information required to perform the job well.

One of the first things you should do is make sure that you have provided the employee with an assigned office or space in which to put personal belongings—a space the employee can call his or her own. This area should be selected well in advance of the employee's arrival and should be clean and neat. A welcome sign or bouquet of flowers can add a warm welcome to a new employee's work area. Once the new employee has been shown his or her personal area, you can tour the work place to give the new employee a sense of place and belonging. Be sure to introduce the employee to the rest of the staff, who should have been previously notified of when to expect the new person.

After you have made the first introductions, it is helpful to have a seasoned worker spend the next few days with the new employee, explaining the job and helping him or her become acclimated to the work place. Your role in the orientation process is far from over, however. You will want to make sure the employee receives concise and clear information about the new work situation. An orientation checklist can serve as a reminder of the kinds of information you need to cover about the new employee's job, work unit, and organization.

Even if the city or county personnel office provides an orientation, you should make sure that you personally review with your new employee all the information that is particular to your work unit. It is very important that what the employee learns first is accurate and relevant.

Your team members can be a big help in designing an orientation program—after all, they were new employees once themselves.

Discussing expectations

Early in the orientation period two points should be made clear: what you expect of the employee, and what the employee expects from the job. Sometimes employees quit or are fired because nothing they do seems to please the supervisor. However, these employees may not have found out until the day they left that they were supposed to volunteer for overtime—the supervisor had never told them that overtime was expected.

Misunderstandings can also arise if employees fail to mention their own expectations; then employees may become dissatisfied and disappointed with the job.

Since situations change, and expectations change with them, both supervisors and workers should continue to keep each other informed about what each expects from the other.

Explaining and informing

The new employee needs to know where things are, how things are done, and who does what. When orienting a new worker, give that employee a good start by taking the following steps:

■ Write down when and where workers should report to work on their first day, who will greet them, and who will give them their first instructions.

■ Introduce new employees to everyone they will come into contact with during the first week.

■ Give new workers a tour of the work area. Point out where tools, equipment, and supplies are stored, and where they will find restrooms, drinking fountains, places to clean up, and other offices and work areas they should know about.

■ Explain the rules and regulations of the organization—especially those that deal with safety, smoking, parking, transportation, working hours, absence from work, work breaks, lunch hours, and paydays.

■ Give the new employees an employee handbook if your government publishes one. Set aside some time during the first week to explain important sections and answer questions.

- Explain the steps employees must follow to clear up misunderstandings or get action on complaints.

- Explain how supplies and equipment should be used, including the telephone system, fax machines, computers, copying machines, tools of the trade, and forms that are filled out routinely.

- During the first week explain how each employee's job fits in with the work of the department and the local government. Show how the job, no matter how simple or small, helps provide services to citizens and is an essential part of a well-run organization.

Orientation will be expedited if you assign one or two experienced and helpful employees to assist each new worker for the first several weeks. Be sure that new employees understand that these persons have been assigned to help them and to answer their questions.

The first work assignment for the new worker should be a simple one, but the work should be useful. It should not be practice work unless the job is so hazardous that practice is necessary. Be sure to check back at the end of the day to see that the task that was assigned has been done correctly.

Setting up a check-back system

For the first three to six months the person on a new job is under some pressure. Everything—and everyone—is new and strange. Almost everything is being done for the first time. Most new employees have moments when they wonder, "Can I really do this job?"

The understanding, supportive supervisor will help new employees get adjusted by using the check-back system. This means setting aside time for the new employee to ask questions and time for the supervisor to tell the employee what he or she is doing right and what needs improving or changing.

The new worker needs this kind of check-back at the end of the first day and the first week. After that, the supervisor can schedule a monthly review of the employee's work for the first six months at least.

This type of stocktaking keeps employee morale high. It reassures newcomers as to whether they are doing a good job. It also keeps them informed about the supervisor's expectations.

Setting up a training program

Training workers for their jobs and developing their skills and abilities are important responsibilities of the supervisor.

In the course of the training period it is a good point to remember that some employees may have unpleasant memories of their school days. Part of your job, then, will be to create a climate for learning by endorsing training activities, encouraging employees to take advantage of them, and helping them in every way to grow on the job. It will be helpful for you to recall those training programs that have been most valuable to you and why.

You might discuss with workers some of the following benefits of on-the-job training:

- It gives new employees information on how to do their work the way the organization wants it done.

- It gives all employees a chance to find out whether they are doing their jobs correctly. Incorrect or inefficient work practices can be changed before there is lasting damage or before the wrong method is taught to someone else.

- It gives all employees a chance to learn new and better ways of doing their jobs; to use new, improved equipment; and to keep up with the rapid changes that are taking place in every line of work.

- It gives all employees a chance to grow on the job through learning new skills and taking on added responsibilities. This also pays off in promotions and salary raises.

These benefits to employees can also be considered benefits to the organization, and they make the supervisor's job easier and more productive. Supervisors can spend more time on planning ahead and preventing problems if the routine work is handled by capable, well-trained workers.

In addition to creating the right climate for learning, you will probably have to do some of the training. In most organizations the supervisor has at least some responsibility for planning and designing on-the-job training programs and for teaching and evaluating them.

Planning a training program

There are a number of points you need to consider in the early planning stages. You might begin by asking yourself the following basic questions:

■ What do I want employees to know or to do, and at what level of skill?

■ What skills should they learn? What attitudes?

■ How soon do employees need this training?

■ What do employees already know? What skills do they have at present?

■ What do the employees themselves think they need to learn? (Ask them.)

When you have answered these questions, then ask yourself:

■ What is needed to provide this training? Equipment? Tools? Teaching aids? Money? Instructors?

■ How much time will be needed? How should the instruction be scheduled?

Before you start designing the training program, remember that you are designing it for a group of adults. It is important to stop and consider what we know about how adults learn best.

How adults learn

Adults should be given information spaced over a period of time. The period between classes should be long enough to give workers time to absorb the material but short enough so that they will not forget it from one session to the next. Weekly one-hour sessions would be better, for example, than monthly three-hour sessions. Training sessions should be scheduled far enough ahead so as not to conflict with work schedules or personal plans.

In any training session, individual involvement is important. Such involvement may be as simple as a question-and-answer period, or as complex as large groups breaking up into smaller groups for extended periods of discussion.

The kind of training also determines the size of the group. For example, specialized job instruction might be more effective in small groups of two or three, to allow for an informal flow of questions, answers, and discussion. In training sessions on areas such as building communication skills, larger groups of up to twenty will provide the opportunity for relating to a variety of backgrounds and experiences.

People learn at a steady pace. But after a while they come to a point where they seem to make little or no progress. Do not become discouraged if this happens. Before long, you will find that your students will begin learning again.

Remember that adults learn best when involved in a process. Words can be forgotten quickly, but when words go hand in hand with actions—with doing and participating—your employees are more likely to learn and retain.

For this reason, training sessions should appeal to people's senses. People learn by hearing words; by seeing words, charts, pictures, demonstrations; and by doing things. Thus, you will want to plan for a variety of teaching techniques (where practical), including lectures, case studies, role playing, demonstrations, and discussions.

You might also use a variety of materials, such as blackboards, charts, graphs, slides, maps, films, and other visual aids. Some local governments may have videotaping equipment. If your organization has a training officer, that individual can be very helpful in providing ideas and assistance.

In order to remember what they learn, students must have a chance to practice. Studies show that if there is no time to practice 55 percent of the instruction is forgotten one hour after a task is learned, 65 percent is forgotten one day later, and 75 percent is forgotten one week later.

Instruction should follow a logical pattern. It should teach steps in the order in which they are actually done on the job. It should progress from the easiest idea to the most difficult. This permits students to build confidence while learning easy material and prepares them for the difficult tasks ahead.

Following a logical pattern also means giving reasons for what is done. Explain why it is done. Show the connection between facts and the ideas behind them. Employees will remember *how* something is done if they know *why* it is done that way.

Adults also learn best if they are at ease. In fact, we could say that a tense, frightened person scarcely learns at all. It is important, then, to create an atmosphere in which everyone is free to make mistakes and can learn from mistakes without feeling clumsy or ignorant. Be at ease yourself so that employees will feel free to experiment and to ask questions.

Plan to hold training sessions in a place that has a pleasant, comfortable atmosphere. It should be away from the everyday work area, if possible, to provide a change of scene and to keep interruptions at a minimum.

Comfortable chairs and tables and adequate lighting should be provided. The room should be well ventilated, especially if people are allowed to smoke.

Teaching strategies for different learning styles

Much research in recent years has revealed how the human brain works, including the various ways people process information. Knowing that people learn in different ways can help you design your training workshops, or work with a professional trainer, to present material in a way that appeals to all learning styles.

These studies show the need to present information so that the left and right sides of the brain are stimulated. By using the whole brain, an individual is able to learn and retain more information. In *Frames of Mind: The Theory of Multiple Intelligences*, Howard Gardner identified seven different kinds of intelligence or ability that individuals may have. The chart on this page, compiled by training consultants Chris Schwenker and Muffy Winkelman, shows characteristics, applications, and implications for learning of these various types of intelligence.

From these studies a variety of training methods, often referred to as integrative learning

Multiple intelligences

Intelligence	Characteristics	Applications	Implications for learning
Spatial	Ability to perceive and reproduce shapes and their placement, even in the absence of concrete examples	Painters, sculptors, designers, architects, navigators, air-traffic controllers, carpenters, etc.	Use color, pictures, graphs, charts.
Linguistic	Sensitivity to words, their meaning, and order (grammar)	Poets, writers, politicians, lawyers	Explain by using words. Write or speak about the subject.
Logical-mathematical	Ability to symbolize relationships between separate phenomena, to calculate, to test a theory against criteria	Scientists, mathematicians, computer scientists	Present concepts in logical order; use flow charts to help explain a process.
Musical	Sensitivity to sound and pitch; ability to express emotion through sound	Composers, musicians, advertisers	Use background music. Make up some kind of tune to help the learner remember.
Interpersonal	Sensitivity to the moods, temperament, and feelings of others	Leaders, people who work in care-giving professions, team members	Use team-learning exercises. Work with others and talk about new learning.
Intrapersonal	Sensitivity to one's own moods, feelings, and reactions	Therapists and their patients, writers who reflect on their own experiences	Design exercises that can be done independently. Spend some time on your own in order to reflect on new learning.
Kinesthetic	Ability to use the body in work, sports, and artistic expression	Dancers, athletes, skilled technicians and crafts people who use tools	Develop a skill by practicing it; get exercise; take breaks.

Source: Howard Gardner, *Frames of Mind: The Theory of Multiple Intelligences.* © 1983 by Howard Gardner. Reprinted by permission of Basic Books, a division of Harper Collins.

techniques, have been developed that appeal to the different ways people process information and stimulate whole-brain thinking. For example, integrative learning encourages small group discussion rather than the more typical training lecture. Classical music is often played softly in the background because music stimulates creativity. In *The Everyday Genius*, Peter Kline provides an excellent how-to and why of using many different teaching strategies to enrich the learning environment.

Other teaching tips

During the 1940s the Job Instruction Training (JIT) system was designed to train industrial workers quickly and thoroughly for work in plants geared up for the war effort. Some of the techniques used in the JIT system are as applicable to local government workers today as they were to industrial workers then.

The JIT system recommends teaching a task by breaking it down into its individual parts and then demonstrating it one step at a time. After each step has been demonstrated, provide time for questions and further explanation before going on to the next step.

A work sheet can be used to show the what, how, and why of each step in a task. The sheet names the task and shows, step by step, what is done, how it is done, and why it is done that way. In addition, special tips about timing, safety, and efficiency can be added to the sheet.

It is often useful for supervisor and employees to trade places at this point. Have the employees tell you how to do each part of the task while you follow their instructions. Correct any mistaken ideas employees have about any part of the operation. And do not forget to praise them when they do the work correctly!

Then ask employees to explain the what, how, and why of each step and actually do the task. Watch for mistakes and correct them on the spot.

At the end of each training session it may be helpful to have employees summarize the key points learned while you write them on a blackboard or flip chart. You then fill in any missing information and correct any misunderstandings.

After the employees are doing these jobs on their own, it is critical that the supervisor check back periodically to see how the jobs are being done. This provides employees with another opportunity to correct errors and the supervisor with an opportunity to give recognition for tasks done correctly.

To have your employees learn how to correctly perform a specific task, you (or a member of your work team) should demonstrate how the task should be performed. The elements of an effective demonstration are:

■ Tell the employee how to do the task, first at your regular rate of speech. Then repeat the directions more slowly, step by step. Then repeat the directions again.

■ As you are verbally explaining the task, you should also be physically demonstrating the operation. You might also want to show slides or a video, diagram, or picture of how the task is performed. People learn in many different ways, so you should demonstrate how the work is performed in a variety of methods that match a person's auditory, tactile, or visual style of learning.

■ Finally, have the employee show you how the task is to be performed. At this point it is likely that you may have to repeat your directions and provide another demonstration. This part of the training may need to be repeated several times until you are satisfied that the employee knows how to perform the task.

Patience is an important ingredient in successful training. You will also need to provide your employee with ample time to practice the task. Practice makes perfect—and so does feedback from you.

After the training program has been completed it is important to try to measure what effect it has had. If the instruction did not accomplish all that it was designed to do, try to find out what went wrong so that the next program can be planned more successfully.

Ask yourself such questions as "Was the material too complex? Was it presented in an interesting, understandable way? Did the instructor use too many unfamiliar words? Did the instructor intimidate or bore the employ-

In a rapidly changing environment, training is a process that will continue throughout a person's working life.

ees? Were enough visual aids used? Was too much taught in too short a time?"

If, as a supervisor, you are good at selecting well-qualified employees; orienting new employees so they understand their responsibilities and feel comfortable with the organization; developing and maintaining a well-rounded training program—then you are well on the way to becoming a first-rate supervisor who elicits good work from employees—your most valuable resource.

Checklist

Have an accurate, up-to-date job description ready for hiring new workers.

Be well prepared for interviewing each applicant.

Be sure that you have clearly identified your personal preferences about people and how they relate to the qualifications listed on the job description.

Put job applicants at ease during the interview, and be at ease yourself.

When a new person is hired, state clearly what is expected on the job.

Listen to the new employee's expectations of the job.

Check back with the new employee regularly on job performance and on his or her reactions to the job.

Explain the written and unwritten rules of the organization to the new employee.

Encourage employees to participate in training programs.

Select or design training programs that meet the needs of adult learners and address the various ways in which they process information.

After each training program is completed, carefully evaluate its strengths and weaknesses in order to enhance future programs.

Supervisory situation 7/1

Bill Dunn, head of the purchasing office, was forty-five years old and had been with the city in one capacity or another for some twenty years. Much of that period had been spent with the department of public works in inventory and stores.

For the past two years, Bill had been in charge of the city's purchasing office. His staff consisted of ten persons, five of whom were clerical staff whose functions included keying purchasing orders, posting bills, filing records, and the like. The duties of the other five were professional in nature and consisted of writing purchase specifications, meeting departmental representatives on purchasing needs, and in general keeping in touch with contractors and commercial establishments that did business with the city. These positions were classified as purchasing agents.

On Monday morning, 20 June, at 10:00 a.m., Bill had an appointment with Nancy, a candidate for one of the purchasing agent positions. Under the city's personnel policies, the top three candidates who had successfully completed the personnel office's examination procedures were always interviewed. Nancy was the third candidate Bill

had seen. When she came into his office, Bill was talking on the telephone so Nancy stood looking out the window. Holding his hand over the phone, Bill nodded and said, "Sit down, Miss, I'll be with you in a minute."

The telephone conversation took longer than Bill had expected and almost ten minutes had passed before he put down the phone. "Sorry about that, Miss, but you know how hard it is to stop some of these guys. I always tell my boys that the public pays our salaries and if the public wants to talk, then let them talk. But you are not here to listen to me; let's talk about you. Have you had any experience in writing purchasing specifications? While you are thinking about that, let me check with my secretary for just a second. We are trying to get our annual report in tomorrow and she is typing the final draft now."

After a brief discussion with his secretary, Bill turned back to Nancy and asked, "Would you anticipate any difficulty getting along with salesmen? You're a good-looking girl and you know the stories about traveling salesmen."

Nancy smiled and without answering the question said, "Mr. Dunn, can you tell me more about the purchasing office? I know the basic facts, but I wonder if you would go a

little further. For example, does the office have a training program? Is there a career development program?"

"Well," said Bill, "you really should ask personnel about that. I'm more interested in what my men do on a day-to-day basis. Are they on the ball in keeping my office in line? If you don't watch those guys, they'll buy chrome-plated johns for their restrooms. I want men who are out there on the loading platforms helping unload supplies so they can check their quality to make certain the city isn't cheated. I want them to drive those trucks, try out the backhoes, get out there on the street with the crews, and see that those paving machines actually work. By the way, Miss, have you ever driven a truck?"

The phone rang and Bill reached for it but before he could say hello Nancy answered his question:

"No, Mr. Dunn. I haven't driven a truck, or lifted a bale, or toted a barge." And with that Nancy got up and walked out.

"Just like a woman," Bill snorted, and yelled to his secretary to get personnel on the phone.

1. *What things did Bill do wrong during this interview?*

Supervisory situation 7/2

At the orientation meeting for all new employees of the city one hour was set aside to discuss the city's safety program. This portion of the orientation was normally handled by the personnel director, who first discussed the importance of safety and then handed out a mimeographed statement of do's and don'ts. For example, the statement contained such statements as: "Do report every accident that results in lost time"; "Do make certain you know where the emergency medical kits are located"; "Don't assume that you will never be involved in a serious emergency." She emphasized that all supervisors had been directed to enforce all city safety regulations.

Safety concerns were especially important at the central garage. Not only was there the constant problem of accumulation of carbon monoxide fumes in certain closed areas, but, in addition, the noise level was very high in some sections. Tyrone, a supervisor in the garage, was extremely sensitive to the noise problem since he had been called on the carpet twice when safety inspectors had observed workers without earplugs in a high noise area. Earplugs were furnished to all employees at the garage and the workers were instructed to wear them "at all times when working in an area where the noise level is so high as to represent a danger to health."

At the last meeting with his supervisor, Tyrone had been told *in no uncertain terms* that it was his responsibility to enforce the safety regulations. In fact, Tyrone could remember the exact words his supervisor used: "I don't care whether the safety rules make any sense to you. The rules are the rules and they will be enforced. I'm getting heat on this thing from upstairs and when I get heat, you feel the burn. So get on their backs and see that they wear those earplugs."

Tyrone had risen to the supervisory ranks primarily by carrying out orders as they were given. He had long ago found out that "the boss might not always be right, but he was always the boss." Tyrone was not going to let his workers threaten his career so he set about putting into operation his plan to carry out his orders concerning safety rules. He decided that, since his supervisor was most immediately concerned with earplugs, that was where he would start.

The next morning Tyrone visited the body shop, making himself very visible and checking each of the workers to see that earplugs were being used. Shouting, "See you later," to several workers, he walked out of the building, waited a few minutes, went around to the back door, opened it quietly, and stepped in.

Sure enough, Bill and Rita, two new employees in the area, were in the act of removing their earplugs even though the noise level was very high.

Tyrone stepped forward, put his hand on Bill's shoulder, and said, "Okay, Bill, both you and Rita can just take the rest of the day off and I'll see that your pay is docked. Maybe this way you two will learn that when we tell you to use earplugs, we mean it."

The next day Tyrone was called in by his supervisor, who was livid with rage. "What have you been doing down in that garage? I've got a delegation of workers in my office and they are hopping mad."

1. *What did Tyrone do that was wrong?*

2. *How would you have handled Tyrone's situation?*

3. *What are some ways Tyrone could provide safety training for his employees, in addition to the personnel department's one-hour training session?*

4. *How could Tyrone have helped ensure that Bill and Rita, as new employees, would follow the instructions about wearing earplugs?*

EVALUATING PERFORMANCE

By the work one knows the worker.

Jean de la Fontaine

EVALUATING PERFORMANCE

Almost all employees are anxious to know how well they are doing in their jobs, but many dread those sessions with the supervisor when their work is evaluated. It is like report card time in school. Many expect the worst and worry about it.

Most supervisors do not look forward to evaluation sessions themselves. Many feel reluctant to tell employees that they are not doing satisfactory work. Yet work evaluation is needed in government as it is in every other work situation. Does this mean that supervisors must grit their teeth and force themselves to evaluate workers? Does evaluation have to be a nasty, unpleasant job?

Fortunately, the answer is no—not if it is done correctly. You should be familiar with your local government's personnel policy regarding evaluation. There are several types of evaluation systems in general use in local government today.

Under one system the supervisor looks at a list of personal traits (such as dependability, cooperativeness, responsibility, creativity) and rates the employee from "unsatisfactory" to "outstanding" according to behavior on the job. Another system is more job-oriented: the supervisor measures an employee's work performance against a list of predetermined job tasks or objectives, which have been agreed to by both the supervisor and the employee. Other approaches combine elements of both these systems.

While it is your responsibility to carry out completely the system your local government requires in its personnel policies, there is a method you may be able to use to enhance and expand the evaluation process, which will make it a less painful and more productive experience for both you and the worker.

What is this method? Briefly, it is a problem-solving approach to evaluation, as opposed to the older, critical, "here's-what-is-wrong-with-you" approach. Evaluation today is aimed at working out better methods of doing the job in the future instead of emphasizing and dwelling on what happened in the past.

This means that the supervisor is less like a judge and more like a coach, playing movies of the last game in order to show team members how they can score more points (or lose fewer) in the next game. Supervisor and employee are no longer on opposite sides of the fence, with the supervisor making accusations and the employee making excuses. The supervisor is on the employee's side. Both are trying to find ways to make changes that are needed and to reach goals both have agreed upon.

This chapter will discuss how this kind of evaluation works, but first let us address a more fundamental question: Why evaluate employees?

Why evaluate?

Evaluations are an important part of your efforts to help employees fully develop their work potential. The evaluation process establishes benchmarks for you and the employee to use to measure performance and provides valuable feedback for both you and the worker. A formal process enables you to develop criteria and job standards that can be analyzed objectively. A formal process also helps standardize how you and employees evaluate performance. It can help remove any tendencies toward subjective analysis and also removes any perception of favoritism.

A formal evaluation follows established guidelines that everyone in the organization can have some input into developing and also adhere to. Regularly scheduled evaluations (usually annual) help to ensure that reviews will in fact occur. They can be put off if there is no organizational commitment or standardized procedures for everyone to follow.

Formal evaluations also provide an opportunity for employees to give their supervisors feedback about the supervisors' own performance. Effective supervisors welcome the chance to hear from employees about ways they can be more supportive of their workers.

If you make evaluations based only on informal impressions of people, you may be wrong most of the time.

In addition, evaluation of an employee's performance is expected and needed in local government for the following reasons:

■ Elected officials want evaluation because they believe it will encourage good performers to do better and will help poor performers to improve.

■ Department heads want evaluation to identify those who should be transferred to other work and those who should be promoted.

■ Other managers, and personnel officers, may want information for making decisions on salary increases, promotions, and transfers.

■ Supervisors need a system for motivating workers or for making decisions about salary increases and additional training, among various other factors.

■ Employees themselves like to know how well they are doing in their work, how well their supervisors think they are doing, and what the future holds for them.

Formal evaluations are needed for another reason, one that is not as obvious but is just as important. Even if there were no formal methods, people would continue to evaluate each other's work. The reason is simple. We all size each other up in a spontaneous, informal way as part of everyday living. Each person in a group has formed an opinion about the others in a group, without formally evaluating them. But the difficulty is this: If supervisors make decisions on the basis of these informal impressions, they will be wrong most of the time!

Not only are first impressions frequently wrong, but often second, third, fourth, and even tenth impressions can be wrong as well. This is because we can confuse our own values, needs, and attitudes with the behavior we observe in others. In addition, we do not observe carefully enough when we make informal evaluations.

Because mistakes about people's abilities are often very damaging and hard to correct, we owe it to others to conduct a careful, formal evaluation of their work.

Let us look at some general principles for making the kind of fair, constructive evaluation we have been talking about. Specific methods may differ from one local government to another, but the ideas behind them remain the same.

When do we begin evaluation?

We tend to think of evaluation as something that takes place toward the end of a period of time—the end of a week, a month, or a year. But it should begin the day a person accepts a job and a personnel file is opened. Into it should go a brief description of the job and the job specifications, the major responsibilities assigned to the employee, how the job fits in with others in the organization, and the new employee's qualifications.

During the first three to six months the supervisor should help a new employee understand his or her responsibilities, assignments, authority, and relationships with other departments and people. Do not underestimate the amount of information and explanation new employees need. Most supervisors do not provide enough information, while most new employees fail to ask enough questions because they are afraid to admit how much they need to learn.

During this first half year, information about major work assignments, how well these are carried out, and any new information that comes to light about the person's abilities should be recorded in the files of a new employee. This should be shared with the employee.

Employees and the evaluation process

Evaluation should not be imposed on an employee from outside or from above. Employees and supervisors together should set goals, standards, and criteria for measuring employee performance.

Setting goals

After an employee has been on the job for about three to six months, goals for the next three to six months should be developed and stated. The employee should contribute as much as possible to the process at that stage. Of course, the supervisor must guide the goal-setting process to make sure that goals fit in with the realities of the work group, department, and government. But even an employee whose job is very precisely defined and limited can—and should—be given the chance to express the goals in his or her own words.

Among the goals set should be actions designed to fulfill the responsibilities spelled out in the job description. Goals should also cover actions—such as training or counseling—needed to help the worker meet these responsibilities.

Goals should be challenging but at the same time realistic. Supervisor and employee should agree that all the goals stated are relevant to the employee's job and are set forth in the right order of importance, and that enough time is available to reach them. The supervisor should be able to place this document in the employee's file with a feeling of confidence.

Specific goals for a three-month period for a police officer, for example, might be written down in this way:

■ Will report on time to all roll calls on duty days

■ Will participate in at least twenty hours of training

■ Will not have to be corrected about personal appearance more than once

■ Will not have more than two complaints regarding language or demeanor from motorists given citations for moving violations

■ Will have car in proper working order and serviced when necessary

■ Will check interior of assigned vehicle at the beginning of each tour of duty for weapons or contraband that may have been concealed therein by arrested persons

■ Will advise all persons arrested of their applicable constitutional rights

■ Will know danger areas and trouble spots in assigned patrol zone

■ Will complete written reports with sufficient accuracy and thoroughness for 95 percent to be accepted without comment by the reviewing authority

■ Will appear on time prepared to testify competently at all judicial proceedings for which the officer has been issued a subpoena

■ Will develop and submit information from four new informants on criminal activity pertaining to *Uniform Crime Reports* Part I offenses

■ Will submit one detailed written suggestion on how operations may be improved and the anticipated quantified benefits if the suggestion is implemented.

Setting standards

The employee now works with the supervisor to decide how well the job should be done—what will be considered satisfactory performance and how it will be measured. Employees may not agree with all the standards, but the fact that they have had some say in them will

make for fewer disagreements or disappointments later on.

In any case, the supervisor has now placed in the personnel file information about the worker's job responsibilities and job qualifications, as well as a list of the goals that must be reached.

Evaluating performance

Many organizations schedule evaluations only once a year—on the anniversary of the worker's hiring, at the beginning of the calendar year, or at the start of the government's fiscal year. Unfortunately, this method does not work well if that is the only time performance is discussed. Many of the actions that are discussed at an annual evaluation are old and perhaps forgotten, having taken place months earlier.

When an employee is told that he or she did something improperly eleven months ago it is too late to do very much about it. The supervisor simply finds fault with the worker, the worker feels rebuked, and no constructive action takes place. Perhaps the worker has repeated a mistake twenty times since last February. It is much better to point out a mistake (and improve the worker's performance) when it first happens.

That is why supervisor and employee should review goals frequently during the first three to six months. No fancy forms or complicated paperwork are required to show them where

Setting goals is basic.

they are in relation to where they hoped to be. The right attitude on the part of the supervisor is far more important. Above all, the supervisor must be helpful and supportive. It must be clear in word and tone that the supervisor has confidence in the employee's ability and wants to help the employee get the job done correctly.

If the goals are stated clearly and the employee has kept good records of work done, the supervisor will not have to point out which goals have not been met. The employee will see this without help.

During this assessment process the emphasis must be on *results*—not on personality traits of the employee, nor the employee's shortcomings and failures. The employee should be praised for all jobs completed satisfactorily and on schedule. Next the supervisor should help the employee decide what the problems were when goals were not met, and how these problems can be overcome.

Finally, new goals should be set for the next three to six months. Notes on the new action plan should go into the personnel file along with information on how successful the worker was in reaching the previous goals.

The formal evaluation interview

Each supervisor should have at least one formal evaluation interview each year with his or her workers. When accompanied by periodic, informal discussions throughout the year to measure progress and give feedback on problems, an annual (or six-month) evaluation can be a valuable time to reflect on an employee's overall job performance.

Discussing past performance and planning for the future can be a positive, constructive, and even enjoyable experience for both the supervisor and the employee. If a major improvement in job performance is needed, it is critical to have a formal evaluation interview. This evaluation process may determine whether any changes will occur in the employee's attitude and work habits. But it isn't easy. The ability to conduct a productive evaluation interview, particularly when an employee must make substantial changes or improvements in performance, requires careful planning.

Planning the interview

Start by reviewing your first evaluation of the employee's performance and consider your reasons for that evaluation. Your main objective in the interview should be to improve the employee's performance and motivation. Think about how you want to accomplish this. What is it about the employee's work that needs improving? How can it be improved?

Picking the right day, time, and place is also important. The right place is a *private* place. The right time is not too soon after a disciplinary action. And the right day is one on which you are in a good mood and the employee seems also to be in a good mood.

Your responsibility is to be *for* the employee regardless of whether you like the employee and regardless of the kind or number of mistakes the employee is making. Remind yourself that your job is to help, not criticize; to support, not disapprove; to encourage change, not to place blame.

Conducting the interview

If this is the employee's first formal interview (and even when it is not) be prepared to reduce the tension, anxiety, and fear that the employee probably feels. You can do this by talking about the employee's strengths first, covering each point in some detail.

Explain that the interview is designed to be constructive—that your main interest is the employee's development and growth in the job. Explain, too, that the process is a cooperative one—that is, you don't expect to do all the talking and when you do talk you will be talking *with*, not *at*, the employee.

Next, let the employee talk while you listen. And be sure that you are listening with an open mind. Be willing to learn about the employee. Do not interrupt or cross-examine. Avoid argument. Let the employee bring out both facts and feelings. Perhaps the employee will identify all the areas where improvement is needed and suggest plans for accomplishing necessary change. This could certainly happen if you have been evaluating frequently. But you will never know unless you give the employee a chance to talk.

If the employee does not mention shortcomings or outright failures, and these exist, you will have to discuss them openly—what they are and what can be done about them. Introduce your recommendations for a specific improvement program and let the employee add his or her ideas. Then, together, you should work out a new set of goals.

Some interviews will be particularly difficult, no matter how well prepared you are. It's especially hard to talk with certain kinds of employees—for example, those who are defensive about their work, those whose high opinion of their work does not match up with your evaluation of reality, or those who have unpleasant personalities. In some cases, there is just no hope that both the supervisor and the employee will leave the evaluation interview happy. But don't give up too quickly.

Show you are concerned and interested in your employee's point of view. Keep the discussion focused on job-related issues. Back up any criticism with facts and examples. Be firm if you have critical comments to make. You may be able to prompt positive changes in even your most difficult employees.

End the interview when you have made all the points you intended to make and the employee has done the same. Employees should not be tense or defensive at this point. Their emotions should have been expressed by now, and you should have developed a joint plan of action. Just before the employee leaves reassure him or her that you are interested in his or her progress and also that you are quite willing to discuss it again at any time.

Keeping the employee's record

Whether you are making informal evaluations or formal ones, factual information about the worker's progress should always be documented and placed in the personnel file. No elaborate system of record keeping is required, but all significant facts should be written down (they do not need to be typed), kept up to date, and shared with the employee.

All *actions* should be recorded: goals that are set, job production, specific achievements on the job, action taken by the supervisor to help the employee, and recognition given for accomplishments.

In addition, supervisors should write down *impressions* of how the employee and the supervisor feel about these actions. For example, was it easy or hard for the employee to reach the goals that were set? How did the employee respond to the supervisor's suggestions for improvement or training? How does the supervisor feel about the employee's long-term career interests?

If the employee moves on to another supervisor you should go through the personnel record and take out all the impressions you have written down. Send along the facts about the employee, but omit the guesses and the judgments you have made. Remember that the law

Reduce tension in the evaluation interview by talking about the employee's strengths first.

protects all individuals against certain violations of their personal privacy (see Chapter 13 for a further discussion of this matter).

Let the new supervisor make his or her own estimate of the worker's ability on the basis of the facts in the file. The new supervisor may have standards that are quite different from yours. Besides, the new job may require a different set of abilities, so that your opinions would be out of place.

While this type of record is kept mainly for supervisory evaluation of the employee, it is important to have these facts recorded for other reasons. For example, if they are not recorded an employee could file a grievance or discrimination suit and the supervisor would be unable to justify a decision made months ago. If there is no written evidence of the facts that the decision was based on, the supervisor will not have any defense.

Remember, too, that when the time comes to make a decision or recommendation about an employee (and that time could come with very little advance notice) it is too late for the supervisor to begin collecting information. With good record keeping, all the supervisor has to do is review the file and come to a conclusion based on facts.

And when you consider the many different types of information that must be recorded for different employees in different jobs, you can see that keeping a file of facts is much more useful than trying to use a single rigid, all-purpose performance evaluation system for all employees. You cannot make all employees fit the same evaluation system any more than all police officers will fit into the same size uniform.

While accurate and complete documentation is critical, it is also just as important to be sure to inform the employee of any positive or negative observations you are making. Your goal is to always do what will help your work team members improve performance. Constant feedback—including written notice of a job well done—will assist the employee in improving job performance.

Your best approach, then, is to be conscientious about collecting information and flexible about how you use it to evaluate different types of performance in different jobs. To come up with an evaluation system tailor-made for each employee, ask yourself the following questions:

- What is the purpose of this evaluation?

- What do I need to know to achieve this purpose?

- What information do I need to collect to support the evaluation?

At this point you will know what kinds of facts and impressions you need to keep in the employee's personnel file. Then, when it comes time to make an evaluation, ask yourself: Do I have enough of the kind of information I need to make a sound decision about this employee?

Team evaluations

Another step in the evaluation process is to evaluate the performance of your work team as a whole. This concept means that in addition to evaluating individual team member performance, you assess how well the team is doing in meeting its team goals and objectives. Team evaluations can be done in a variety of ways. Team members can each offer an appraisal of how well they think their team is doing, or the supervisor can offer feedback to the team as a whole just as he or she does for individual team members.

Effective supervisors realize that too much emphasis on individual performance can be detrimental to how the team as a whole performs. While a team is as good (or as poor) as its individual members, it is also an organic whole. Just as a basketball team has individual star players, those stars cannot function without the actions of all team members playing together in a synchronized fashion.

Providing performance feedback for your work team will help it move forward as a productive and efficient unit. It also helps forge stronger bonds as team members realize "we're all in this together." The more you as a supervisor treat your work unit as a team, the more its members will begin to think and act collectively.

Evaluation and compensation

Two questions are often asked about the evaluation of work performance. The first of these is: Should an employee's wage or salary be based solely or largely on his or her performance evaluation? This question causes considerable debate among personnel specialists. Some claim that it is not proper to adjust a person's pay without basing it on evaluation of performance—that those who do more and better work should get greater compensation than those who do less—and perhaps not so well. And they are right.

Many personnel specialists, however, believe that most supervisors do not have control over a sufficient number of factors in the pay area to allow them to make this direct link between what a person does and what is received as pay. They, too, are right—for compensation does involve such considerations as the financial conditions of the local government, the amount budgeted for increases, and changes in the cost of living. This, of course, makes it hard for the supervisor to choose which practice to follow.

The second question is: Should a supervisor's reviews of employee performance be conducted separately from reviews for wage or salary adjustment?

The practical path for dealing with both of these questions seems to be to conduct frequent performance evaluations to give each employee the opportunity to improve performance as he or she goes along. Then at some specific point—perhaps once a year, but separate from the annual evaluation interview—the supervisor should sit down with the employee to discuss wages or salary. All of the aspects that have an effect on compensation should be considered at this time. Within the limits created by all of these factors (including those over which the supervisor has little or no direct control), the supervisor can recommend an adjustment in the employee's pay to reflect his or her overall performance. Obviously, the employee's overall performance is determined by weighing the results of all the performance evaluations since the last compensation adjustment.

Most of the discussions a supervisor has with employees about performance, then, should be developmental in nature—focused on improving performance in the future. Wage or salary adjustments are primarily designed to recognize and reward past performance and to keep the person's rate of pay at a level that is appropriate and fair for the services rendered. When the two evaluation activities are kept separate and distinct, the supervisor and the employee can concentrate on the specific purpose of the discussion.

Remember, though, that your local government's personnel policies may require these activities to be done in a particular way. Your role in determining compensation may be very broad or very limited.

In some local governments, those with more authority in the work group than the supervisor, such as the supervisor's boss or department head, may conduct evaluations. This may be an especially frustrating situation for the supervisor, and it is important for the supervisor to keep these individuals informed about each employee before evaluations are made.

Legal considerations

Recent court decisions have emphasized the following factors, which should be carefully considered in evaluating an employee's work performance:

■ Evaluation must be significantly related to important elements of work behavior specifically associated with the employee's job.

■ Even if the evaluation is clearly based on the best judgments and opinions of the supervisor, it will not be held sufficient unless it also includes definite identifiable criteria based on quality or quantity of work or specific performances supported by some kind of record.

■ Evaluation cannot be based solely on the supervisor's subjective observations.

■ Documentary evidence supporting evaluation elements is required.

The evaluation process is full of pitfalls for the biased supervisor. You should make each evaluation as if you were going to justify it to the employee, your boss, a judge, and a jury.

One final point should be made. As has been mentioned before, as a supervisor you want to help people so that their work will improve. But you should remember this: No one can change another person. The desire and will to change must come from inside that person.

It follows, then, that you should try to create the atmosphere that makes change possible, using methods of working with employees that make it comfortable and even easy for them to change, grow, and develop.

Checklist

Be sure that employees understand their authority, responsibility, and place in the work group.

Let the employee take part in setting his or her goals, standards of performance, and ways of measuring accomplishment.

Compare work results frequently with the goals you have set and agreed on.

Do not evaluate until you have enough of the right kind of information to do a fair and thorough job.

Work with the employee to make the evaluation, devise ways of improving work performance, and set new goals.

Use a formal interview process if a great deal of change in job performance is needed.

Keep written records on all actions and on all impressions.

Keep performance evaluations separate from salary adjustment evaluations.

Supervisory situation 8/1

Tom liked his job as a supervisor. He liked the responsibilities, the status, and the authority to get things done. And he liked the people who worked for him. He believed that each of them was honest and hardworking and would live up to his expectations. When he had been named to his supervisory position, Tom had participated in a supervisory training workshop. One of the topics discussed was performance evaluation, and great emphasis was placed on the importance of setting goals and being positive and affirmative rather than negative and critical in evaluation conferences, and on having a continuous evaluation process.

As Tom was finishing his third month as supervisor, he thought he should begin the evaluation process. He had been told by his department head that the county's personnel officer had said the county's appraisal process was very flexible and any supervisor should feel free to develop his or her own approach to the appraisal process.

Tom's first interview was with an old-timer whose reaction when Tom began to talk about participatory goal setting was one of complete disbelief. He said, "You just tell me what you want and I'll do it." When Tom tried to explain that goal setting should be a mutual effort, the older man shook his head and muttered something about young supervisors.

The next interview was with a young woman who spent most of the interview time complaining about being overqualified for the position she held.

A third employee had a rather dismal record of arriving fifteen minutes late at least twice a week. When Tom suggested that a good goal for the next quarter would be to be late no more than once a month, the employee inquired, "Does that mean it is OK to be late once a month? My old supervisor said I was not supposed to be late at all."

At the end of the day Tom was confused. Some of the things he thought he had learned at his supervisory training course had not worked. None of the workers had acted the way those people in the films had acted and he had many questions about what to do next. He had been told by several people, "That's not the way Mr. Ames [Tom's predecessor] did it." Some of his pleasure at being a supervisor began to fade.

1. How should Tom improve the evaluation process with his employees?

Supervisory situation 8/2

Maria is the supervisor in the payroll department and manages a work unit of ten employees. Every six months she reviews the work plan with her team and each member suggests ways they might personally improve the team's effectiveness and productivity. In addition, team members give feedback on each other's performance. Maria also gives her team members the opportunity to evaluate her performance as supervisor. The feedback she receives has helped her in dealing more effectively with the team as a whole, as well as with individual team members.

1. *What are some ways Maria is likely to give—and receive—feedback in order to make it a positive experience for herself and her team?*

2. *In what ways does team members' feedback to one another build team spirit? How might this process create ill-feeling among team members? What are some ways to avoid ill-feeling?*

COMMUNICATING WITH EMPLOYEES

Word is not crystal, transparent and unchanged; it is the skin of a living thought and may vary greatly in color and content according to the circumstances and the time in which it is used.

Oliver Wendell Holmes

COMMUNICATING WITH EMPLOYEES

"Those guys never do what's expected of them."

"It seems that Susan can't follow my simplest instructions."

"I can't figure out where they got an idea like that!"

"How was I to know Ray was upset? He said he was okay."

"Why didn't someone tell me there was a problem?"

We are frustrated and surprised when people misinterpret or do not understand what we say. Because we have been expressing ourselves all our lives, we assume that we communicate well, almost as easily and naturally as we breathe. The truth is that although we may be talking, we may not be communicating effectively. Effective communication usually demands a great deal of effort, practice, and understanding.

If the supervisor's job is to get work done through others, then communication is a necessary part of supervision. In fact, supervisory relationships could not exist without effective communication. Whenever workers join together to accomplish given tasks, they must communicate.

Most supervisors probably spend more than half their time communicating in some way—training employees, giving work assignments, demonstrating procedures or equipment, conducting staff meetings, answering questions, listening to employee concerns, helping citizens with problems, giving directions, and discussing plans and operations with managers and other supervisors. In fact, studies show that we spend up to 80 percent of our day communicating.

Supervisors communicate in many different ways. They may talk face to face to groups or individual employees; they may use a telephone or a two-way radio; they may write letters, memos, or bulletins. They may also communicate through gestures or signals, facial expressions, or silence. Regardless of the extent or method, without effective communication, supervisors and work teams or individual workers may find themselves acting at cross purposes, pursuing competing objectives, duplicating one another's efforts, and failing to complete necessary jobs.

What is communication?

One definition of communication is "behavior that transmits meaning from one person to another." This definition seems simple enough, but actually it is very complex. Let's look closely at its individual parts.

"Behavior that transmits meaning" can be more than words—much more. Facial expressions, posture, tone of voice, and even silence tell a person about the feelings, thoughts, and attitudes of another person. Through one of many methods, we can transfer, share, or convey *meaning from one person to another*. The definition says that any transmission that exchanges meaning is communication, but it does not say whether the meaning is clear or unclear.

Communication is a process because it involves activity. We must do something in order to exchange feelings, facts, ideas, and meaning. Something must happen between two or more people. But what exactly happens?

Elements of communications

To answer this question, let's look at the elements of the communication process. These are the *sender*, the *message*, the *medium*, the *receiver*, the *feedback*, and the *environment*.

When we transmit feelings, facts, or ideas to others, we become *senders*. The sender initiates the transfer of meaning. A sender appearing before a group of people may be referred to as the talker, speaker, or presenter. During one-on-one conversations, both the parties alternate as senders.

The *message* is the feeling, fact, or idea the sender conveys to the receiver. Because we cannot directly exchange with someone else what we are experiencing, we translate the experience into symbols. Symbols such as words and gestures permit us to describe, explain, and share with others what we feel, know, or think so that it has meaning to them.

The *medium* is the means the sender uses to transmit the message. Although the most commonly used means are speaking and writing, physical touch and body movement also serve as ways to transfer a message from one person to another. Often the sender uses more than one medium at the same time and sends the message through more than one of the receiver's five senses. In fact, using two or more senses may enhance the communication process (seeing and hearing, plus touch—a handshake—for instance).

The person who gets the message is called the *receiver*. A group of receivers may be called the audience or the listeners. In one-on-one conversations, both parties become receivers. In seeing, hearing, or feeling, receivers create a frame of reference and change messages into experiences with meaning for themselves.

As the receiver attempts to understand the message, he or she usually reacts in some manner. This reaction is called *feedback*. Nodding the head, for instance, may signal agreement or understanding while shaking the head may indicate disagreement or frustration. Facial expressions and body movements may show pleasure, discomfort, boredom, or confusion. Feedback tells the sender how well the message is being received.

The *environment* is both the physical location and the conditions existing when communication occurs. Noise, temperature, lighting, and time of day may improve or hinder communication. In fact, the environment itself—colors, seating arrangements, lighting—may communicate a great deal to the receiver. It is very important for the sender to consider the impact a particular setting or certain conditions can have on communication.

Effective communication

We see, then, that communication is actually a process involving a number of steps. Using this process, a person can communicate meaning to another person. However, what the sender means and what the receiver "hears" or understands may be very different. Even if we do a very good job of sending our message, how do we know that others receive it correctly? Our communication efforts may not always be very effective!

Let's carry our discussion a little further. Effective communication is behavior that transmits a meaning (message) from one person (sender) to another (receiver) so that it is mutually understood. By *mutually understood*, we mean the receiver understands the same message the sender understands.

Many breakdowns in communication occur when the sender gives a message one meaning and the receiver gives it another. Misreading "simple" instructions in assembling a child's toy or getting lost following "you-can't-miss-it" directions are examples of communication breakdowns.

A shared understanding of the message is critical for effective communication. Expressing feelings, facts, or ideas to our own satisfaction is not enough because what seems clear to us may not be clear to those with whom we are trying to communicate. We must say what we mean so that others understand us.

Feedback is a crucial part of effective communication. It enables the sender to know what message the receiver understands. Feedback enables the sender to change, adapt, revise, or clarify communication to the receiver, thereby improving the likelihood that the receiver will understand the meaning intended.

Symbols

We communicate meaning to one another through symbols representing a message. A supervisor who wants to communicate with an employee in order to discipline, explain, praise, or recognize that person may do so verbally or nonverbally. Verbal communication is the most obvious kind of symbolic communication. Most supervisors would say they usually communicate verbally with employees. However, much of the communication between supervisors and employees does not involve words. Because of the subtle ways that we continually communicate nonverbally, it may be impossible not to communicate when we are with others. Let's examine some of those ways.

Paralanguage, or voice characteristics, is closely related to verbal communication, but it concerns

How you say something is just as important as what you say.

how something is said, rather than *what* is said. It involves the tone of voice, pitch, emphasis, speed, loudness, and pauses we use in speaking. The same words may communicate various meanings depending on how these words are expressed. For example, a supervisor who says, "I am not upset with your work," may give the statement many different meanings by saying it many different ways.

Often, how something is said is just as important as what is said in communication between supervisors and employees. Paralanguage can communicate meanings in ways that words alone cannot.

Body language, another type of nonverbal communication, involves the position or movement of the body—posture, gestures, and facial expressions. Unintentionally, a supervisor may communicate much to an employee through body language. A clenched fist may signal anger, worry, or tension. Eye contact may communicate honesty, attention, or interest. Playing with a pencil, tapping fingers on a desk, or gazing out the window when an employee is talking may communicate lack of interest or boredom.

Physical space around and between people also communicates meaning. Personal space is the physical distance revealing emotional distance between people. We permit those close to us emotionally to be close to us physically, and we tend to be uncomfortable when crowded into an elevator or seated next to strangers.

If we move too close when approaching someone, that person may back away. If we stop too far away, the other person may come closer. We each have our own idea of personal space and we expect most types of communication to take place at a "normal" distance. A supervisor who stands "in an employee's face" may be threatening the employee. In the same way, a supervisor who stands so that he or she couldn't touch the employee "with a ten-foot pole" may be communicating dislike or disapproval.

The furniture arrangement in an office is an example of semi-fixed space as a means of communication. If a supervisor sits behind a desk and employees sit in front, the desk becomes a barrier representing formality, superiority, or authority. If the supervisor moves to a chair next to the employee, the desk barrier is removed and both parties are on an equal basis. The employee may relax somewhat because the situation seems friendly and informal.

Nonverbal communication, with symbols, is exchanged in a variety of other ways. Some years ago, the Broadway production *Hair* dealt in part with the 1960s conflict over hair length. Like parents and teenagers, supervisors and employees have argued about hair styles. As the play indicated, the real issue is not hair, but what it communicates and symbolizes.

Much of what we communicate is based on such symbols, in our personal lives as well as in work situations. The symbols of our jobs—the vehicles we drive, the clothes we wear, the equipment we use, the way we carry out our duties—communicate a great deal about us and our work for local government to citizens and other employees.

The supervisor, therefore, must consider nonverbal as well as verbal communication. The supervisor should be aware that such things as intonation, inflection, actions, setting, behavior, personal space, and personal appearance can communicate meaning.

Channels of communication

The expression "you have to go through the proper channels" applies to communication because messages are translated through channels into symbols others can receive. Channels are the medium for transferring messages from the supervisor to others in the organization.

Oral channels include face-to-face communication as well as the loudspeaker, telephone, radio, and other electronic media. Written channels include letters, memos, bulletins, manuals, handbooks, brochures, and pamphlets.

The channel we choose is important: communicating with someone face to face is different from telephoning or writing a letter, even when the same words are used. Receiving a memo from the supervisor is obviously different from being called to his or her office about the same issue.

Face-to-face communication usually conveys nonverbal symbols such as body language, as

You communicate by your appearance and facial expression as well as by what you say.

well as verbal symbols. The receiver can hear the speaker's tone of voice and emphasis on certain words and can give immediate feedback through facial expressions, gestures, or words. Telephoning also has the advantage of producing immediate (verbal) feedback.

Written communication, however, depends almost entirely on understanding of printed words. Feedback for written communication is limited. For example, someone reading this page is less likely to give the author feedback (by writing a letter or telephoning) than a person listening to the author speak in a classroom.

In every local government or organization, there are two different, important kinds of communication channels: the formal or official channels and the informal channels known sometimes as the "grapevine."

Formal channels, established to permit information to flow through the organization, take three forms.

Downward communication comes from people in positions of authority within the organization, such as department heads, the city or county manager, or the mayor. This type of communication conveys the official message of the organization, generally in the form of a memo, executive order, or administrative rule, and it directs the work effort. Goals and objectives designed at the top level of the organization are passed down to managers, supervisors, and finally to workers. This process links the various levels together in pursuit of the organization's mission. Policies, orders, procedures, and assignments are carried out through downward communication.

Upward communication keeps those at higher levels informed about the work effort. Essentially, it yields feedback about what is taking place at the various levels of the organization. Supervisors play a critical role in upward and downward communication because they link managers and employees.

Horizontal communication takes place between people on the same level in different areas or departments. Its primary purpose is to coordinate effort and work assignments. To avoid downtime or duplication, to improve the efficiency and effectiveness of local government service delivery, supervisors use horizontal communication.

The democratization of the work place is beginning to change the formal way organizations communicate internally. The top-down, hierarchical form of management that is reflected in upward and downward communication is changing to a "flattening out" of the organizational structure. This means that horizontal communication is becoming far more common. That is, as work teams become increasingly responsible for making decisions, communication is shared among team members and between various work units. Policies, procedures, goals, and objectives are developed through a team approach and not exclusively passed down from upper management.

This process of including more of the work force in decision making means that employees are better informed about what is occurring throughout the organization.

Informal channels exist outside the organization's formal channels. The continual interaction of employees and work teams is a vital part of the total communication process that makes local government organizations function effectively. Informal communication tends to be quick and believable—that is, information moves quickly through informal channels and is often more readily accepted than official messages.

The informal channels may become busier when formal channels don't provide enough information or don't provide it when it is expected or needed. Sometimes it is easier for management to be heard and understood if the message is shared informally rather than sent through the formal system. An effective manager knows that many important messages—some of them accurate, official, or sanctioned, some not—flow through the informal system.

Informal channels become far less busy and necessary as an organization flattens its organizational structure and increases its use of horizontal communication.

Generally, a manager or supervisor has more control and influence over the formal channels of communication than over the informal system. One person or a few people decide what information goes into the formal system, when,

and in what format. But a message that will travel unchanged through the formal channels may be reworked, filtered, or distorted as it works its way through the informal system. Therefore, it is important for you to be receptive to both channels, regardless of your position in the organization.

Barriers to effective communication

One metaphor depicts communication as a conveyor belt moving packages: a bundle transported along a conveyor belt from Point A to Point B arrives as the same package, unchanged. Unfortunately, communication does not work this way. The message we package in symbols and send to our receiver may become something entirely different when the receiver interprets the message.

We have all used expressions such as "I don't see things your way" or "I see the situation somewhat differently from you." What we mean is that our perception is different. We know, for instance, that if ten different people witness an accident, each one will have a slightly different impression of what happened. And if participants in a training class are asked to look out a window and to describe in a paragraph what they see, each one will describe the same scene in a different way.

Perception is the way we "see" things. It is based on environment, experience, and motivation. No two people will have the same perception because perception is as unique and

Hierarchical Organization

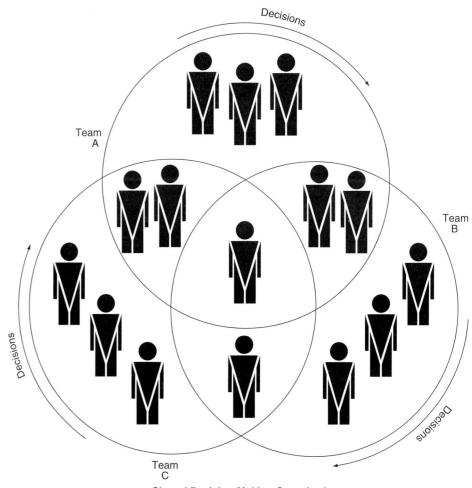

Shared Decision-Making Organization

In the hierarchical or pyramid style of management, decisions are made from the top down. In a team-centered organization, decisions are made by members of work teams who may share members for certain projects and programs. Supervisors act as coaches to facilitate the decision-making process.

individual as the employees in a work group. Each worker grows up in a different family, experiences different events in life, processes information differently based on temperament and personality, and has individual needs and goals. For this reason, employees will have various perceptions of their supervisor, their work, and their co-workers.

For example, an employee reared in a permissive family environment may resent the rules and orders of a supervisor with years of military experience who thinks "standard operating procedure" is important. On the other hand, a worker strongly committed to authority and "chain-of-command" principles may perceive a supervisor seeking input and participation as wishy-washy, uncertain, or unknowledgeable.

Prejudice—prejudging—is an example of the possible negative impact of perception. It may cause us to see and hear only what we want to see and hear, producing false ideas about others and what they want to communicate. Even before a female, African-American, or foreign-born worker speaks, some supervisors have already determined the value of what that worker will say.

Problems in perception may be the primary reason communication between people sometimes breaks down. We use common symbols as a means for communicating, but these symbols are still subject to individual interpretation. And our interpretation depends on our perception of ourselves, others, and the world around us.

Many other barriers to effective communication exist, some of which are closely related to perception. Useful as they are, words still create a variety of problems. As mentioned earlier, words are merely symbols with attached meanings. And while we have a general or common understanding about the meaning of most words, the meaning is often vague or imprecise. What a word means to one person may not be exactly what it means to someone else. The meaning of words may change with time or between cultural groups.

Words such as "awesome," "not," "cool," and "tough" have different meanings for today's young people than for those of other generations. New words like "CD-ROM," "e-mail," and "Internet" weren't even used by earlier generations. Terms such as "ergonomics," "information highway," and "global village" have become increasingly popular, while others like "phonograph," "outhouse," and "buggy" are no longer common.

Words can mean different things to different people even though those people are the same age and have had similar experiences. For example, let's say a supervisor tells Maria to "run over" to the supply room for a spare part. Does this mean that Maria is to run or just walk briskly? And if the supervisor says "hurry," should Maria go as quickly as possible, throwing caution to the wind, or only as fast as safety permits? Is it okay for her to stop and speak to someone else "for just a second" while hurrying?

Suppose that a supervisor evaluating Jim's performance says that a poor work attitude is obvious—what does the comment mean to Jim? That Jim's performance is poor? That, though Jim's performance is good, he seems unhappy? Or that Jim seems not to like the supervisor, or vice versa?

The difficulty with words, then, is that because we give them individual meanings or use them differently, what we communicate often depends on the other person's interpretation. This situation is similar to the game "Password," in which people take turns trying to understand messages from each other.

Another barrier to effective communication is noise. Noise, in terms of communication, is defined as a distraction or interference that disrupts the transfer of messages between people. Obviously, carrying on a conversation is difficult in a busy office where people are typing and phones are ringing, or at a work site where machinery is operating or traffic is moving. The noise may be so loud that we cannot "hear ourselves think," much less communicate with someone else. Physical noise prevents us from receiving.

However, noise can be internal as well as external. Internal noises include personal problems, conflicts, daydreams—whatever occupies a person's mind when you are attempting to communicate with that person. Instead of hearing what you have to say, the person is, in a very real sense, hearing something else.

No two people hear things the same way.

For example, a supervisor may want to remind Bob of something that needs to be done first thing Monday morning. The supervisor mentions this to Bob just before the workday ends on Friday. Bob, however, is already thinking about a weekend trip and consciously or unconsciously tunes out his supervisor. Bob "hears" but he just doesn't listen. Conversely, suppose Bob tries to discuss a problem with his supervisor. The supervisor at that moment is more concerned with an upcoming purchase order or a meeting with the department head, and listening to Bob is difficult for the supervisor.

Noise, both internal and external, may cause numerous messages to be missed or misunderstood. Good communicators try to eliminate such distractions by choosing a time and place that will enhance listening and thus be conducive to effective communication.

Finally, a sender can create another barrier by using a one-way communication channel. It is typical for us to place the responsibility for listening on the receiver of a message. In fact, the receiver is commonly referred to as the listener, while the sender is called the speaker. This is accurate, however, only if we view communication as a one-way process.

If a person assumes that the sender's job is to express the message and the receiver's job is to hear it, that person ignores the role that feedback plays in communication. This would be equivalent to ignoring someone who asks a question. If a sender uses one-way

Noise distorts the message from sender...to receiver...to sender.

communication only, the opportunity is missed to provide further information, to clarify a point, or to correct an error.

Unfortunately, this situation is exactly what sometimes unfolds when supervisors and employees try to communicate. Some supervisors miss feedback—facial expressions, tone of voice, oral statements and questions, or plain silence—simply because they are too busy communicating on a one-way channel.

Improving communication skills

Improving communication skills is of particular importance to supervisors because communication is so closely related to supervisory effectiveness. A good supervisor is also a good communicator. Through feedback, active listening, and the use of formal channels, a supervisor can improve communication.

Feedback

No matter how well supervisors and employees express themselves (or think they do), many barriers to communication can still exist. Obtaining feedback is the best way to overcome the barriers because it lets us check what we said or heard. The supervisor, as a good communicator, must both *give* and *receive* feedback.

Supervisors should give employees feedback to tell them how they are doing. Feedback can be used to discipline, correct, inform, or praise the performance of employees. Often employees really do not know whether they are doing good

work or poor work. Why? Because they are not receiving feedback about their jobs.

Many supervisors mistakenly assume that employees know both how well they are doing and how well their supervisors think they are doing. It is the supervisor's responsibility to tell employees about their performance through feedback.

Giving feedback to all employees—good and poor—is important. If we offer feedback just to poor performers, we ignore the needs of good employees who should be recognized for their efforts. It is human nature to want praise for a job well done. And giving positive feedback is worth the supervisor's time.

Although it is not easy to offer negative comments, constructive criticism is important for less productive workers who may think you are satisfied with their work. By not disciplining or correcting them through feedback, you may be implying that you are pleased with their poor performance.

An evaluation once or twice a year should not be the only time when a supervisor gives employees feedback. Remarks should be offered at appropriate times and locations. For example, do not give an employee negative feedback in front of co-workers—your primary purpose is to help, not to embarrass, your employees. Whether positive or negative, feedback can and should be used to help employees know where they stand and adjust their performances accordingly.

It is just as important that supervisors receive feedback. Have you ever ended a workday wondering whether your employees think you are doing a good job? Or agonized over a tough personnel decision and then tried to guess whether the jury (your employees) judged you innocent or guilty? Have you disciplined a worker and then tried to imagine how that person felt? Or have you ever conducted a training session on new equipment or procedures and wondered whether your employees really understood what you explained? Supervisors who receive feedback from their employees are more likely to have answers to these and similar questions.

Receiving feedback is sometimes difficult for supervisors because of the barrier created by their positions. Supervisors who are good communicators can overcome this problem to some degree. They encourage feedback by being receptive and open to their workers' complaints and concerns. These supervisors also do another very important thing: they solicit feedback.

The feedback a supervisor receives, however, largely depends on how he or she requests it. For example, suppose a supervisor explains a new work method to an employee and then asks, "Do you understand?" We know the answer is likely to be "yes." If the supervisor asks instead, "What do you understand?" the feedback will be much more informative.

It is important for supervisors to realize that when they ask for feedback they might just get it! And although all feedback from employees may not be positive, all of it can be helpful. The kind of feedback your employees give you will be influenced by how willing you seem to be to accept it.

In both giving and receiving feedback, supervisors should deal with feelings as well as thoughts. Supervisors must be willing to express their feelings to employees and to give employees a chance to share their reactions and feelings. Feelings are real. Supervisors and employees will find that dealing openly with feelings is the best practice.

Active listening

Being a good listener is the best way for supervisors to encourage feedback. Listening is another ability of supervisors who are good communicators.

To improve our communication skills, we have to become active listeners. Too many of us think listening is a passive, easy activity demanding little from us. Active listening is hard work. It requires us to give our undivided attention to another person and to attempt to understand what is being communicated. As a supervisor, you can communicate that you are actively listening in several ways:

- Face the worker and look at him or her attentively. If your gaze moves to the clock or around the room, the worker may interpret these actions as displaying lack of interest.

- Show that you are following the conversation by making facial expressions, by nodding occasionally, or by saying, "I see."

- Wait patiently if the worker talks slowly or becomes silent—this gives the person time to collect thoughts and to consider what has been said.

- Avoid interrupting the worker by talking, finishing sentences for him or her, or answering calls.

- Listen not only to what the person is saying but also to the feelings being expressed.

When workers come to you to discuss difficulties, they are telling you more than just facts. They are telling you not only what happened but also how they feel about it and they are doing so through verbal and nonverbal means. You should notice facial expressions, body stance, tone of voice, position, and hand movements.

Many people are uncomfortable when talking about feelings—yours as well as their own. They may think that being angry, jealous, or depressed is wrong, and they may find it difficult to admit these feelings even to themselves. However, ignoring feelings is overlooking information needed to solve problems.

To "listen" for feelings, you should pay attention not only to what the worker is saying but also to how he or she is saying it. If Rita insists she is not upset, but her face is red, her fists are clenched, and her gaze is unsteady, you may guess that she is not being completely candid.

Active listening helps supervisors "hear" more than the words of their employees. Feedback becomes an integral part of the active listening process. It lets your workers know you are truly listening. Sometimes it is helpful to paraphrase the worker's message by beginning with a statement such as "What you're saying is…" or "Sounds like you're feeling…"

The basic principles of active listening are to

- Listen to what the employee is saying without making any judgments

- Try to identify and acknowledge the employee's feelings

- Paraphrase—use your own words to restate what you heard the employee say

- Ask questions to find out how to meet the employee's needs.

Listening to the person you're communicating with can sometimes require a great deal of self-restraint. We often want to share our own ideas before the other person has completed his or her thoughts. One helpful technique is to count to ten after the other person has stopped talking—this gives the person a chance to continue in case he or she wants to add more, and it also slows you down so that you don't interrupt.

To identify and acknowledge feelings, first try to sense how the employee feels and then "check out" that perception by actually telling your employee how you think he or she might be feeling: verbalize your perceptions so that you can verify them. This also helps your employee to feel that he or she has been heard.

When you paraphrase you repeat in your own words what the employee has said in order to make sure that you correctly understood what he or she said. This also gives employees the opportunity to make themselves clear.

When you ask questions you are being a detective. You want to figure out exactly what your employee is trying to communicate so that you can attempt to meet his or her needs, as well as your own. Open-ended questions will provide the most information. Close-ended questions will give you less useful "yes" or "no" answers. An example of an open-ended question is "In what way does this work procedure make the job safer?" In contrast, a close-ended question would be "Does this work procedure make the job safer?"

By listening attentively and actively, supervisors may come to appreciate their workers' concerns and may be able to help resolve them. Consider the following situation:

Abdul, a worker, says to his supervisor, "This job really depresses me. I no sooner finish one thing than they bring me something else to do. Sometimes I think they think I'm a machine."

A supervisor who considers only Abdul's words might immediately try to devise a way for Abdul to do his job faster or might get someone to help Abdul do his work. A supervisor who is listening to the feelings in Abdul's message may suspect that he is complaining about more than just the work load. Abdul may be saying indirectly that his only reward for doing his work is receiving more work. He may be frustrated because his supervisor has not recognized his efforts with a word of praise or appreciation.

A supervisor who wants to discover what sparked Abdul's comment will check out an array of possible reasons, perhaps saying, "You know, Abdul, we *have* been very busy lately. I can see how it would be frustrating to you and I haven't even been by here lately to let you know how much I appreciate the fine job you're doing."

This kind of response opens the door for the worker to share what is really on his or her mind and gives you a chance to listen further. The supervisor, then, has an opportunity to learn whether the employee feels that the work load is really too great or that the amount of praise is too small, or a combination of both. That you can learn more by listening than by talking may be true—supervisors would do well to practice their listening skills.

Supervisors must also improve their skills of expression. There is no need to impress employees with your command of the English language or your technical expertise. It is important that your employees realize that *you* know what you are talking about, but it may be even more important that *they* understand what you are saying.

Your workers will undoubtedly have various cultural and educational backgrounds and work experiences. Supervisors who are good communicators try to take these differences into account when communicating with their workers. Some workers may understand an explanation that only confuses others.

As a supervisor, you will spend a good part of your time trying to make sure that all your workers understand what you are saying. The following considerations may help you in your efforts at effective communication:

- Keep in mind that each worker is different and that what succeeds with one may fail with another.

- Use simple and direct language. Just because something is easy for some to understand does not mean that everyone can understand it.

- Repeat what is important for your workers to understand. Remember that much of what we learn is based on repetition.

- Communicate the same message in different ways. For example, in training employees, you may use discussions, written materials, demonstrations, and visual aids to communicate your message.

- Use open-ended questions. Open-ended questions, those which cannot be responded to with a simple "yes" or "no," tell us whether employees are understanding us.

- Remember that face-to-face communication works best because it provides an opportunity for direct, immediate interaction between supervisor and employee.

Formal channels

Supervisors who are good communicators use the formal channels of communication in their local government. Their participation is critical for facilitating effective communication between employees and management.

Supervisors should use downward communication to keep their employees informed. Workers want to know about decisions being made that directly affect them. They want to know what changes they can anticipate. Such information should always be presented to workers in a positive and constructive way. The supervisor has a duty to support directives from above and to communicate his or her support to workers. If you tell your workers, "I don't like these changes, but...," or "I can't agree with their decision, but...," or "I know this isn't going to work because...," you are actually encouraging your workers to gripe and complain and to carry out the directive with a less than wholehearted effort. The success or failure of many management directives depends on the supervisor's willingness to present them in a favorable light to workers.

Supervisors also have a responsibility to communicate upward. Management wants and needs to know how well workers are doing their jobs and how workers feel about their work. One of the primary concerns expressed by workers is that no one listens to their problems or does anything about them. Employees' problems and concerns can be resolved only if management addresses them. However, management (or the governing body) must first become aware of the problems. It is important that workers feel that their supervisor is concerned about them and is willing to express their problems for them.

You should give thoughtful consideration to the means you use to communicate information upward. It can be done face to face in a meeting or one on one by telephone. Or, you may decide to put information in writing, in a memo, letter, or formal report. Time, importance of the information, its accuracy, and its sensitivity all weigh upon the means of communicating the information. If having an accurate, permanent record of the message is important, for example, putting it in writing is essential. However, if confidentiality is important, then communicating the message in person may be critical.

In any event, it is important to be prepared. Plan what you intend to say and decide how best to say it. Organize your information—whether it represents facts, ideas, or impressions—so that it is clear and understandable. Present the information in the way that you feel will best accomplish your purpose.

Some supervisors think that if management knows the employees' concerns it reflects poorly on them as supervisors. They feel they aren't doing a good job. However, many problems and issues cannot be solved at the supervisory level. Legitimate employee concerns should be communicated upward for the benefit of both employees and management.

Communicating with a diverse work force

Another aspect of communicating effectively with your work unit is to recognize the diversity of your employees. As mentioned in Chapter 2, the U.S. work force is composed of workers from other cultures, younger workers and older ones, larger numbers of women and people of color, as well as workers with disabilities. Supervisors need to be sensitive to the needs of all members of such a widely heterogenous group. Building effective communication skills is critical to overcoming any barriers that might keep you from creating a strong, closely knit work team.

Intercultural communications

In order to communicate effectively with workers from cultural or ethnic backgrounds that are different from your own, you need to have patience and show respect for workers by treating them as individuals. You must be nonjudgmental. You'll also need to be aware of differences in language, sense of time and personal place, and nonverbal communications among various cultures.

The first step in developing communication skills to meet the demands of diversity is to know your own outlook and perspective. It is much easier to be nonjudgmental and open to different ways of thinking and doing things when you understand fully your own point of view.

Next, you need to exercise patience. Dealing with workers with different cultural or gender perspectives requires giving them—and you—time to get used to each other. Respecting differences is a critical step. Most supervisors, when they fully realize the richness that diversity brings to their work team, highly respect and value the differences among their workers.

There are several aspects of intercultural communication that you need to be aware of:

Language. When listening to employees who have an accent, have them repeat themselves if you do not clearly understand what they said. Guesswork can lead to embarrassment for both you and the worker. And never underestimate the intelligence or skill level of workers because they do not speak English clearly or have an accent different from yours.

Nonverbal communication. Always remember that both you and the worker you are communicating with are sending signals through body language. However, someone from a different culture may have different ways of interpreting the same gestures. For example, in Native American tribes, to give someone a firm handshake is to show disrespect, while in the dominant American culture, a firm handshake indicates assertiveness and sincerity. In Native American culture, to look someone directly in the eye can be a sign of disrespect, while the dominant culture insists upon making eye contact, again as a way of showing assertiveness and sincerity.

Physical distance. Cultures vary in what is considered the norm for physical distances between people who are communicating. It is important to remember that members of your work force who are from different cultural backgrounds may feel more or less comfortable with the distances you may be used to maintaining. To avoid misunderstandings with employees, be aware of your own feelings about acceptable distance and find out what their comfort level is by observing—or by just asking.

Gender differences

The different ways in which men and women communicate, stemming in part from the different ways in which they are brought up in our culture, can at times be comical. But they can also cause real confusion in the work place. Deborah Tannen, in her book *You Just Don't Understand*, has recorded numerous examples of misunderstanding that have their basis in what she sees as a fundamental difference in the communication styles of men and women. A work-related example follows:

> Morton, a psychologist on the staff of a private clinic, has a problem with the clinic director, Roberta. At staff meetings, Roberta generally opens discussion of issues by asking all staff members for their opinions. She invites debate about the pros and cons of proposals, but somehow, when the meeting ends, they always end up deciding—by consensus—to do what Roberta thinks best. The women on the staff are happy with Roberta as a director. They feel she listens to their points of view, and they like the rule by consensus rather than fiat. But

Morton feels Roberta is manipulative. If they are going to do what she wants anyway, why does she make them waste their breath expressing their opinions? He would prefer she just lay down the law, since she is the boss.

Morton's impression that Roberta does not act like a boss is the result of style differences. She *is* acting like a boss—a woman boss.

Although Morton considered Roberta's behavior manipulative, when a female supervisor seeks consensus, her actions also may be interpreted—by other women as well as men—as evidence of her incompetence, inability to make independent decisions, or lack of authority. When a male supervisor seeks consensus, however, he may be seen approvingly as someone who is so sure of his authority that he is willing to relinquish some of it to others.

Tannen also points out the reluctance of many women to express themselves at mixed-gender meetings because they are not accustomed to competing with men for the floor. This reluctance could be mistakenly interpreted to mean that these women have nothing to add to the discussion, when they may have valid observations and helpful suggestions to offer.

Tannen says that both men and women can make adjustments in these situations. A woman, for example, can push herself to speak without being asked or without waiting for a polite interval before beginning. A man can recognize that a woman may not feel as free to speak as he does and allow a bit more time for her to respond or ask her directly what she thinks. It is particularly important for supervisors to understand these differences in style because they ultimately affect the contribution that members make to the work team. Supervisors must be attentive to gender differences in communication style and—as with all differences—respect and make room for them.

Communicating with disabled employees

Whether you are supervising a new employee with a disability, or a seasoned employee who has become disabled, it is important to communicate with sensitivity to the disabled person's needs. For example, when talking to a person with severe vision loss, identify yourself and others in the group. Do not shout at a hearing- impaired person but look directly at him or her and speak clearly. In a conversation with a person in a wheelchair, never lean on the person's wheelchair. If possible, don't remain standing; sitting at the same level as the person in the wheelchair will make eye contact and conversation easier and more natural.

While being sensitive to a disabled person's particular needs, be sure to treat the person as you would any other competent adult employee. Be careful to avoid any behavior that might appear patronizing.

As a supervisor, you need to be aware of the ways in which a specific disability should be accommodated in the work place. Your Equal Employment Opportunity (EEO) officer or ADA coordinator is an excellent resource for this type of information.

To be an effective supervisor of a person with a disability, it is critical to understand the implications of the particular disability. For example, if a hearing impaired person is part of your work unit, you need to know the extent of impairment, what the person's preferences are for communicating (sign language, lip reading, speaking), and any special needs he or she may have in order to carry out work assignments (such as a special phone and phone lines for the hearing impaired called a Telecommunications Device for the Deaf, or TDD).

However you communicate with a disabled worker, it is imperative that you communicate with respect. Never underestimate a disabled worker's capabilities. You can fully expect, with the proper equipment and facility design, that he or she will meet the requirements of the job.

Summary

It is easy to see why communication is so much a part of good supervision. Communication is the process supervisors use to get work done through others.

Supervisors must be aware that they do not communicate merely by sending out various types of messages—these messages may have little meaning in themselves because messages are merely symbols of meanings. If a receiver does not attach the same meaning to the message that the sender does, no communication occurs between them.

As we have said, effective communication is a two-way process. It requires a willingness to change or to be changed—essentially, it demands an open mind. We have to be willing not only to express ourselves but also to hear what others have to say and to give their messages thoughtful consideration.

Good communication between supervisors and workers can help your work unit function better as a team in completing tasks. And good communication can help the supervisor gain the trust and respect of workers—something that is basic to developing effective supervisory practices.

Checklist

Be aware of the importance of effective communication.

Recognize that communication is a process and involves a number of parts.

Understand the various ways of communicating verbally and nonverbally.

Learn to use both the formal and informal channels of communication in your organization.

Recognize the major barriers to effective communication.

Understand the importance of giving and receiving feedback.

Remember the significance of active listening in effective communication.

Appreciate the relationship between good communication and good supervision.

Be sensitive to the diverse communication styles in your organization that result from differences in gender and culture.

Supervisory situation 9/1

John has been a supervisor in the purchasing department for the past four years. Jim and Miguel are buyers in his division who have had problems working together. Jim is fifty-two years old and has been involved in various aspects of purchasing for the past twenty years. Jim prides himself on having worked his way up to senior buyer in charge of coordinating all capital purchases for the city.

Miguel was hired by John two years ago. Miguel speaks with a strong Spanish accent and his English is sometimes hard to understand; at John's urging he is taking courses in English at night school. John assigned Miguel to work with Jim as an assistant buyer. However, they have not been able to work cooperatively together. Both have continually complained to John about the other. Jim's major complaint is that Miguel does not follow directions and often turns in work that Jim has to redo. Miguel, on the other hand, complains that Jim is far too demanding and impatient. "I don't think Jim likes me at all," Miguel has said.

When John called these two employees into his office he was determined to resolve the longstanding issue between them. John requested that both employees sit down and face each other. He then told each he wanted to help them resolve their argument by laying some ground rules for discussion. John stated that each employee was to take five minutes to tell the other exactly how he was feeling about the issue. When one was speaking the other was to actively listen.

Jim began by telling Miguel that he liked his sense of humor and unassuming manner. He then told Miguel that what he really didn't understand was why Miguel didn't follow his directions. Jim's voice grew louder as he recounted the latest incident, when Miguel had been instructed to contact the police department to clarify questions about the police sedan specifications that the department had submitted: "You did not contact the department and consequently, several items included in the specifications were inaccurate. Your lack of follow-through could cost the city an extra $2,500 per police vehicle. That's a waste of the taxpayers' money," Jim fumed.

When it was Miguel's turn, he first said that it sounded as though Jim was really angry and frustrated. "You feel that I don't follow directions and that I did not contact the police department as you had told me to do. I guess you're right. I didn't follow through. But that's because I thought you told me to check the police sedan specifications and to call them if I had any questions. I read the specs and didn't see anything wrong with them. But, I will admit there were a few phrases I had trouble understanding. I felt that if I asked you to explain them, you would be angry. You don't like me, do you, Jim?" Miguel asked.

After the session, Jim and Miguel admitted they had at least a better understanding of the other's point of view.

1. *What were the active listening steps that each employee was asked to follow?*

2. *How do you think active listening may have helped in this case?*

Supervisory situation 9/2

Claude was administrative assistant to the head of the accounting division of the finance department. Both Claude and his supervisor constantly emphasized that Claude was not in the chain of command, but, instead, aided the division head in all his operations. It was known to all, however, that Claude was the chief's eyes and ears in employee relations. To carry out this function, Claude made it a point to have coffee and lunch with the personnel in the various sections on a regular basis.

At coffee one morning the conversation turned to the computer system recently installed to handle most of the bookkeeping and check writing functions of the division. The computer had been purchased by the city for this purpose, and the task of restructuring the office and its procedures in order to utilize the equipment was being discussed.

In the course of the conversation two young men from another division raised the possibility of combining several accounting and reporting systems to more efficiently utilize computer time. The discussion soon turned to the possibility of setting up a data processing center for joint use by the city, the county, and the independent school system.

The next morning at coffee Claude raised the problem of the computer discussion again, interjecting some specific questions that had occurred to him since the previous meeting. The topic was so interesting to the participants that Claude asked to group to serve as a team to work on the project; he then received permission from the accounting division to establish the group as a formal project team.

Meetings of the group continued for several weeks and a recommendation was prepared on restructuring the office and revising necessary procedures. The day after the recommendation was finalized, an idea began to form in Claude's mind. Why not write up the recommendation and turn it in to the city suggestion system?

Under the suggestion system, which had been in operation for some time, employees were given cash awards based on a sliding scale of from 1 to 10 percent of the annual savings accruing from acceptable suggestions. While Claude knew that because of his staff position he could not receive a cash award, he knew he could receive formal recognition for any acceptable suggestion.

A short time after Claude turned the suggestion in, he was told that his suggestion had been approved and he was to be recognized at a rather impressive ceremony during the next city council meeting. Among the spectators at the ceremony were several members of Claude's project team.

On the morning following the presentation of the award Claude again joined the coffee group. The reception he received was less than friendly. Indeed, one of the women in the group told Claude that his presence was no longer welcome since the group did not feel that he had acted fairly in not sharing recognition with the group. When Claude tried to defend himself, stating that each member of the group had had the same opportunity to submit the suggestion that he had had, and that, further, he had used a great deal of his own time in writing up the suggestion, he got nowhere.

But this was not the end of the matter. Word of the "suggestion case" spread rapidly through the entire division and Claude found that the welcome mat was no longer out for him when he tried to join other coffee and luncheon groups. The seriousness of the situation hit his supervisor in two different but equally important ways. First, Claude's efficiency level began to drop rapidly. Second, and perhaps more important, Claude's function as a channel of communication between the division head and his employees disappeared almost completely.

Claude realized that he must rebuild his relationship with the group in order to have an effective team.

1. What should Claude do?

aspects of the game. They fail because they can't translate their ideas and plans into action by their players. The best plans and decisions in game situations are useless if the players can't or won't follow them. Winning coaches are those who can direct players toward a goal that they themselves are interested in achieving. Players usually respond to coaches who show confidence in them. They are more likely to succeed in game situations when coaches have demonstrated day-to-day support and encouragement. The great coach assumes responsibility for teaching the players the skills they need—and for encouraging the players to excel.

There are times when the supervisory coach will be severely challenged. It may be by the employee who feels he or she is more qualified for the supervisor's position, or by the marginal worker who does just enough to get by, or by the employee who possesses excellent technical skills but is not able to get along with his or her co-workers.

In the face of these challenges, the supervisor is responsible for getting the work out—for results and productivity. He or she must direct the individual's work and that of the crew or team, yet still have a vision of the big picture, the goals the department must accomplish. It is the job of the effective supervisory coach to find ways to cope with human demands and to inspire commitment among employees. After all, the true test of a successful coach is not only the day-to-day performance record—it is the bonds of trust and respect created

Players respond to the coach who shows confidence in them.

within the team that produce consistent winning results over a long period of time.

The supervisory coach

Your actions as a supervisory coach can either encourage an employee to perform to the best of his or her abilities, or cause him or her to resent you and work against you. Successful coaching in most cases involves the psychological aspect of dealing effectively with people—not the psychology presented in textbooks, but plain, commonsense psychology.

It is important to remember that different coaching actions will almost certainly produce different reactions among your employees. No two people are alike. For instance, you may successfully correct one employee who has just made a mistake by mildly calling attention to the mistake and requesting that he or she try not to let it happen again. On the other hand, with a different employee, you may need to be much more severe and explicit in dealing with mistakes.

The line in the song that says "different strokes for different folks" is a fitting lesson in coaching psychology. Knowing the individual, his or her needs, and knowing which of your coaching actions will be perceived by the employee as a reward or as a punishment is a very important aspect of coaching. A point to remember is that what serves as a reward or punishment for you, the supervisor, may not do the same for your employees.

An illustration of this is the older supervisor who comes to work in local government after a long military career. For a long time he has served in an organization where directives, orders, inspections, and discipline are a major part of daily activities. He motivates his employees in the way that he is accustomed to being motivated—by using his authority and threatening punishment for wrongdoing. He may feel that most of his subordinates hate work and that they will try to get away with doing the least amount of work possible. Because of his attitude, morale in the work unit falls, the employees resent him for his iron-fisted techniques, and they do only what they are told to do and not a bit more. This supervisor fails to realize that fear and threat of punishment can carry you only so far—and that if they do not produce the desired behavior once they are used, they become ineffective management techniques (after all, what else can you do to the employee once he or she is fired?).

More important, he fails to realize that different people in his unit and different situations require different coaching actions. For example, one employee works well for him and is eager to learn new skills. However, once he learns them he becomes bored and his work deteriorates. In the place of threatening this employee with disciplinary action for poor work, an effective coaching action would be to point out to the employee how much the employee's eagerness to learn is appreciated. Then the supervisor can point out that the employee is having a problem staying with a job until it is satisfactorily completed. The

supervisor lets the employee know how this problem is affecting the entire unit, and enlists the employee's support in finding ways to correct the problem. Successful coaching supervisors treat employees as responsible adults who can help find solutions to problems.

Effective coaching

The effective coaching supervisor builds a strong one-to-one relationship, or one-to-small-group relationship, with his or her workers. In basketball, for example, the real coaching takes place among the subunits of the team, such as guards and forwards. Nothing is more essential in directing and motivating the activities of others than the bonds of trust and mutual support that develop in a strong one-to-one relationship. The coach must take a close look at each person and try to figure out: How can I get across to this person what I want done? How can I bring out this person's best work efforts? Then you must constantly evaluate what he or she has learned and how the new skills and knowledge are being used in the performance of the job.

Praise and encouragement are the most effective coaching tools. They enable the supervisory coach to define exactly what he or she expects in a *positive* way. Also, the good behaviors and performance of employees are reinforced through praise and encouragement. However, some employees may respond better to criticism—and it is the supervisory coach's responsibility to observe which workers need praise and which workers may respond better to criticism.

Remember, though, that a person must possess a very good self-image before criticism can stimulate desired behavior. Most people want to know how they are doing and want to be told if they are not doing the job right. However, ineffective supervisors are apt to criticize a subordinate too harshly, or to focus criticism on the person rather than on the problem. Criticism should always be directed at correcting a problem, not at demeaning an individual's personality. For example, if a cashier in the tax department is wearing clothing inappropriate for the job, avoid saying, "Your taste in clothes is horrible for a person who has to meet the public much of the time." Instead, you might say, "I think the citizens we serve may be put off by the clothes you've been wearing on the job lately. Let's sit down and talk about how we can remedy the problem."

A good coach tries to be a "people developer"—and you can't develop people by tearing them down. The point to consider is that you need to direct your criticisms and actions at correcting the mistake or solving the problem, not at calling attention to defects in an individual's personality.

Think of a supervisor you may have worked for whom you considered to be effective. What characteristics of that person's coaching style do you recall? Do you remember how he or she treated you and how you felt? Some comments probably are:

"He was a motivator—I always found myself wanting to give my best."

"She was a diplomat—always tactful in letting me know what needed to be done or how I had messed up."

"A real smooth communicator—I never realized how hard he worked to have me understand exactly what he wanted me to do."

"She was firm, but fair—always treated everyone consistently and you knew exactly where you stood."

You may remember many other things about how you felt working for an effective supervisory coach. There are several coaching actions that can contribute to effective supervision. They are as follows:

▪ Provide your employees with positive encouragement—employees will respond favorably when they feel they are being supported.

▪ When you have to criticize, focus on the mistake or the problem, not the individual's personality. A problem-solving approach will result in less hostility and increased performance.

▪ Give your employees both positive and negative feedback—they want and expect information about their performance. It will help them to develop and become better at what they do.

▪ Build and maintain strong relationships with your employees—there is no substitute for face-to-face contact. Be accessible to them, and be attentive to their problems.

▪ Confront employees with problems in their performance. Be honest with them about your feelings when their behavior is unacceptable—a constructive attitude and a sincere desire to help the employee will help you increase the batting average of poor performers.

▪ Use active listening skills.

▪ Listen more than you talk. Ask questions designed to give you information you need to solve the problem together. Don't ask a question if you are not going to listen to the answer.

Ineffective coaching

Have you ever worked for someone who was totally ineffective at supervising people? What characteristics of that person's work behavior made that person an ineffective supervisor? Some responses probably are:

"He took all the credit for the work *I* did!"

"She didn't take the time to really get to know people."

"She didn't think you had a brain and could think for yourself....She was always telling you where, when, and how the work should be done....She treated me like a child."

"He put himself on a pedestal once he made supervisor....You couldn't even talk to him."

"He was so unappreciative. He felt that you were paid to do a job and that you should just do it. The funny thing is that he was always complaining to me about how the department head didn't appreciate all the things he did to make the department look good."

Sound familiar? You may have thought of these and a number of other characteristics. In fact, you probably told yourself more than once that if you were ever promoted to supervisor, you would try your best not to be like that ineffective supervisor.

There are many specific supervisory coaching actions that can keep you from getting work accomplished through people—that can make you an ineffective coach. If you are on the receiving end of the following coaching actions, you probably react negatively and consider your supervisor ineffective:

- *Threatening.* "You better do this, or else...!"
- *Commanding.* "You *must* do this!" "I order you to do this."
- *Attacking.* "What a stupid thing to do!" "You've always been so lazy."
- *Moralizing.* "Believe me, I know what's best for you."
- *Ridiculing or shaming.* "You think you have it rough? You should have been around when I first came to the city." "They just don't make workers the way they used to!"
- *Blaming.* "You're the reason why so many things go wrong around here."

These coaching actions will almost invariably draw defensive reactions from workers. Think

about it...if you thought someone was threatening you physically—say, going to punch you—what would be your first reaction? It would be to protect yourself. Well, the same thing happens to us when we feel threatened psychologically. If we feel our well-being, our self-esteem, or our self-worth is being attacked, we are likely to react by protecting ourselves.

When threatened most people will defend themselves. For instance, if a supervisor threatens an employee with harsh disciplinary action the employee might deny that he or she has a problem or rationalize, making excuses for the undesirable behavior. The employee might counterattack by acting flippant or equally aggressive toward the supervisor. Or the employee might just take the threat of punishment and withdraw, like a turtle protecting itself from harm.

The sad fact is that productivity suffers, feelings are hurt, future work is jeopardized, and it will take a long time for the supervisor and the worker to patch up their relationship after a conflict. The supervisor will probably label the employee a problem employee with a bad attitude. The employee, in turn, will probably be disgruntled and feel that he or she has been treated too harshly—and the supervisor may soon be looking for a new employee. However, an effective supervisory coach might prevent all this trouble from happening by developing and using a plan for coaching employees.

A coaching plan

As an effective supervisor-coach you'll need to know when to coach and what to coach. Generally you will need to assume the role of coach when a member of your work team does not know how to do an assigned task, performs a job task incorrectly, or does not perform to prescribed standards. The specific subject matter of your coaching sessions will be the difference between what is being done and what should be done.

Generally if the performance problem is one of attitude or motivation, you need to counsel the employee. Once you identify a performance problem that requires coaching, either through personal observation or an employee's direct request for help, you can develop a coaching plan based on good coaching actions. Elements of a plan follow:

- Let employees know what's expected of them by setting standards and clearly defining job responsibilities. Develop a work plan with agreed-upon tasks and completion dates.

- Let employees know how they are doing, through positive and negative feedback, evaluation of the workers' performance and documentation of their strengths and weaknesses, and a performance interview at least once a year.

- Mutually develop a plan for improvement, by monitoring employees' progress in areas that may need strengthening and suggesting appropriate training. Recognize and praise performance improvement.

Give or withhold rewards based on employees' performance.

Finally, remember the principles of effective communication discussed in Chapter 9. How you get your message across is as important as what you say. Your enthusiasm, eye contact, nonverbal behavior, gestures, voice inflection, all are powerful coaching tools at your disposal. You have the opportunity to convey encouragement, trust, and support, or to convey hostility, dissatisfaction, and disapproval. Don't lose the opportunity to be an effective supervisory coach!

What is counseling?

Counseling is another application of good communication principles that you can use on the job. Counseling skills can help you develop your employees and build a positive relationship with them. Most of all, counseling skills can help you be more effective as a supervisory coach. Most employees want to feel the sense of accomplishment and satisfaction that comes from doing a good job. They want your approval, and they want to be able to come to you for help. Counseling skills help you to capitalize on these needs. Employees can and do change through the supervisor's effective use of counseling techniques.

Counseling is a face-to-face communication or interview that can be used in a wide range of

Basic coaching: Look at the employee, measure the employee, and work with the employee.

situations: for performance appraisal, for work progress review, for dealing with employees with personal problems, and for addressing employee performance problems. For example, counseling may be the first thing you do with an employee who wastes time, who has a record of being late or absent, who is careless, who has a drinking problem, or who seems to be going through a personal crisis at home. Think of counseling as the first step you take toward solving performance-related problems. Sometimes counseling is the step you take before taking disciplinary action.

The difference between coaching and counseling

The essence of counseling is that you

- Help your employee identify a problem

- Help your employee figure out alternative ways to deal with the problem

- Help your employee to arrive at a solution to the problem—or, if not a solution, at least a decision on what needs to be done

- Hold your employee accountable and responsible for the decision.

To do these things you must resist being judgmental about the person and the decision made and resist the temptation to make the decision for the person—you must avoid letting the person know what you would do. You can only hold the person accountable for correcting a problem if it is his or her decision to correct it.

This is what distinguishes counseling from coaching: when coaching, you direct the activities of others, while in your role as a supervisory counselor, you act as a reporter, an observer, someone who can help the employee to help himself or herself and to manage his or her own life better, without directing how he or she should manage—that needs to come from the individual. Most adults strive to gain more control over their lives and situations. Self-control makes us feel more secure and gives us a sense of well-being. If you put yourself in the position of making personal decisions for an employee, you are likely to damage that person's self-esteem. In effect, you are treating the person as a child rather than as a mature adult. Your role as a counselor is to try to help your employees solve their problems for themselves—they win because they experience more control over their lives, and you win because performance problems will be corrected!

Counseling skills

Counseling skills are behaviors a supervisor can use to help an employee find solutions to problems that might affect their work performance. The counseling skills that we will talk about here are:

- Empathy

- Caring

- Questioning

- Listening

- Understanding

- Responding helpfully.

Each of these skills may seem obvious and simple, but they are not so easy to practice. To ask a question and really listen to the response rather than merely appear to listen, to really understand rather than to go through the motions of understanding, requires effort, concentration, and know-how.

While some people seem by nature to be more helpful than others, anyone who wants to be more helpful can improve his or her ability to care, question, listen, understand, and respond helpfully, by learning what to do and then practicing.

Why counsel?

It may be difficult for you as a supervisor concerned with output and deadlines to counsel your employees and try to help them solve their problems. You might well ask yourself, "Why should I bother with counseling skills? I'm not a minister or a social worker."

A most obvious and important answer is this: Your position as supervisor gives you great influence in the work setting. In the same way that workers will look to you as their coach, they will look to you also for support, understanding, and direction in dealing with their problems of working and living.

If you can listen and be helpful in these situations you are also doing yourself a favor. When you take time to listen to and understand your employees, you are demonstrating to them that you are the kind of person they can talk to and trust. Therefore, they will be more likely to come to you with difficulties in the work setting while such difficulties are still manageable problems and not catastrophes.

Your department's productivity is affected by the attitudes and moods of all the workers. Workers who are spending time and energy worrying are putting less of themselves into their jobs. Similarly, workers involved in a misunderstanding with each other can disrupt the cooperation of the work team. The supervisor who takes a few minutes to talk over such concerns with workers is usually able to help relieve their minds and get them back on the track.

Taking an interest in your employees by showing them that you appreciate them and want to listen to them helps them to find satisfaction in their jobs. Recent studies have shown that these behaviors are far more important to workers than most supervisors realize. It should not surprise us. We all have the need to respect ourselves and have others respect and appreciate us. When you take the time to understand employees it helps to satisfy this need. Employees will usually repay you for your interest with loyalty and hard work.

Empathy

Empathy is an attribute that is very helpful in counseling. The supervisor who is empathetic is not only aware of how an individual worker feels, but is also able to feel the same way. For example, if an employee is stressed because she has difficulty delivering and picking up her child at a day-care facility within regular working hours, you, as an empathetic supervisor, can actually feel the stress too. In other words, you do not just understand your worker's anxiety, you experience it.

Why is this skill so valuable to you as a supervisor? There are several important reasons: empathy can propel you to find a creative solution to a problem. You are more apt to take the employee's point of view seriously and to think of immediate resolutions. You may build a stronger bond with an employee, which can enhance morale. Empathy also enhances your ability to treat the members of your work team as significant human beings, not just as elements in the production or delivery of a service. Employees want and need to know that someone understands them and takes their feelings seriously.

In the example of the employee who had a problem with day-care, the empathetic supervisor would feel the employee's anxiety and take seriously the need to find a solution. The effective supervisor might work out a flex-time schedule so that the employee is able to drop off and pick up her child at the day-care facility and still work the number of hours that the job requires.

To be empathetic requires practice, as does any other interpersonal communication skill. The first step in developing empathy is to realize your own prejudgments and assessments about situations, because they can affect your objectivity. You need to set aside your feelings about a particular situation in order to free yourself to feel the way someone else might. Next, you need to listen actively to your employee to understand accurately his or her situation and viewpoint. Open-ended questions that begin with why or how can help you get a complete picture of the issue at hand. Next, you need to accept the employee's feelings and perceptions. That doesn't mean you necessarily agree with them, but it does mean that you acknowledge the way that person perceives his or her reality. Once you rid yourself of your perceptions of how the situation should be viewed and you fully accept your employee's viewpoint, you are fully prepared to approach the situation in an empathetic way. You are prepared to move forward with that employee to develop a resolution that is both understanding and caring.

Caring

Caring—or taking an interest in the worker—is any behavior on the supervisor's part that lets the worker know the supervisor respects him or her as an individual with rights, feelings, values, and a life outside the work setting.

Caring may be as simple as telling a worker he or she has done a good job or reassuring a worker that you know he or she can do a new task well. It can also be the following:

■ Going out of your way to tell a worker you are concerned when you learn he or she has had a death in the family, an accident, or some other upsetting event

▪ Congratulating a worker who has been promoted

▪ Asking a worker to show you a picture of his or her new baby or grandchild

▪ Following through on a worker's suggestion or complaint.

A supervisor can also show caring in situations that are difficult or unpleasant. When a supervisor has to discipline a worker for a violation of a regulation the supervisor can ask to hear the worker's side of the story. When workers feel that a supervisor understands why they broke a rule and does not hold it against them, it is easier for them to accept that supervisor's warning or disciplinary action.

There are times when a supervisor must let a worker know that his or her behavior is affecting job performance and could result in dismissal. Again, if a supervisor is willing to listen to the worker and look at the situation from the worker's point of view, the worker may be more willing to hear the supervisor's recommendations. In the case of alcoholism, for example, a worker may be less defensive about the problem and may be more willing to seek help if the supervisor is understanding and helpful, not judging or condemning.

Caring also means respecting the workers. That does not mean the supervisor must *like* each and every worker. It does mean that the supervisor is willing to regard each worker as an individual with a right to his or her own ideas, values, attitudes, and life-style. This statement could be expanded:

▪ Respect is listening to your workers and attempting to understand their viewpoints even when they are quite different from yours.

▪ Respect is treating all employees fairly, regardless of their politics, race, national origin, religion, age, or appearance. It is giving yourself a chance to know people before you judge them on the basis of their hair, their politics, or the color of their skin.

▪ Respect is accepting people who are different from you. It takes a person who is mature, who is satisfied to be himself or herself and is willing to let others be themselves. Remember that when people think or act in ways very different from yours, it can be threatening. You may take the difference as a criticism or mockery of beliefs that are important to you. You may feel threatened because you must take a second look at your own attitudes and beliefs.

An attitude of acceptance and respect for people *as they are* is essential if you are to be effective as a counselor. It allows you to be effective as a helper. It allows people to feel comfortable with you and talk about things that are difficult to admit, even to themselves. If your workers feel you will listen to them without judging them or holding what they say against them, they may be able to look at their

Showing interest in and concern for people is a simple thing to do.

problems more honestly, to admit more readily their responsibility, and to deal with problems more realistically.

Questioning and listening

One of the most important communication skills is listening. Listening to a worker and trying to understand what he or she has to say is a visible demonstration of your caring and respect for that person. In effective counseling, listening and questioning go hand in hand. Once you have asked a question and the worker is prepared to give you information, you should practice listening.

The supervisor should try very hard to listen and understand what the other person is saying. Hear the person out. Don't interrupt. Be patient. Hear the other person's feelings as well as his or her arguments.

Use appropriate listening responses that convey to the other person that you are interested and want him or her to continue:

■ Show you are listening by facing the employee and looking him or her square in the eye.

■ A gentle nod of your head, with eyes fixed on the speaker, provides encouragement but does not necessarily indicate agreement with what is being said.

■ A casual remark such as "I see" or "Mmmm" lets the employee know you are following the conversation.

The use of questions closely relates to listening. It is what you do when you want the employee to provide you with further information, or when you want to clarify points already made. The skill is to be listening well enough to pick up key points needing further clarification without interrupting.

Important aspects of questioning are the tone of your voice and the phrasing of the question itself. Your phrasing and the tone of your voice will often influence the attitude and responses of the employee. For example, the following question is likely to bring about a very defensive or antagonistic response:

"Why did you mess up so badly on that report I asked you to do?"

A softer line of questioning focusing specifically on what you found wrong with the report is more likely to solve the problem. The supervisor could say: "I called you in here today to talk with you about the report you submitted. There were some points I didn't quite understand. Also, you may need to check some of your calculations because I found some errors. Let's talk about how this report can be improved. First, did you have problems doing it?"

This problem-solving approach appeals to a person's sense of responsibility and maturity. You are more likely to solve the problem than if you humiliate or embarrass the employee.

You can ask closed questions, those that invite a one-word answer, such as, "Is that what really happened?" Or you can ask open, probing questions, inviting a more lengthy response, such as, "I understand you were involved in an accident. Can you tell me exactly what happened?" Above all, *don't* ask a question if you are not prepared to listen to the employee's response.

Understanding

Understanding is putting yourself in the other person's shoes, seeing the problem or situation from the other person's point of view. You do this by listening to the worker's words and feelings. As you listen, you attempt to think and feel with the worker and imagine what the situation the worker is describing *means to him or her.* Very often it is helpful to call on your own experiences to help appreciate what the worker is thinking and feeling. If a worker is describing resentment toward another worker, for example, you might recall occasions when you felt resentment yourself.

Sometimes when you are trying very hard to understand someone you not only remember what the feeling is like but you actually go through that feeling along with the person. As discussed earlier, this empathy can be very helpful to the other person. When you are feeling *with* a worker, everything about you—the expression on your face, the words you use, your tone of voice—tells the worker you really *do* understand just what he or she is saying.

Seeing a problem or situation from another's point of view can be difficult because each person reacts to a situation according to his or her own beliefs, attitudes, and past experiences.

Take the case of a parking ticket. You walk up to your car and see the red flag in the parking meter proclaiming "Violation," and under the windshield wiper is the parking ticket.

Do you respond calmly and logically in this situation, recognizing that you are at fault, and take your $15 to the police station? Some people do—and some even find a bit of humor in the situation.

But there are also individuals among us who are outraged at being ticketed. They feel that the police should be tracking down muggers and burglars instead of ticketing parked cars. Some people are angry at themselves for returning late, and some feel guilty when they think about their spouses finding out about the ticket. Some people are embarrassed at being caught violating the law. They walk up beside the car, glance around to see if anyone is looking, and snatch the ticket from under the wiper.

In each case, the situation is the same but people experience the situation differently. When you are trying to understand someone, then, you cannot take it for granted that they will react as you would in the same situation. If a worker is promoted you probably assume that he or she is excited, proud, and happy about the extra money. It is possible, however, that the worker actually has mixed feelings, is worried about handling the new responsibility,

or feels guilty about a friend he or she thought more deserving.

The only way you can be sure you have really understood a worker is to check it out face to face. To do this, you can repeat in your own words what you think the worker is saying and feeling. If you have misunderstood either the facts or the feelings, the worker has a chance to tell you.

In your attempt to understand a worker, do not hesitate to ask questions about things that are not clear to you. Questions often tell a worker you are interested and want to make the effort to understand. Be sure, however, that your questions are important to an understanding of the worker's viewpoint. Questions that seem aimed at irrelevant details may tell the worker you are curious or inattentive rather than concerned.

The greatest blocks to understanding are our biases, prejudices, and stereotypes. We all have them. A person with an "open mind" is not someone without biases or prejudices. He or she is someone who knows his or her blind spots and works to keep them from interfering with understanding another's viewpoint.

You can work to overcome your biases and prejudices, but first you must learn what they are. You can do this by noticing such things as the kinds of people you take an instant liking to, or by noticing the topics that you find it difficult to talk about without arguing.

Once you know your problem areas you can work on them. To fight prejudice, you use your energy to understand another's point of view instead of thinking up arguments to support your own. When you deal with a worker toward whom you feel prejudice, you should look for the worker's good points instead of focusing on faults.

Responding helpfully

Responding helpfully is any action the supervisor takes to help a worker with a problem. It can be as simple as a word of praise or reassurance given at the right time. In some cases, the helpful response is listening and letting the worker know he or she is understood; in others, it may be helping a worker explore feelings that are difficult to face.

Responding helpfully often requires helping the worker sort through the alternatives he or she has to solve the problem. Discussing alternatives is different from giving advice or telling a person, "This is how you should do it." It involves talking over the pros and cons of different courses of action with the worker—and then leaving it to the worker to make the choice of what is best in his or her own situation.

It is not helpful to brush aside or minimize a worker's problem. In an attempt to cheer up someone who is upset, people often will respond, "Come on, now, it's not as bad as that," or, "You'll feel better after a good night's sleep." While these remarks are intended to be helpful, they usually leave the person feeling frustrated and misunderstood. When a worker comes to you with some difficulty, he or she is serious about it and wants you to take it seriously.

Referring a worker for professional help

There are times when a supervisor needs to refer an employee for professional help. Employees who recognize that they need help for themselves or a member of their family may approach a supervisor and ask for a referral to an appropriate professional helper. In other cases, employees may not voluntarily seek help but the supervisor may feel that professional assistance is needed. Referral may be necessary when alcoholism, emotional problems, or various similar stresses are seriously affecting job performance.

In such situations the supervisor may have to bring to the worker's attention the supervisor's own knowledge of the employee's problem and its effects on job performance. The supervisor must then attempt to gain the employee's cooperation in seeking the help needed.

It is not your job as supervisor to resolve an employee problem that requires professional counseling. You are not a trained therapist. However, many organizations do have an employee assistance program (EAP) that offers professional, confidential counseling for troubled employees. This service is an invaluable tool for you as a supervisor, since you can refer an employee for professional help once

you have determined that an employee has a serious problem that is affecting job performance. Your initial counseling sessions can determine the level of intervention that is necessary to get the employee back on track. If the problem is severe, such as substance abuse, you may require referral to the employee assistance program. It is best to check with your organization's guidelines so that you know when you can require an employee to seek professional help through the EAP.

Remember that in most cases you cannot force an employee to seek help. Your role as supervisor is to

- Confront the employee with the problem and with how you see it affecting his or her work

- Advise the employee of any consequences that will occur if the behavior continues to affect work

- Recommend that you work together to see that he or she receives the needed help.

The following steps are intended to guide you in making a referral once the worker has agreed to seek help in this way:

- Seek the worker's confidence by listening and by assuring him or her that you want to help.

- Have as complete an understanding as possible of the worker's problem so that you will know which person or agency is the most appropriate source of help.

- Encourage the worker to take part in the referral process by asking for his or her suggestions and talking over possible alternative sources of help.

The following agencies and other agencies like them in your community can probably help workers:

- Community mental health centers (for people with emotional problems; many operate drug and alcohol clinics as well)

- Vocational rehabilitation services (for people with physical or emotional disabilities)

- The U.S. Social Security Administration (for disabled workers)

- Family counseling agencies (for parents having difficulties with children)

- County children's services (for parents interested in adoption, or parents having difficulties with their children; such problems as runaway children and child abuse are also handled)

- State employment services (for people changing careers or jobs)

- Area adult vocational and technical schools (for people changing careers or jobs, or those interested in learning or updating skills)

- Public health departments (clinics for communicable diseases, heart disease, cancer, diabetes, etc.; family planning clinics)

- Alcoholics Anonymous (nonprofessional group that provides support for alcoholics and their families).

Confidentiality

If you are involved in a counseling relationship with a worker, *you are ethically bound to keep all your communications confidential.* You may not reveal to a third party what a worker has told you in trust and confidence, with two exceptions. One is in the case of a referral of a worker for professional help. In this instance you need to talk about the worker and his or her problem to the referral person or agency. However, you must secure the worker's permission to do this. The other exception is in the case of a worker who is a danger to himself or herself or to other people. In this instance you need to share the information with the proper authority or agency.

Checklist

Coaching:

Take an interest in your workers: show them they are important as individuals.

Use positive encouragement as the first step in coaching.

When coaching, focus criticism on the problem, not on the individual.

Develop a coaching plan—adapt your style and the plan to each individual and each situation.

What you say is less important than how you say it—be aware of your tone, your inflection, and your body language—think how they affect other people.

Confront employees with problems in their performance. Be honest.

Listen more than you talk.

Counseling:

When you are listening to a worker's problem, give that person your undivided attention.

Give each worker the respect due anyone, regardless of beliefs, attitudes, gender, race, religion, life-style, or physical ability.

Put yourself in the worker's place and try to see the problem from his or her point of view.

Do not assume that a worker would react to a situation in the way that you would.

Help the worker explore feelings, since feelings are an important part of every problem.

Repeat what you think the worker is saying and feeling so that he or she can tell you whether you have understood.

Help a worker sort through various alternatives to solve a problem; then let the worker decide which is best.

Do not minimize a worker's problem: he or she takes it seriously and wants you to do the same.

When a worker asks for professional help, or when a worker's problems are seriously affecting

performance on the job, work with him or her to arrange a referral for professional help.

Keep all communications between you and your worker in the course of your counseling strictly confidential.

Supervisory situation 10/1

As the supervisor of the vehicle maintenance division, Hassan finds it necessary to constantly take courses in various aspects of vehicle maintenance. Electrical systems, hydraulics, and fuel injection engines are changing so rapidly that he finds it difficult to stay on top of things. Hassan also finds it necessary to make sure that his work unit is informed so that they are able to be as effective and productive as they can be. Lately, Hassan has tried to have daily meetings with his crew to discuss innovations in vehicle maintenance.

However, Hassan has noticed that even though he is taking the time to read to the crew from the maintenance manuals and to show training videos, his crew seems to stick to their own ways of doing things. Hassan is surprised that none of the crew ever tries any of the new methods that he reads to them. In fact, most of the time they seem bored with the tailgate sessions.

1. *What are some coaching tips that may help Hassan teach his crew new techniques?*

2. *How can Hassan motivate his crew to participate more fully in his daily meetings?*

Supervisory situation 10/2

Sandy has noticed that Leo has been late for work the past four Mondays. Leo's wife called in on each occasion to say that he was sick. In reviewing Leo's work file, Sandy was reminded that in the past month Leo had an accident in one of the city cars when driving to a meeting across town. As his immediate supervisor, Sandy has called Leo into her office to discuss her observations.

1. *If you were Sandy, how would you begin your discussion with Leo?*

2. *What type of questions might help you determine more clearly whether Leo has a problem and how you might help remedy it?*

MOTIVATING EMPLOYEES

Our chief want in life is somebody who shall make us do what we can.

Ralph Waldo Emerson

11

MOTIVATING EMPLOYEES

When we talk about motivation we are really talking about the amount of physical and mental energy that a worker is willing to invest in his or her job. Note that this definition of motivation covers three points:

■ Motivation is already within people. The task of the supervisor is not to provide motivation. What is important for the supervisor is to know how to *release* higher levels of motivation to do the work.

■ Different people are willing to invest different amounts of energy and enthusiasm in their work. Not everyone is a rate buster, an overachiever. On the other hand, not everyone is lazy or poorly motivated.

■ The return in personal satisfaction that an employee receives from an investment of energy in the job affects the level of that employee's motivation. In other words, a low return in need satisfaction results in a low level of motivation; a high return in need satisfaction results in a high level of motivation.

In supervisory staff meetings you may have heard comments such as these: "We could get a lot more work done if our people were better motivated." "If you don't have employees who are motivated, a work group can never do a good job." "The reason these people don't do a good job is that they aren't paid enough."

People state these "facts" so often that we come to believe they are true. We now know, after many years of research into human behavior, some revealing facts about how and why people work. Here are three important findings on what makes people do their best or something less than their best.

First, scientists tell us that whatever people do they do to satisfy a physical need (such as the need for food) or an emotional need (such as the need for acceptance, recognition, or achievement).

A second important point is this: raises, bonuses, or fringe benefits are not the only way or even the best way of encouraging people to do more and better work. Of course, a fair wage or salary and other benefits are necessary, but we have tended to exaggerate the power of money in motivating workers to perform. Instead, it is our understanding of and ability to satisfy workers' human needs that count most, because having the chance to satisfy needs is what motivates a person to get the job done— and done well.

Third, the attitudes workers have toward work and their jobs are to a substantial degree the result of the experiences these workers have had at work or in life. They may have *learned* that hard or quality work does not pay off.

The needs levels of human motivation. This illustration is based on the work of Abraham Maslow, especially his book Motivation and Personality. *This ranking of needs has been highly influential in the field of management.*

SELF-ACTUALIZATION: Full development of abilities; creativity; fulfilled personal life

ESTEEM NEEDS: self-respect and the respect of others

SOCIAL NEEDS: Sense of belonging; group membership; love; acceptance by others

SECURITY NEEDS: absence of threats to life, health, and safety; orderly environment

PHYSIOLOGICAL NEEDS: food, shelter, and clothing; environment that sustains life

What makes people work hard?

What really motivates people on the job? There are many theories about motivation that are based on thorough studies of human behavior. The important idea to remember in the face of these sometimes complex theories is that each member of your work team is different—and that what will motivate one member of your work team to be a productive member of the unit will not necessarily motivate another person. It is also important to realize that each of your workers is motivated to satisfy his or her individual needs. The trick is to align workers' individual needs and their efforts to satisfy those needs with the goals of the organization, so that individuals' needs are taken care of as they pursue the organization's goals.

As human beings we have certain needs, which include those necessary to sustain life itself, such as the need for food, clothing, and shelter. Our needs also include, among other things, recognition for what we do, and the chance to do those things that we think are important and that we can do well.

Psychologist Abraham Maslow suggests that our needs fall into the five categories shown at left as a ladder of priorities. You should remember that the needs higher on the ladder are not more important than those lower on the ladder. It is simply that if a need lower on the ladder is not satisfied, a person will be motivated to satisfy that need first and will be "blocked" from releasing higher-level motives.

Maslow tells us that when a person is truly hungry or really in need of clothing for warmth, that person will be strongly motivated to satisfy that need first of all. Once such bodily needs are satisfied, however, the person will seek satisfaction at the next level of need—the need for safety and security—until this level also is satisfied. Then the person is motivated by the next level of need, and so on.

The important thing which Maslow is saying is this: *once a human need has been satisfied, it no longer motivates a person.* For example, if a worker is able to satisfy all needs except the need for *self-actualization*, then what that worker considers most important is to be able to feel that he or she is doing something important that he or she wants to do personally, and to feel that that activity is being done well. The worker thereby feels fulfilled as a person.

When human needs are unsatisfied in the job situation, a person's work motivation will be at the level at which there is an unsatisfied need. The supervisor's job, then, is to free this blockage in order to release higher levels of motivation in each of his or her workers.

Changes in the work situation—for example, a new and easier way of doing the job—may threaten some employees. They may be afraid of losing their jobs. Explaining the new procedures in advance and convincing these workers that there is no reason for concern will help satisfy their need for security and let them move to a higher level of motivation.

While Maslow's ladder of human needs helps supervisors to understand why most people behave the way they do, we also need to recognize that for some people the ladder has fewer than five steps. Many of us have heard about artists who aren't concerned with economic security or acceptance or recognition by others. Of course they need satisfaction of their bodily requirements for enough food, shelter, and clothing to survive. But their real motivator is their need to be creative and to fully develop their abilities. It isn't that such people don't have all five levels of need. Rather, it is that, for them, security and acceptance and recognition aren't very important needs.

Maslow's view that a satisfied need no longer spurs a person on brings us to a point that is important for all supervisors. Once a person's needs for a decent income and good working conditions have been satisfied, improving these elements of the job will cease to motivate the worker. This is an idea that many supervisors find hard to accept.

To satisfy the lingering doubts of many people, a number of studies have been made in different organizations. In one study both workers and supervisors were given a list of ten job-related factors. Supervisors were asked to rank these factors in the order in which they thought these were important *to their workers*. The employees were also asked to rank the items in order of importance to themselves. In other words, both supervisors and workers were asked what workers want from their jobs. The table shows how they answered that question. The numbers show the importance that supervisors and workers gave to each item (1 being most important).

Job-related factors	Supervisors	Workers
Good working conditions	4	9
Feeling "in" on things	10	2
Tactful disciplining of workers	7	10
Full appreciation for work done	8	1
Management loyalty to workers	6	8
Good wages	1	5
Promotion and growth in the company	3	7
Understanding of personal problems	9	3
Job security	2	4
Interesting work	5	6

Source: Lawrence Lindahl, "What Makes a Good Job?" Reprinted by permission of the publisher from *Personnel* (January 1949) © 1949 American Management Association, New York. All rights reserved.

Note that the factors the workers ranked 1–2–3 were the ones that the supervisors ranked 8–9–10!

Workers gave highest rank to appreciation for their work, being in on things, and sympathy for personal problems, while supervisors thought that good wages, job security, and promotion would be most important to their workers.

Other studies have told us that supervisors often overlook the fact that most workers in the United States have enough of life's necessities and enough job security to be reasonably well satisfied as regards both of these job-related factors.

Today many employees—especially younger ones, as discussed in Chapter 2—believe that having interesting work to do is of great importance. Many of us probably know people who work harder and better for their church or club or community as unpaid volunteers than they do for their employer who pays them for working. This is because they gain more satisfaction of their higher-level human needs from their unpaid work than they do from their paid jobs. Their volunteer work provides more motivators—interesting work or challenge, real responsibility, or personal fulfillment—than their employment provides.

The money we are paid for working is a basic necessity (we need it to buy food, shelter, and clothing) but for most people it is not a motivator. Higher pay does not automatically

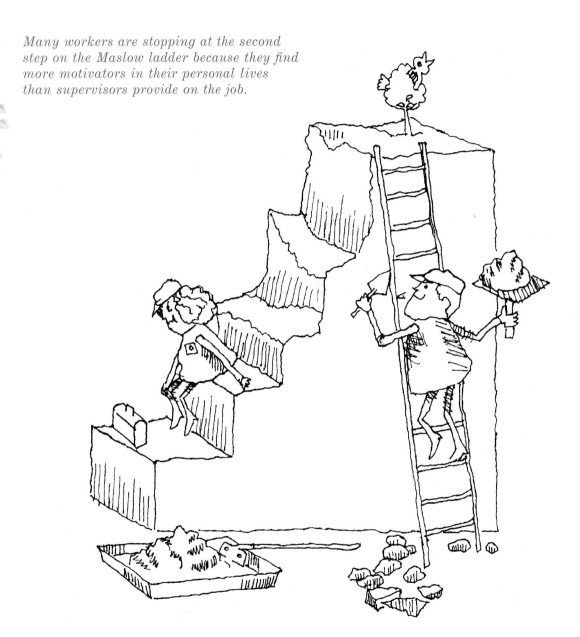

Many workers are stopping at the second step on the Maslow ladder because they find more motivators in their personal lives than supervisors provide on the job.

motivate employees, especially those whose basic needs are met, to work harder or better.

Unless the supervisor tries hard to provide motivators that make a job interesting and meaningful, many workers are unlikely to find much satisfaction in their jobs. When workers are not motivated by their work—when they do not find it stimulating or challenging or fulfilling—then they focus on other factors of the work environment, such as pay and benefits. One of the important challenges for today's supervisor is to help workers find more interest and satisfaction in their jobs to fill needs for accomplishment and self-fulfillment.

One of the best ways to discover what specific needs, desires, or expectations your individual team members have is simply to ask them. Asking the question "What motivates you to work here?" will give you some surprisingly straightforward answers. For example, if you discover that your employee Bob wants to learn more and more each day, you should make sure that his work assignments offer him an opportunity to pick up new skills. You should give him training opportunities, and perhaps arrange for him to be cross-trained in another worker's job.

Or, if you find out from Emily that she wants to make a lot of money, you should encourage her to prove her value to the organization and give her opportunities for job growth so that she will be eligible for promotional opportunities as they come along. Perhaps Cecilia tells you that she wants a job that leaves enough

time for her family life. You may want to explore job-sharing or flex-time and help arrange for vacations that coincide with her children's school vacations.

You should also find out what your employees expect from you and how you can best support them. Again, just pose questions directly to each member of your work team: "How can I, as your supervisor, help you be a productive member of our team? What am I doing that might keep you from doing your best on the job?"

Remember to be open to the feedback you receive—and to take positive action to correct any of your own behaviors that inhibit your workers' on-the-job performance.

The supervisor's role

The skillful supervisor, therefore, watches for each worker's needs, examines the extent to which they are being met, and then seeks ways of enriching the job to help each worker better satisfy those needs.

Your attitude sets the tone

For better or for worse, conditions in a work unit tend to reflect the personality and attitudes of the supervisor. Your own attitudes toward people in general are important because they will be translated into actions on the job.

In his book *The Human Side of Enterprise*, Douglas McGregor described some important ideas regarding the attitudes of supervisors toward people. McGregor suggested that two different sets of beliefs about work and workers can lead to two different methods of supervising people.

The listings below present McGregor's two sets of beliefs. He referred to them as Theory X and Theory Y.

Theory X supervisors adhere to the following beliefs:

■ Most people think work is unpleasant and try to avoid it.

■ Most people must be supervised a lot and must often be forced to do their work.

■ Most people are motivated only by their desire for basic necessities and security.

■ Most people do not want to get ahead, do not want responsibility, and like to be told what to do.

■ Most people are incapable of thinking of answers to problems in the work unit or the organization.

Theory Y supervisors, on the other hand, believe the following to be true:

■ Work is as natural as play or rest. If workers think work is unpleasant it is probably because of the way it is done in the organization.

- Self-control in workers is necessary if work is to be done properly.

- People are motivated by their needs for social acceptance, recognition, and a sense of achievement, as well as their needs for money to provide the basic necessities and for security.

- Given good supervision, most people will accept and even seek responsibility.

- Many people have the ability to come up with creative solutions to organizational problems.

It is easy to see why Theory X supervisors might use methods of getting the job done different from those used by Theory Y supervisors. Theory X supervisors think of workers largely as tools of production, motivated by fear of punishment or by desire for money and security. Supervisors with this outlook tend to watch workers closely, make and enforce strict rules, and use punishment and the threat of punishment as motivators.

Theory Y supervisors take an opposite view. They see workers as having varied needs. They see their own job as one of organizing and managing work so that both the organization and the workers can satisfy their needs. The Theory Y supervisor therefore works with workers to set goals for the unit, encourages workers to share in decision making, and strengthens workers' desire to do a good job.

Since McGregor wrote his book, research has shown that people really are more complex than either Theory X or Theory Y assumed them to be. Some people really are lazy and do try to avoid work, just as Theory X said. Other people truly enjoy working, as Theory Y held. Some workers must be supervised a lot, while others require almost no supervision. Some need to be closely controlled; others will control themselves more effectively than their supervisors can control them. In other words, there are Theory X workers and there are Theory Y workers. And there are some who behave according to Theory X one day, and according to Theory Y the very next day.

This research strongly suggests that supervisors need to understand not only McGregor's Theory X and Theory Y, but also a "Theory Z." Edgar Schein describes this "complex person" theory as follows:

- People are complex, and also highly variable. They have many motives, which are arranged in a ladder of importance for them, and the order of importance changes from time to time and from situation to situation.

- A person's motives interact with each other, and combine into a complex motivational pattern. A person might work hard for money, for example, in order to be able to spend a week skiing at Aspen.

- People bring their motives with them to work. The experiences they have on the job teach them new motives. For example, people may come to a job strongly motivated to work. The experiences they have at work may teach them to dislike working.

- A person's motivation is not the only element in determining how much work is done and how well. The skill of the person also is important. A very unskilled but highly motivated worker may be as effective as a highly skilled but poorly motivated worker.

- There is, therefore, no one correct supervisory strategy that will work for all people at all times.

Your actions release motivation

Regardless of how complex people are or what their prior work experiences have been, it is clear that if your objective is to release higher levels of motivation in employees you need to do the following:

- Enlist the help of workers in setting goals for the work unit.

- Make rules and set conditions that help people get the job done, rather than hinder and frustrate them.

- Regularly talk with and listen to other work team members to make sure they have a chance to tell you what they think.

- Learn what "fuels" each team member's behavior; then positively reinforce behaviors that result in good work.

- Involve your work team in decisions that directly affect quality of work life.

In short, today's supervisor must understand just what it is that makes each person tick and what is important to him or her.

Experience and research tell us that certain types of supervisor are better than other supervisors at releasing high levels of motivation in their workers. Successful supervisors usually do the following things:

■ They let their workers know that they are confident that the workers will produce good work. They provide positive reinforcement of productive behavior.

■ They always praise good work, rather than taking it for granted and noticing only mistakes.

■ They are easy to talk to and are willing to listen to new ideas. They try to make a worker feel good about making a suggestion even if the suggestion cannot be used.

■ They look at tasks, projects, and activities from the worker's point of view and explain to workers how their jobs fit in with the work of the whole department and of the entire local government.

■ They pay attention to how other people feel and correct workers' errors without making them feel discouraged, frustrated, or angry.

The job of the supervisor is to help release higher levels of motivation in employees.

They are empathetic and make an attempt to share workers' feelings.

This adds up to a healthy climate in the work group, and a healthy organizational climate results in high productivity and a high quality of work.

Let us now look at some specific supervisory actions that will help put this understanding to use—actions that will improve employee motivation, employee productivity, and job satisfaction.

One management technique that can be very helpful to supervisors in meeting this challenge is *job redesign.* Job redesign involves things like giving employees additional responsibility for planning their own work, allowing them to set their own work pace within broad guidelines, changing the types of tasks an employee does on a regular basis, or allowing more direct contact with the public. For example, you might ask an employee to set up a work schedule for a specific assignment with reporting dates that you will review together, rather than simply telling the employee when the work is due.

The motivators provided in this example would be at Maslow's fourth and fifth levels: recognition, and personal achievement and responsibility. We could provide another motivator at the fifth level, self-actualization through growth and learning, by giving an employee the opportunity to learn and perform new and more difficult and challenging tasks. Opportu-

nities for job growth can be identified by both you and your work team as you review individual and team work plans.

Another management technique that is sometimes used to provide motivation is *job rotation.* This involves asking employees to trade jobs for a specific period. It may involve cross-training, mentioned in Chapter 3. Job rotation is different from job redesign because you don't change anything about the job other than who does it. It can be helpful in motivating bored employees by giving them something new to do and broadening their perspective on what your work unit does. But if we merely substitute a job that contains few if any motivators for another that also has few motivators, rotation will not have lasting motivational value.

Supervisors must try especially hard today to develop and use the skills of successful supervision to motivate employees, because the 1982 study referred to earlier—a study of nearly 100,000 employees conducted by the Opinion Research Corporation—indicates rising employee dissatisfaction, which is a real threat to progress in productivity. While many managers and supervisors have gone back to a "tough" approach with their employees—perhaps because of recent economic conditions and tight budgets—getting tough appears to result in worker anger and frustration, which is exactly the opposite of what these managers and supervisors expect.

There are some general methods that you can use to develop positive behavior among your work team members:

- Satisfy team members' basic needs before you try to motivate them at a higher level.

- The more you reward a result the more likely you'll get that result.

- Reward must almost immediately follow the desired behavior and must be connected with the desired behavior.

- People perform most effectively when tasks are challenging but not too hard. That is, when their efforts are likely to result in success but success is not absolutely certain.

- Criticism, failure, and discouragement damage self-confidence and severely dampen any desire to continue an activity or task.

- Approach your role of supervisor as enabler, facilitating the work of your team, not directing or dictating.

- Celebrate quality performance of individual work team members and your work team as a whole.

Checklist

Accept the concept that the capacity for motivation, like growth, is already within people. The task of the supervisor is not to provide motivation to others but rather to release and help channel the capacity that is there.

Learn how to recognize frustrations in individual workers and how to remove the causes, in order to allow each employee to move to the highest possible level of motivation.

Recognize that the assumptions you make about others affect your supervisory relations with them. Be sure your assumptions are correct.

Since many employees want more interesting and challenging work, learn how to make jobs more challenging. Be willing to spend time thinking about job changes and let your employees help in the thinking and planning processes.

Remember not to judge a person's ability on the basis of what that person is now doing. Most people are able to do much more.

Supervisory situation 11/1

As the supervisor of the summer recreation program, Huang is responsible for over thirty seasonal workers and ten regular, full-time employees. Sometimes he feels overwhelmed with his job since there are so many schedules to maintain and programs to track.

Cathy, one of the seasonal workers, provides the clerical support for the summer recreation program. She is responsible for handling walk-in registrations and answers all incoming telephone calls. She also prepares the weekly payroll. This is the second summer that Cathy has worked for Huang.

Cathy is thirty-four years old and the single mother of two small children, ages one-and-a-half and four years. She is hoping to do a good job so that Huang might offer her a permanent position. Cathy is eager to earn more money at a steady job she can count on, with working hours that fit the demands of caring for her children.

However, Huang has been unable to change Cathy's habit of coming to work late and often requesting to leave work before normal quitting time. He has had little chance to talk with Cathy about her attendance and tardiness, but he has given her both verbal and written warnings.

At this point, Huang is considering terminating Cathy since he feels he cannot count on her and she does not seem motivated to change her work habits. With such a heavy summer workload, Huang doesn't feel he can afford to have an employee who refuses to pull her own weight.

1. *Are there any other approaches, short of termination, that Huang might try in order to motivate Cathy?*

2. *What are some techniques Huang could use to identify Cathy's motivational needs?*

Supervisory situation 11/2

Ed has supervised his street maintenance crew for over ten years. He continually has to give verbal and written warnings to three or four of the same workers, who repeatedly avoid doing the work they are assigned. Ed believes that this group will never change their behavior, but he will not give up the fight. "This is a war they're waging— and I'm going to be the winner," Ed says. He closely monitors the activities of these workers and consistently threatens punishment in order to keep them in line.

1. *How may Ed's attitudes contribute to unproductive behavior among the "problem" members of his crew?*

2. *How would a "Theory Y" supervisor's attitudes and actions be different from Ed's?*

3. *What are some ways you might handle Ed's crew?*

MANAGING CHANGE EFFECTIVELY

There is nothing more difficult to take in hand, more perilous to conduct, or more uncertain in its success, than to take the lead in the introduction of a new order of things.

Niccolò Machiavelli

MANAGING CHANGE EFFECTIVELY

If we listened in on some comments from employees to their supervisors we might hear something like this:

"Why do we grind valves in the same old way?" asks Bill, the mechanic in the county garage. "I know the garage in Tannersville has a much faster, easier way of doing their valve-grinding jobs and they cut their costs by 20 percent. Why don't we give their way a try?"

"Do you know it takes three days to process an application for a building permit for a small one-story building?" asks Ann, a counter clerk in the building permit office. "A woman was in the office this morning. She wants to put up a building that is going to provide twenty jobs for people in this city. She was furious when she found out how long she'd have to wait for the permit! Do we need to make people wait so long to get an application processed?"

Effective supervisors know that suggestions like these from employees or citizens should be followed up by efforts to improve a service. Today, when local governments have more people demanding more services, and fewer tax dollars are available, efficiency and economy are top priorities.

Listed below are four solutions that many supervisors resort to under the above circumstances. Which of them do you think would work best to save time and money for your group?

- Let's ask everybody to do some overtime.

- Everybody will just have to work a little harder and a little faster.

- Let's get another set of tools and a new and bigger machine.

- What we really need are two more clerk typists, a receptionist, and an answering service.

You are right: none of these suggestions is necessarily the best answer. All of them require that something be added: more work, more effort, more machines, more people, more money. But adding more of something does not always mean better service. Problems of productivity are usually due to the processes and systems that employees are asked to follow to perform their work. The supervisor's first choice should be to get people to work *smarter*, not harder, and to make *better use* of the equipment and people already on the job.

Organizations that are successfully meeting the challenges of global competition mentioned in Chapter 2 have freed their employees to take risks and to introduce new ideas. As a supervisor, you are an agent for change. You can enable your work team to develop new and creative solutions for improving work methods by creating a climate for innovation.

In order to help your employees be creative, it is important to understand the nature of change and how the creative process works.

This chapter deals with four important aspects of improving work methods: creating a climate for change, analyzing work systems and tasks, planning change, and implementing change.

Creating a climate for change

As a supervisor in local government you constantly face the challenge of implementing change. The environments you work in today—political, social, technological, and economic—are changing, sometimes very rapidly. In order to be effective and to survive, governments must learn to adapt to change. The supervisor plays a key role in helping workers to respond and adapt to necessary changes.

The supervisor's most important task is to make sure that employees participate in every part of the change process. The suggestions, and especially the support, of your own employees is vital to the success of your plan. Failing to involve your employees can seriously hurt the morale of your unit.

If you have ever attempted to introduce a change in your work area you may have been surprised at the way people responded. You were only trying to be helpful, to make life easier for your people. What you got in response to your good intentions was anger, misunderstandings, work slow-downs, absenteeism, grievances—perhaps even deliberate foul-ups of the new, improved system. What went wrong? After all, you explained how helpful the change would be.

What you encountered was a normal human response to change. People are creatures of habit. We don't like to change our comfortable ways of doing things, even when someone we trust promises us the new way to do things will be better. Adjusting to the "new way" requires using some energy and will be physically and psychologically uncomfortable until the "new way" becomes a habit. Some people call this uncomfortable feeling while we adjust to change "stress."

There are many reasons why people resist change. Some of the most common are the following:

■ The "cost" seems too high. People believe (whether it's true or not) that the change will lower their income, or reduce their status in the organization.

■ People are afraid that they won't be able to learn a new skill required by the change and might lose their job because of it.

■ People do not trust the person introducing the change. This person may be considered an outsider or may be someone whose skills are not respected.

■ People don't understand the purpose of the change. People like to know the reasons for making a change. They want the change to make sense.

■ People really like the way they are doing things now. Most of us don't like to give up doing things we enjoy.

■ People's basic values are challenged by the change and they are asked to do something they don't believe in or feel they must give up something they believe in.

■ People anticipate that they must give up their established patterns of friendship and get to know new people. If you like the people you work with, you won't like a change that makes you leave them behind.

For these reasons many people would rather live with a problem that is familiar than try to adopt a solution that is unfamiliar. As a means of self-protection many people will try to avoid the stress of making changes. If you insist that employees make a change that results in their feeling uncomfortable you may expect some negative reactions. Some of these negative reactions may be directed toward you, others may be directed at the change itself.

Among the people in your work group you may have some people who will strongly resist any change. They may actually be afraid to make changes. Other people may be more willing to try something new. They may enjoy the challenge that change can offer. To effectively manage the change that must take place at

Some will change, no matter what the obstacles. Others will stay put, no matter how bad the situation.

work you must know your people well enough to understand how each employee will respond. By understanding and anticipating their responses you can be more helpful to your people as they adjust to the new way of doing things.

Reducing stress

There are also some guidelines you can follow that can help reduce the stress caused by changes in the work place. When you are considering a change in the work place you must always consider what changes will occur in the lives of your employees and in all other people who will feel the impact of the change. This includes the public and employees in other departments of your organization as well.

You know that change creates stress and that the faster a change takes place the greater is the stress placed on the people involved. As a supervisor you need to consider: How fast does this change need to take place? Can it be introduced slowly or must it happen overnight? People will adjust better if the change can be introduced gradually. You should also consider how long the change will last. Is this change permanent or temporary? You should let your people know.

The greater the magnitude of the change the more stress and resistance it will generate. You should ask yourself: How different will things be after the change takes place from the way they were before? Can this change be made in small steps rather than in one big step?

We also know that people adjust to change much better if they know the change is coming and have some time to prepare themselves. You should therefore do your best to involve people in planning for change and keep everyone informed of changes that you know are being planned by others in the organization. You should ask yourself: What changes are coming that will affect my work group?

The stress of making a change is reduced if people know as much as possible about the change before it takes effect. You should ask yourself: Is there something I can do to educate my workers about the change before they have to implement it? Can I provide training in the new procedure? Can I send them to see this new piece of equipment in use in another department? Are there video tapes or manuals that discuss the use of this newly designed tool?

We have learned that the greater the number of different changes that people must make in a short period of time the greater the stress they will feel. You may have noticed that your work crew begins to feel overwhelmed when asked to make many changes, even if the changes are small ones. You should ask yourself: Are we asking our people to make changes in other areas of their work environment right now? Do all these changes have to take place right now or can some of them wait? You will find less resistance to changes if you spread them out instead of piling them up.

Finally, we know that people will experience less stress if they feel good about the change they are making. People like to know why a change must take place. You should ask yourself: What can I do to explain the need for this change? How can I involve people in planning so they can understand why we need to make this change?

Sometimes organizational changes are mandated by someone above you and you are told to comply with the changes immediately. The principles of introducing change effectively must be violated and you know it will create stress for your workers. In these situations you can explain to your employees the reasons for the changes as you understand them. Giving your people a chance to talk about how the change is affecting them will help reduce some of the stress that the change creates.

Many times top management mandates a change in response to a crisis, not realizing the effect the change will have on the people who actually implement it. Since you are aware of these effects you can point them out to top management in a helpful way, out of concern for the organization's long-range success. After all, winning the battle but losing the war has never been sound management practice, and we know that people under great stress are less productive. You could point out some ways to reduce the stress of making a change. Top management may be responsive to your ideas when they recognize that you are concerned about long-range productivity.

Involving your employees

As you introduce the need for change to your work unit and the public, you want to help people develop a *commitment* to change rather than force them into *compliance* with your demands. "Commitment" means people *want* to make the change. "Compliance" means people feel they *have to* make the change. Changes that grow out of commitment last longer and will work better.

Another equally important reason for involving people in the change process is related to effective problem solving. In most cases all of us together are smarter than any of us alone. Almost always the people who are actually doing a job will have the best ideas about how to improve the way the job is done. Supervisors frequently say that they could improve the way the government is managed if the administration would just listen to their suggestions. The same principle holds true for your workers. You need to listen to their suggestions and ask for their input in order to discover new and better ways of getting the job done.

Finally, people who have been involved in planning for a change that they must implement can enjoy the pride and satisfaction that comes with making a successful change. Things are working better now and it's because of their ideas and effort. Everyone can be proud of the group's accomplishment because everyone helped plan for it and do it.

There are many ways a supervisor can go about involving people in the process of change. In recent years the quality improvement process (described earlier in Chapter 6) has been used

Participation means teamwork. Everyone should help keep the ball in the air.

in private companies and local governments to get employees involved in solving problems. This process involves the people who work on a task in the development of strategies to improve the quality of work done. Quality improvement is not a "quick fix" solution to overcoming employee resistance to change. The basic elements of the approach are recognizing the expertise of workers, treating workers with respect, and involving them in planning for change.

Any approach to employee participation will work if and only if management is sincere about allowing *real* involvement and participation in planning for change. Management must realize that allowing employees to participate in planning changes means that management must be willing to share some of its power. If management is not sincere in involving employees in planning, resistance to change will undoubtedly occur. Quality improvement and other participatory processes should not be utilized as gimmicks to pacify employees. If a decision has already been made, or if management will accept only one decision, then this decision should be presented honestly to the employees.

Management that is truly interested in employee involvement will use the participatory approach throughout the year. Since progress and growth require change, your employees should be constantly thinking of how work can be improved. Don't wait for a crisis to occur before involving people in the change process. Continuous evaluation ("How well are we doing our job in the department?") will help identify potential problems before they become crises. Your employees will also know that their ideas are valued and respected. When change occurs they will be more willing to tolerate the stress of making the change. They will also be more willing to give the innovation a fair chance to work. They will be able to take pride in their

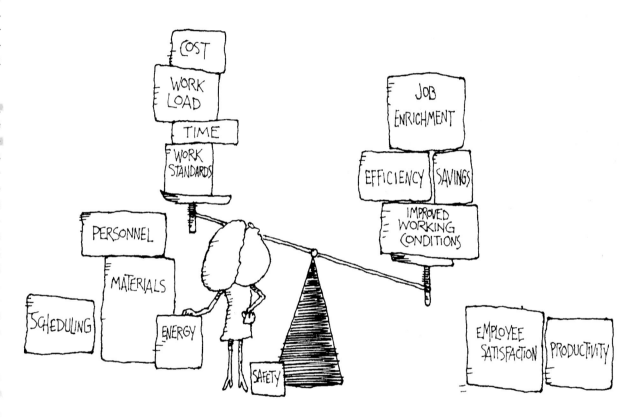

The decision to change a job procedure requires balancing work load, personnel requirements, and other costs against productivity gains, job enrichment, and other benefits.

success and they will be more likely to support their supervisor in implementing a change because they have helped decide what the change will be and how it will take place.

Analyzing work systems and tasks

In most cases when we improve the way we do a job we simplify it—we change it so that it can be done more easily, more quickly, and with fewer tax dollars.

Before making changes, you may need to analyze how you and your team perform specific work tasks. There are two approaches that you can use to do this. One is focused on problem solving and the other is focused on opportunity.

Problem solving means following specific steps to resolve an issue. Pursuing opportunities means responding quickly to a favorable combination of circumstances. To be an effective supervisor it is helpful to have both problem-solving skills and the ability to both recognize and create opportunities.

A standard method for problem solving/decision making includes the following steps:

Step 1: Name the problem.

This can be the most important step in problem solving. It has been shown that if you can accurately define the problem, you are more than 60 percent on the way to resolving it. One way to help your work team define the problem is to have the team describe exactly what it is—and what it is not.

Step 2: Brainstorm causes.

In this step your work team throws out all sorts of ideas about what is causing the problem. The principal rule to follow in brainstorming is to accept all ideas and record them exactly as stated.

Step 3: Select the cause.

One technique for selecting the cause of the problem is to have participants vote on what each one feels are the major causes of the problem. Each team member receives the number of votes equal to 20 percent of the number of options. For example, if there are five options to choose from: 5 x .20 = 1 vote per person. (Round up if the multiplication results in a decimal.) This method reflects the "80/20 rule," which states that 80 percent of a problem comes from 20 percent of the factors. So, if the 20 percent of the factors that are causing the problem are identified, the problem can be 80 percent solved.

Step 4: Brainstorm a solution.

Follow the same rules as in Step 2.

Step 5: Choose a solution.

During this step the team discusses various solutions, giving sufficient time for each member to voice his or her opinion and for all team members to understand the opinion given. Members work toward arriving at consensus, which means that everyone can agree on the decision reached by the team, not that the decision is everyone's first choice. It simply represents a course of action that all members can support. Although reaching a win-win situation can take a long time, in the long run it actually saves time and energy, because members feel that they have been heard throughout the decision-making process.

Step 6: Write an action plan.

Team members now develop specific ways to carry out the solution. They identify who will be responsible for carrying out the solution, when and how the solution will be implemented, and how they will know whether the solution is successful.

Step 7: Implement the action plan.

As the supervisor you will want to ensure that the plan is properly implemented.

Step 8: Evaluate the solution.

Check the criteria that were used to select the solution. Does the solution still meet these criteria? How effective was it? Does the solution resolve the problem effectively? Evaluate the circumstances to see whether anything has changed that may affect the solution that was implemented. The problem-solving process is a dynamic one, so be prepared to review the process until the problem is satisfactorily solved.

Opportunities for innovation

Another way of analyzing the systems by which your work is accomplished is to look for opportunities for change. You need to be receptive to opportunities, open to taking risks, and able to see possibilities that exist—even in problem situations.

In *Innovation and Entrepreneurship: Practices and Principles*, Peter Drucker outlines unexpected places where opportunities might appear. For example, having to reduce your budget in a tight fiscal year may create the opportunity for you and your work unit to discover improved ways to deliver a service, or it may help you to eliminate ineffective programs that were merely carried over from year to year. You may have a project that has funding for just one year, or an intern who is available for just six months. The time-crunch these situations present can provide an opportunity to harness the energy that comes through a sense of urgency.

The following questions should be considered when you want to streamline the work methods in your unit:

- Which methods need improving?
- What are the steps involved in the job?
- What is a better method?
- Should this change be made now?

Which methods need improving?

Let us assume that you are the kind of supervisor who encourages employees to make suggestions and to discuss work problems with you. If so, you may have had complaints that the job is not set up as efficiently as it might be. (After all, there is hardly a job in the world that could not be improved by some streamlining.)

How do you and your employees decide which problems to tackle first? And which ones need most attention? The team will decide which are your most serious problems, but the checklist below can help the team make the decision.

- Does the work involve a large expenditure of money, work hours, or machines?
- Does the job make up a large portion of the work load in your department?
- Does the job involve many workers?
- Does the job involve a large number of highly skilled people?
- Will the job last for a long period of time— more than a few weeks or months?
- Do you often have trouble scheduling the job? Do you have backlogs, overtime, and missed deadlines?
- Is the work produced not meeting quality standards?
- Does the job result in numerous accidents or near accidents?
- Does the work involve excessive physical exertion or tension, or require frequent rest periods?
- Does the job create unpleasant or unhealthy conditions, such as excessive dust, noise, smells, heat, or cold?
- Will change reduce tension, lessen fatigue, and relieve employees of the boredom of doing the same thing day in and day out?
- Will change result in job enrichment for employees? Will it give them more satisfaction and a greater sense of worth and accomplishment?
- Will change result in greater productivity, better quality work, or a cost reduction?

One final word of caution about choosing the job methods that need improving: Don't overlook the jobs that have been done the same way for a long time. The oldest methods may be the ones that need improvement most.

What are the steps involved in the job?

Once the team has chosen a job to work on, you should take a closer look at the steps involved in getting it done. You will want to refer to your unit's work procedures manual—or start to put one together, if none exists.

Remember that any job has three basic parts: the preparation part; the actual doing of the job; and the cleanup or put-away part. Preparation and cleanup are especially important to consider because they are often more time-consuming than the actual doing of the job.

Two helpful rules for breaking down the job into steps are: (1) Pick a subject and stick to it; and (2) Write a brief description of every step.

As far as the first rule is concerned, remember that most jobs involve a person, an object, or a printed form. When you make a study of the job, choose from these three the one that is most important to the job and then make a detailed list of what happens to that person, object, or form—where it goes, who handles it, how long each step takes. It is important to remember that if you start tracing the path of a printed form, for example, you should not leave that path to follow that of another printed form. In other words, stick with the subject you started with.

In writing a brief description of every step, you should physically follow the person or object you are describing. Do not try to do the job sitting at your desk. Bear in mind, too, that you should list all the steps in a job in the order in which these steps actually take place.

Keep your description brief and list only one step at a time. Do not combine two steps, using the word *and* between them. "She takes the form to Room 112 and then files it," should read: (1) "She takes the form to Room 112," followed by (2) "She files the form in the permanent file."

Whenever possible use action verbs and specific words that tell what actually happens: "Walks up two flights of stairs to the fourth-floor filing room" is better than "Goes to the filing room." "Types up information on four-page form" tells you more than "Fills out the form."

Finally, record both time and distance for all steps. To estimate the time a job takes, watch it being done several times, time it, talk with the person who does the job and be sure this was an average situation, and then figure out an average time. In most cases time will be recorded in minutes and distances will be recorded in feet.

Here is a sample breakdown of steps involved in making an application for a building permit. The route of the application form was followed in the analysis.

- Citizen fills out two-page application form (10 min.).

- Clerk looks over application (5 min.).

- Form and plans are carried to inspection department by citizen (2 min./120 ft.).

- Form waits on inspector's desk (2 days).

- Form is checked by inspector (10 min.).

- Inspector writes changes needed on form and gives initial approval (20.5 min.).

- Form is carried to clerk's desk (0.5 min./ 120 ft.).

- Form waits on clerk's desk (1 day).

- Clerk looks over form and discusses it with citizen (20 min.).

- Clerk types permit for application (10 min.).

- Application is filed (0.5 min.).

Total time: 3 days, 1 hr., 18.5 min.

Total distance: 240 ft.

In addition to making a list of the steps involved in doing a job, it is sometimes helpful to actually *see* the movements that must be made to get it done. A flowchart can be a commonsense means of showing them.

What is a better method?

When all the facts are down on paper—on a chart or a list—the team can begin to question and evaluate. Your most important asset will be an open mind.

Begin by challenging the job as a whole. Is the job necessary? Could the procedure be eliminated? Does it help accomplish work goals?

Next it is important to challenge every step of the job, to ask the team why. Why is it done at all? Why is it done at that time? Why is it done in that way? Why is it done in that location? Why does this person do it?

If the team feels the job is necessary, it can begin to think of alternatives—different and better ways of accomplishing the job. The discussion below, in the form of six questions, can help you in your evaluation.

Can we do away with the job or part of it? Doing away with a whole job or step is not easy, especially for people who have been doing it for a long time. But if the only reason given for doing it is "because we've always done it," you should certainly question the need for that job or that step.

Can we combine steps or jobs? Combining two operations will often save time and improve the quality of the work. You may be able to get rid of useless time between steps or you may be able to cut down some of the preparation and put-away time.

Can we change the order of steps or jobs? If parts of a job cannot be eliminated or combined perhaps they can be done in a different order. This can save time if it shortens distances between steps or if it gets rid of backtracking.

Can we change the place where the work is done? Too often work is done in a certain place just because it has always been done there. It may not be the best place. It may just be the place where the job got started. But changing the work location may make the work more pleasant and may save steps and time.

Can a different person do the work? Can someone else perhaps do some or all of the steps in the operation better or more easily than the person doing them now? Does the job need someone with different training or different skills?

Can we improve the equipment or the work environment? This should not be the first question asked, but it *can* be a way of improving work methods when all the other, more basic

The basic parts of every job.

and less costly changes have been considered. Purchasing new equipment without first studying and simplifying the job itself merely means that you are using poor work methods on a new, expensive piece of machinery. Quite often this "solution" can be more costly and more difficult to change than the problem you started with.

Should this change be made now?

Let us assume that you have studied your most troublesome job and have figured out why it was not functioning smoothly and how it could be improved. What do you do next?

Most changes take time and patience. Before you can begin the process of putting the change into effect you need to be sure that it is a change for the better and one that has a good chance of succeeding. At the very least it should not create more problems than it sets out to solve.

Check your proposal again to see that nothing has been overlooked. Does the new method comply with safety regulations? Is it in conflict with working conditions? Will it reduce costs? Increase service? Improve quality? Will the cost of installing the new method be offset by the lower cost of operation in the long run?

Remember, too, that you are part of a large organization. Have you thought of how your improvement will affect the work of other units and departments? (How would a change in meter readings affect the work load in the billing department, for example?) Is it compatible with other systems, schedules, and machines already in use in your department or government?

Timing is another important consideration. Have you thought about how the proposed change would be affected by recent public issues? What about the connection between your change and other recent changes in your jurisdiction? (You would not want to test your new method of installing storm sewers if most of the streets in the area were resurfaced a month ago.)

Do you have the money, materials, and personnel to make this change now? Or have you made too many other changes in work methods lately? Are you making changes more quickly than your department can adjust to them? Would it be better to make this change at a time when another department (or a department in a nearby city) makes a similar change?

Implementing change

When and if your new method is ready to be formally proposed, there are three groups of people you should take into consideration: those who must approve your new plan, those who must be consulted about it, and those who must be informed about it. Let us take a look at the human side of putting your idea across.

Getting your new method approved

You will have to develop a plan for obtaining managerial and legal approval to make the change you are considering. You will need to convince your organization that your idea is a good, workable one. In a governmental environment, checking the legal ramifications of a change is absolutely essential.

First of all, you should present your team's plan to your manager and others in the organization, as necessary, pointing out both the benefits and the shortcomings of the plan. Be prepared to defend it—that is, to prove with facts and figures how it would affect service, schedules, costs, personnel, other departments, management, and the citizens you serve. You may find it effective to have a small representative group of employees go with you to assist in making these presentations. These employees can respond directly to questions to help clarify your plan.

Be sure that you or your department head either checks or has the legal department check laws, ordinances, safety regulations, and timing, as well as other factors that might affect your plan.

In addition, explain to your department head how you plan to introduce your new method to citizens and other employees. Be sure you let your manager know that you are looking not only for approval but for suggestions that will make your plan more workable.

Informing your work unit

Once the change has been agreed upon and approved you will want to announce it to the rest of the employees in your unit. It is important to be sure that everyone understands the reasons for the change and the improvements that can be expected.

Ask for questions and suggestions, but also answer the questions that may not be asked, for example: Will this change have any bad effects on me or my job? Explain, for instance, what the schedule for making the change is. Then ask employees if they feel that it will give them enough time to adjust to the new situation.

If additional training will be provided, explain who will be trained and how it will be done. Will it be on-the-job training? Special training outside the job? Whatever it is, tell them about it; it will help them feel more confident about being able to handle the change.

If people will have to be moved around, explain that every effort will be made to keep them close to their former co-workers. And if the change is a major one it is important to avoid giving people the impression that the old way was completely inefficient. (Employees do not want to be told that they have been doing their work in an inefficient way for years.)

If a change is very sweeping or very threatening to many employees it might be well to take the "let's-try-it-and-see" approach by making the change a pilot program—an experiment to see whether something will work. It means that you expect problems but that the employees as a team will help identify those problems and will help solve them.

You will want to explain to employees that the success of the project depends on their willingness to suggest the changes that are necessary to make the project work. Sometimes it is useful to select a "team quarterback" to "call the signals"—the person on your work team who will do the best job of leading the unit in the new project.

Since a pilot project is an experiment, you will need to decide eventually whether or not the experiment has succeeded. Employees should keep the records you will need to compare the quantity and quality of the work done by the old method and the new.

When the "before and after" figures are in, employees should share in making the decision about the project. Did it save money? Time? Did it help us work faster? Better? Should we continue it? Change it? Or go back to the old system?

Answers to these questions should be written down in a final report for management. If there is a difference of opinion on the results or the recommendation for action, you must include the opinions of the minority as well as the majority on your team.

Informing other work teams and citizens

It is essential that you or your manager notify those who might be affected by your change: for example, employees in other departments who work with your own employees; council members; members of advisory committees;

staff people such as the chief administrative officer, the personnel officer, the city engineer, the finance director, and the mayor.

If your project affects the public, you will need to let citizens know why, when, and how the change will take place, and how long it will last. This is usually done in cooperation with the administrative staff. For example, suppose you are planning to change the routing of several refuse pickup trucks. Citizens will want to know specifically why the change has been made, when the change will take place, how long it will last, and what the new collection dates will be. The time spent involving the community in your change will pay off in citizen help and support. (Chapter 17 discusses in detail the matter of communication with the public.)

Finally, some changes will require that special groups such as vendors who do business with the city, consulting engineers or architects, or county, state, and federal agencies be notified. You will want to discuss this matter with your manager and develop a communications plan.

Planning a follow-up program

An open mind is an important ingredient of any follow-up program today. Supervisors should realize (and should help their employees realize) that no change is really permanent. New techniques and new equipment are developed so quickly today that new ways can become outdated overnight.

An effective supervisor encourages employees to continue to suggest new and better ways of getting things done. For example, the supervisor will continue to ask for suggestions at meetings and to circulate pamphlets, newspaper clippings, and other publications that may contain new ideas.

It is important to be receptive to suggestions. Suggestion forms and directions for their use can be placed near the work area. A committee should be assigned to review the recommendations every month or two and choose those that are most useful. Winners should be mentioned in your newsletter or on your bulletin board. They should receive a personal note of thanks from you as well as someone in higher management.

Indeed, everyone should know that his or her efforts are appreciated. Whenever a change is completed you can show your appreciation for your employees' support in one or more of the following ways:

■ By thanking them individually and in a group meeting

■ By writing them letters with copies to the personnel files

■ By recommending them for merit promotions or pay increases

■ By giving them public recognition in department, government, or community publications.

Employees who are praised for suggesting and making changes are likely to come up with other new ideas. At the very least they will not fear future change because they will think of change as positive and beneficial for government and for themselves.

Checklist

Involve your employees in every step of the change process.

Think about ways of getting people to work more efficiently before you request more personnel for your unit.

Think about new and better ways of using your equipment and supplies before you request more of them.

Choose carefully when selecting the job that most needs improvement. Do not overlook jobs that have been done in the same way for years.

Break the job down into steps and question each step when trying to simplify.

Check for safety hazards, legal problems, and other obstacles, such as those involving money, personnel, or time, before you choose a new way of doing a job or task.

Be sure you have the necessary approval before you make a change.

Explain new ways of doing tasks to everyone inside and outside of local government who will be affected by the change.

Follow up your change by evaluating whether it was worth making.

Let those who helped to make the new plan work know that their efforts are appreciated.

Urge employees to continue to look for new and better ways of doing their jobs.

Supervisory situation 12/1

The administrative officer of Glenview County has just announced that the county will begin a county-wide citizen-service campaign. This means that departmental managers and supervisors will be reviewing county services with their work teams from their customers' perspective. The administrator has announced that she expects many changes in the way that the county performs its operations and delivers its services.

George is a supervisor in the finance department. His work unit is responsible for processing tax bills. When George announced the pending campaign to his staff a look of alarm passed across the faces of several staff members. After the meeting, Sue and Tom approached George. Both asked him whether changes would mean layoffs. Sue was also concerned that her system for filing receipts would be changed. "I have a really good system that works for me, and I resent the thought that it will change," she stated. George was not sure quite how to respond to Sue and Tom.

1. *What are some reasons Sue and Tom might be resisting possible changes in their work processes?*

2. *What are the steps George might follow to analyze his unit's work processes?*

3. *Provide George with some suggestions for reducing the effect of change on his work team.*

Supervisory situation 12/2

Tahoora is the supervisor for the refuse collection division. In reviewing her division's calls for service from city residents, she has noticed a marked increase in the number of households where pick-ups are skipped. In addition, an increased number of accidents, mostly slips and falls, also seem to be occurring. Tahoora suspects that the cause of this situation may be the newly instituted incentive program under which her crew members are permitted to punch out when they have completed their collection routes. Tahoora plans to meet with her crew to discuss the situation.

1. *Apply the problem-solving steps that Tahoora could follow in analyzing this situation.*

2. *Develop a solution based on your analysis.*

DEVELOPING AND MAINTAINING DISCIPLINE

The state of discipline of any group of people depends essentially on the worthiness of its leaders.

Henri Fayol

CHAPTER 13

DEVELOPING AND MAINTAINING DISCIPLINE

The supervisor's responsibility is to maintain discipline. This means maintaining efficiency, cooperation, and proper work conduct among employees to achieve desired goals. At the same time, the supervisor is responsible for protecting the rights of all employees in the group or unit.

For this reason, it helps to know that the word *discipline* comes from the word *disciple*—a person who follows the teachings and example of a respected leader. Like a disciple, the average worker who respects the leader or supervisor follows his or her teachings because they are contributing to meaningful and worthwhile goals. These workers recognize that rules and standards are needed to help everyone get the job done quickly, safely, and well. Discipline does not mean punishment.

Effective supervisors recognize that the average employee wants to do a good job. They help the employee by setting a good example, by matching the right person to the right job, by giving clear instructions, by observing and evaluating everyone's work periodically, and by praising a job well done. They reinforce each employee's self-control and self-respect, and create a well-disciplined and self-disciplined atmosphere.

Unfortunately, not all supervisors employ this positive approach built on mutual respect and self-control. Some supervisors with an old-fashioned outlook practice a negative discipline based on threats of punishment. They believe employees will not obey rules unless they are watched closely and forced to obey. They watch for mistakes and rule violations so that violators can be given the punishment they deserve. They want the employees to know who is boss!

Often such supervisors get the desired behavior from their workers, but usually only when they are looking. Their workers obey rules only to keep out of trouble while the boss is around. Since they fear and dislike their boss, they fear and dislike the rules.

Most employees, however, expect to follow certain rules and regulations that govern their performance on the job, use of equipment and materials, safety and health, and standards of acceptable conduct. Often in a well-disciplined group, if an employee steps out of line, his or her fellow workers will put pressure on him or her to get back on the track. As a supervisor, you can bolster your employees' desire to do what is expected by helping to strengthen each employee's self-discipline and by avoiding typical causes of discipline problems.

"Discipline" comes from the word "disciple"—a person who follows the teachings and example of a respected leader.

Most causes of troublesome behavior can be traced to one of the following:

▪ Discontent, which comes from boredom, idleness (lack of work), or lack of interest in the work

▪ Ignorance, which comes from lack of instruction, guidance, goals, training, or experience, or a misunderstanding of rules and standards

▪ Belief that one has been treated unfairly

▪ Personal problems that cannot be left at home.

Frequently the supervisor has created situations that produce behavior problems. Without realizing it you may be doing one of the following:

▪ Enforcing rules unfairly or inconsistently

▪ Reinforcing poor job performance by ignoring it

▪ Rewarding poor conduct by giving it more attention than good work

▪ Rewarding good work with additional work, thereby overloading the good worker.

Your relationship with your workers is a powerful force for developing commitment to organizational rules. Let's look at some of the steps you can take to build mutual respect and appreciation.

Strengthening self-discipline

Step 1: Issue clear, reasonable rules and regulations.

Begin by reviewing all the rules and regulations that apply to your department and work unit. You should be thoroughly familiar with them. Be sure that each one is needed to create an orderly, efficient, and safe work environment.

If you feel a rule is unfair or poorly written you should recommend to your supervisor and your department head that it be reviewed and changed. Make suggestions on how to improve it. Be sure, too, that all rules can be enforced consistently. If a rule cannot be applied to everyone it should not be made.

Finally, be sure that standards for job performance are set so that the average employee can attain them.

Step 2: Set a good example.

To keep morale and discipline high, you should expect good performance from everyone, especially yourself. Demand good work and good conduct from yourself, so that you can ask for the best from others. Get to work on time. Keep on schedule. Meet performance standards. Submit reports on time.

A supervisor must be self-disciplined and present a good role model as a leader to be able to discipline others effectively.

Step 3: Communicate clearly.

Each employee should know what is expected. Employees should know what work should be done, at what quality level; when it should be finished; and why it is being done. They should also know what acceptable standards of work and of behavior are.

When an employee is hired he or she should be told what the policies and rules of the department are, what the penalties are for breaking the rules, and how these penalties can be appealed.

There are several methods supervisors can use to call attention to the rules and to ensure that employees understand them. Any or all of the following may work for your group:

■ Give each employee a copy of the work procedures manual and of the employee handbook, if there is one, which contains personnel rules and regulations and other applicable rules for the working group.

■ Post the rules and regulations on a bulletin board for easy access.

■ Help the worker understand how his or her job fits in with the whole work group.

■ Have the person in charge of training conduct an orientation program for new workers and refresher sessions for seasoned employees.

■ Conduct a series of meetings with employees to explain the rules and work procedures

and to help employees understand them—especially those employees who have reading difficulties. Encourage employees to make suggestions and ask questions at these meetings, and be sure that they have ample time to do so.

In talking to employees about the rules and procedures in your department, you should use simple, clear language and give specific examples. Remember, too, to tell workers about those regulations that are especially important to your own department and work group—the ones that will be enforced strictly.

When discussing penalties for breaking rules, explain clearly which violations result in severe penalties such as dismissal, demotion, suspension, or reduction in salary.

Supervisors often forget to give information about job standards. The employee should know from the beginning how much work is expected, and what its quality should be.

Hold meetings at regular intervals to review standing rules and regulations, and pass along information about new policies or rule changes.

Careful, patient job training can give employees the skills they need to do a good job. You may want to use procedure manuals, training programs, films, and other aids. Above all, you will need to devote extra time to coaching and encouraging new workers while they are learning.

Step 4: Keep complete records on workers.

As a supervisor, you have the responsibility of keeping records of each person's work and of the work of your unit as a whole. This kind of record keeping is useful to top management and to you in planning and evaluating your work load. It is also an important step in establishing a positive discipline program.

These work records should contain each worker's responsibilities and duties, job goals, and major accomplishments, as well as copies of letters of commendation and records of training courses attended, leave taken, and disciplinary action taken, if any. You may want to furnish a new employee immediately with copies of some of the records going into his or her file.

In keeping this type of personnel information or working files on your employees, you should remember that the law protects all individuals against certain violations of their personal privacy. And interest in protecting the informational privacy of individuals is increasing. For example, in recent years many privacy bills have been introduced in the U.S. Congress and in state legislatures.

It is important, then, that the information you keep in your working files is information that should be there—information that has to do with the job and the employee's performance and behavior on the job. If, for example, you hear from someone that one of your employees

Pressure from fellow employees will often bring a worker who has stepped out of line back on the track.

is having an extramarital affair, that is purely personal information and does not belong in the file on that employee.

In addition, you should be careful as to who can see your files or can have information from those files. The best rule to follow is: Does the person have a legal right to know? Any information relating to an employee's job or performance or behavior on the job should be available only to management or any other individuals in the local government who really need to have such information to do their jobs.

It is a good idea to allow the employee to see the information in his or her own file that relates to performance appraisals, records of awards or letters of commendation, formal disciplinary actions, work assignments, production records, and the like. Then if any information is wrong it can be corrected. But such information as your own notes about an employee's work and work behavior you will probably want to keep to yourself. You also have a right to privacy.

Note that disciplinary action is *only one small part* of the contents of this file. Be sure your employees understand that their work records are not intended as records of their mistakes and rule violations but are balanced accounts of their accomplishments on the job. These records should be open to employees and they should be encouraged to look at the materials regularly.

If and when disciplinary problems do come up, then the work record will help you decide how to handle them in light of the past performance, both good and bad, of employees. It should be borne in mind, however, that if work records are to be used as evidence when employees are being penalized for an offense, the supervisor must be able to show that a record has been kept on *all* employees, not just on one or two problem employees.

Dealing with rule violations

Let us assume that you have built a good relationship with your workers. You have strengthened their desire to do a good job. You have given them clear instructions and have been generous in praising a job well done. Your workers are self-disciplined, productive, and satisfied.

But sooner or later, despite your good efforts, an employee will break a rule or fail to meet the standards that have been set. You will then have the unpleasant but necessary task of dealing with that employee to correct the situation.

The supervisor must strike a balance between ignoring rule violations altogether and pouncing on every mistake. The disciplinary action taken by the supervisor should be aimed at guiding the employee, strengthening the employee's self-discipline, and improving the employee's work behavior. The penalty the supervisor chooses should be the mildest penalty that will accomplish these changes.

Let us look now at the steps that should be taken by the supervisor when a rule has been violated.

Step 1: Act promptly.

When a violation occurs, do something about it immediately. This does not mean that you should reprimand or punish the worker on the spot. It does mean that you should immediately make notes on all important details of the incident.

You should immediately try to find out exactly what happened, and you should be sure that the person who violated the rule knows you are looking into the matter. If you do or say nothing when a rule is broken you are condoning the violation. When workers see that you are not enforcing a rule, they soon stop abiding by it and it ceases to exist for all practical purposes.

Step 2: Get all the facts.

Most disputes about rule violations arise over the facts. This is why supervisors should remember that the most important thing to do when a rule has been broken is to *get all the essential facts, and then write them down.*

You should gather all the facts as quickly as possible for the following reasons:

■ The details will be forgotten if there is a delay.

■ You need the facts to decide whether a rule has been broken.

■ You need the facts to decide who broke the rule.

■ You need the facts to decide what action to take.

■ You need the facts so that your decision making will be objective.

■ You need the facts if your disciplinary action is challenged by a worker who has been penalized.

The facts you gather should give a complete word picture of the situation so that anyone reading them can feel that he or she has been a witness.

Informal memos are often a good way of setting forth the facts. Whatever form your report takes, it should answer the following questions:

■ Who was involved?

■ Exactly what happened?

■ When and where did it happen?

■ Who else was there or nearby?

■ What did you say to the employee?

■ What did the employee answer?

Be sure to ask the employee for an explanation of the incident and record the answer. Do not decide whether the explanation is true until you have investigated it thoroughly. If no explanation is given, this fact could be important, especially if an explanation is made at a later date at a grievance hearing. Pass no judgment until all the facts are in hand and you have had time to review them. Follow your organization's guidelines for reporting accidents. Complete all accident reports thoroughly and in a timely fashion.

For a rule violation: (1) get the facts promptly; (2) get the facts in writing.

Step 3: Decide what action to take.

When you have gathered all the facts you can, have spoken to everyone concerned, and are convinced that the employee did violate a rule, you must use your best judgment to decide what to do.

Take the time you need to make a proper decision, but do not delay too long. Consider all relevant factors and get all the advice you can. You should consult your supervisor and the personnel office at this point. They can help you to be sure that you are following local government policies and legal requirements and that the action you take is not stricter or more lenient than the action that would be taken by other supervisors.

To decide what penalty is necessary (if any), you should first decide how serious the offense was. You should ask yourself the following questions:

- Why did the worker commit the violation?

- Was it a major offense?

- How much trouble did it cause?

- How many people or dollars were involved?

- Was one rule broken? More than one?

- How have previous violations of this rule by other employees been dealt with?

- Does the employee have a good conduct record?

- Does the employee have a good work record?

- How long has the employee worked in the department?

- When was the last disciplinary action (if any) taken against the employee?

- Did the employee understand the possible consequences of the violation?

Keep in mind that the purpose of disciplinary action is *to change an employee's behavior*—not to "get even" with or to humiliate the employee. How a supervisor deals with a disciplinary problem is a question of circumstances, precedent, the supervisor's judgment, and the employee's personality. Strict discipline with an ordinarily stubborn or rebellious employee would probably produce different results than with one of a more compliant nature. Any action you take should be constructive. It should bring about compliance with the rules.

When you are making your decision consider the possible effects—both good and bad—that your action can have on this employee and on other employees. And whatever action you decide to take or to recommend to your manager, you must be prepared to explain it and defend it with facts.

There are two approaches to disciplining employees. Supervisors who take the first approach believe that penalties create feelings of anger and the desire for revenge, and that they actually produce negative behavior in a worker. These supervisors first tell workers who fail to meet standards or obey regulations what the consequences of their problem behavior are and what they must do to improve their conduct. (Of course, workers who commit crimes or such serious offenses as fighting, intentionally damaging property, or drinking or taking drugs while on the job might be fired or otherwise strongly disciplined as soon as all the facts are known.)

Supervisors who take the second approach immediately penalize workers who break rules or fail to meet standards, with the idea that penalties will change the workers' behavior.

Usually there is a range of penalties—from mild to severe—that supervisors can use. Following is a discussion of disciplinary actions in common use. Usually, the appropriate penalty is the least severe penalty that is at the same time strong enough to convince the employee that the behavior that brought about the disciplinary action will not be tolerated. As the penalties become more severe, it is important to document prior problems and the use of a progressive sequence in the discipline used.

Be sure to follow your organization's disciplinary procedures, which are likely to follow this sequence:

An *informal talk* is usually given to employees with good records who have broken a minor rule. They are told that they have violated a rule and are asked for an explanation. They are cautioned about repeating the violation, and the matter ends there. No record is kept of this kind of action.

A *spoken warning* is somewhat more severe. In this case the employee is told that his or her behavior must improve or more serious action will be taken. This warning should always be given in private. A record of the warning should be placed in the employee's work file, but not in his or her permanent record in the central office. If the employee's behavior improves, the report of the warning should be removed from the file after a certain period of time, usually six months.

The *written warning* is similar to the spoken warning but is more severe. It is used for more serious offenses or for employees who have broken the same rule several times.

The written warning should mention any prior warnings given; should describe what the employee has done wrong; should indicate what improvement is expected and the time limit during which the improvement should be made; should state what will happen if improvement is not made; and should offer the supervisor's help in bringing about a change in conduct.

The employee keeps a copy of the warning. Copies are also placed in his or her permanent record as well as in the department's work file. The warning can be removed from these files after a period of time if the offense is not repeated.

Suspension is a far more severe penalty. An employee who is suspended is removed from his or her job—usually from one to thirty days—without pay. This serious disciplinary action is usually subject to review by upper management. You will almost certainly need the approval of your supervisor and the personnel office for such action.

Suspension is used when a major rule is violated or continual warnings have not succeeded in bringing about change. The employee must be interviewed before suspension is decided on. He or she is then notified in a letter delivered personally by the supervisor or by certified mail. The letter should state the reasons for the suspension and the dates on which it begins and ends. It should also tell the employee how, to whom, and by what date he or she can appeal the action.

Salary reduction is another severe penalty. An employee's salary may be reduced when suspension has been tried but the problem behavior has continued. The employee must be notified in a letter stating the reasons for the action and spelling out the exact amount of the reduction. The employee's right of appeal should be explained.

Demotion is another severe form of penalty. Demoting an employee to a lower job level is unlikely to improve his or her attitude and may actually make it worse. For this reason demotion is rarely used as a form of discipline, or is used merely as a last resort before dismissal.

Usually a demotion can be authorized only by a department head or the local government's upper management. (In some cases employees are placed in lower job levels because they are having difficulties coping with their jobs. Then the demotion is not a disciplinary action and should not be treated as punishment.)

Dismissal from the job is the most severe penalty of all—the ultimate penalty. It is, of course, reserved for the most serious offenses, and used only after everything else has failed. In many cases only your department head or the government's upper management can authorize dismissal, after sufficient time has been taken to gather all the facts in order to ensure that the penalty is justified.

Transfer, while it is not a disciplinary action, is sometimes resorted to as a method of solving a problem of employee conduct. Transferring a problem employee to another department or work group is valid only when there is a personality conflict between employee and supervisor that keeps both from working efficiently and affects the morale of the whole unit. It should be emphasized that transfer is inappropriate as a disciplinary action and should not be used as one. Arranging to remove a troublemaker from a particular work group is not a way of solving a problem. It simply passes the problem on to another supervisor.

Step 4: Hold a disciplinary interview.

Suppose you have gathered all the facts about a rule violation and have considered all appro-

priate disciplinary actions. Before you make the final decision you must talk to the employee who violated the rule. The purpose of this interview is to get his or her side of the story, beyond a factual recounting.

The interview should be conducted in private, without interruptions by others in the office or by the telephone. Encourage the employee to talk. Listen carefully to his or her explanation and look for the reasons underlying the employee's actions.

Have all of your facts organized and at hand, and have your questions ready. End the discussion when the employee has been heard in full and when there seem to be no new facts to consider.

At this point you should tell the employee what he or she did wrong and what disciplinary action you have decided to take or to recommend to your supervisor. You should have a good idea of what action seems appropriate when you begin your interview, and you should change your mind only if the employee gives you some valid *facts* that you had not considered or did not know about beforehand. You should not change your mind because the interview makes you feel more or less sympathetic toward the employee.

You should also agree on what the employee must do, and in what specific period of time, to improve his or her behavior. You should be sure that the employee knows what changes are expected, and when, and what will happen if no changes are made. Finally, before the employee leaves, you should inform the employee of his or her right to appeal your decision and you should explain how, when, and where the appeal can be made.

Be calm, neutral, and fair but firm and businesslike throughout the interview. If you find you are losing your temper, interrupt the interview and reschedule it for later in the day. Treat the employee like the adult he or she is and restrict your comments to the employee's behavior; you should not criticize him or her as a person.

After the interview is over, you should write up the main points discussed. Be sure to include the goals for improvement that were agreed upon. The record of the interview should be kept in the employee's work file.

Step 5: Use the appeal procedure.

Under our legal system an accused person cannot be judged by the person who accuses him. But in your position you are both accuser and judge when it comes to disciplining employees. The possibility of wrongly accusing a person is great in this kind of situation and must be guarded against.

This is why in a good disciplinary system the employee is given the right to appeal to a third person. As supervisor you should inform the employee about the procedure for appealing and help him or her with the appeal if necessary.

Typically, the procedure for appealing a disciplinary decision is clearly stated in the local government's personnel policies. If you are not familiar with the procedure, you should contact your department head or the local government's personnel office to determine the steps in the process and how to assist the employee in making the appeal. In many local governments someone in the personnel office is assigned the responsibility of assisting the employee.

As the employee's supervisor you should emphasize to the employee that he or she has complete freedom from reprisal if his or her choice is to appeal the disciplinary decision. Remember, if an employee feels wronged and cannot get justice inside the organization, he or she may decide to take you to court outside the organization—a situation that could be most unpleasant for all concerned.

Special considerations in unionized local governments

In local governments that have bargaining units, the supervisor has a responsibility to discipline employees fairly based on the labor contract procedures, and a labor contract always modifies disciplinary procedures. Most of the points already discussed in this chapter are applicable to union-represented employees; in addition, usually these employees will have a right guaranteed by contract to appeal your disciplinary decision a final step to a neutral third party.

The most severe form of discipline, dismissal, is always discussed in the labor contract. Most contracts state that dismissal can be only "for cause" or "for just cause." The legal effect is to require that the constitutional guarantee of due process as defined by state and federal court decisions be observed in any dismissal action. If you dismiss an employee in a unionized local government, a step-by-step process should be followed before that employee is deprived of his or her job or income:

▪ Decide what has happened and write a letter or a memorandum to the employee explaining your concerns. Include factual allegations in writing and cite the employer rules that were violated. ("Allegation" is a legal term for a statement you intend to prove.)

▪ Give the employee a copy of any written complaint upon which a disciplinary action may be based.

▪ Let the employee know in writing about any disciplinary action you are considering, such as suspension or discharge.

▪ Give the employee a chance to reply to the allegations in writing. Show a specific date and time for his or her reply, and allow at least forty-eight hours from the time of receipt of your allegations.

▪ Give the employee a chance to talk to you personally and present his or her side of the story. Set up a definite date, time, and place for the meeting, usually one day after the employee's written reply.

■ Let the employee know in writing when the decision will be made and when it will be made known to the employee.

■ Allow the employee to resign, but do not suggest or urge the employee to resign, or offer any incentive for the employee to do so.

It is always prudent to check with your supervisor, the personnel office, or the labor relations office to review the steps to be followed for dismissal or other major actions. In addition to being good management practice, this assures a defensible position if your action is appealed.

Checklist

Know the personnel rules and regulations of your organization.

Establish fair work standards.

Brief your employees on the rules and regulations of the local government, the department, and the work team.

Have a regular method for discussing changes in policies and rules with employees.

Maintain a file on all employees on your work team.

Set a good example by following all rules yourself.

Apply rules consistently to employees.

When a disciplinary situation arises try to get all available facts.

When you have to correct an employee's behavior, discuss the problem privately.

Direct your comments toward the problem, not the person.

Let the employee tell his or her side of the story during the disciplinary interview.

Always end the disciplinary interview by telling the employee what, if any, disciplinary action you have taken or have recommended to your supervisor.

Inform the employee of his or her right to appeal, and safeguard that right.

Avoid making an example of the disciplined employee to other members of the work force.

Be consistent in applying penalties on the basis of the severity of the offense.

Always check with your supervisor and the personnel office or upper management, as necessary, before implementing any severe disciplinary action.

Supervisory situation 13/1

Susan is a newly hired planner in the community development office. She has been accepted by most members of the staff; everyone has been very friendly and welcoming, with the exception of Fred, who is also a planner. Fred has been assigned to work on several projects with Susan. He resents working with a woman who he feels was hired because of her gender. "There were plenty of qualified candidates—and several I know had more work experience than the woman they finally settled on," Fred has said.

Susan has reported to her supervisor, Juan, that Fred has made comments about how women have a hard time with directions—how can they be expected to work reliably with maps and planning designs? In addition, Susan has complained that she has overheard Fred making reference to her looks by telling "dumb blonde" jokes.

Juan realizes that this is a situation that can't be allowed to continue. However, he wants to resolve the situation in such a way that both Fred and Susan will be able to work together.

1. What are the steps Juan should follow to correct this situation?

2. Explain what approach to discipline you would suggest that Juan take in this case.

Supervisory situation 13/2

Nancy is the supervisor in the building maintenance division. While Nancy is knowledgeable about technical requirements, she has difficulty communicating effectively. Consequently she rarely if ever holds meetings with her crew. Over the past three years that Nancy has been supervisor, she has issued a number of written reprimands and in some cases given two- and three-day suspensions to members of her work unit who have not followed the rules.

In several of these cases, crew members have filed grievances, reporting that Nancy did not make the work procedures clear to them. Nancy sees this as an excuse, since she always posts any new rules or procedures on the board in the locker room.

In one such instance Nancy had posted a hand-written notice about the effective date for changes in shift times. Each winter, in preparation for snow plowing, her crew goes on a three-shift schedule, which provides 24-hour coverage for snow removal. Martin, a heavy equipment operator, who was newly hired four months earlier, arrived two hours late the first day of the shift change. Nancy was furious and immediately sent Martin home with a two-day suspension. "If a new employee doesn't start out following the rules, who knows where it will end," Nancy grumbled. "My announcement has been posted on the board for the last three days. I won't accept any excuses."

Martin filed a grievance, claiming the supervisor was too harsh since he was a new employee and was not familiar with the shift change. "Nancy didn't inform me about the shift change, and I didn't see the notice on the board," claimed Martin.

1. *Is suspension the appropriate disciplinary action for Martin? If not, what steps might Nancy have taken?*

2. *What are some ways that Nancy might try to communicate more effectively with her work unit so that work rules and procedures are clearly understood by everyone?*

3. *How would you counter Nancy's argument that posting the work rules is adequate?*

RESOLVING EMPLOYEE COMPLAINTS AND GRIEVANCES

The search in the settling of disputes should always be for the best future activities of the parties concerned.

Mary Parker Follett

14

RESOLVING EMPLOYEE COMPLAINTS AND GRIEVANCES

Wherever people work you can expect to hear complaints. Handling employee complaints requires patience, tact, understanding, and sound judgment. But above all it requires a procedure for airing and resolving complaints and an effective supervisor who can make the procedure work.

Supervisors who develop skills in handling complaints build good relations with their workers, improve employee morale, and improve the operating efficiency of their work unit, thereby contributing to their local government as well.

Every gripe that is ignored and allowed to become a formal grievance is costly. You pay for it in low production, absenteeism, high turnover, and loss of support from the community around you.

As gripes, complaints, and grievances are a normal part of living and working, let us take a closer look at what they are, what causes them, how they can be prevented, and how they can be resolved.

Your local government's personnel policies may establish the process you must follow. If your workers are covered by a union-negotiated contract, the contract may require a particular procedure. In either case, as a supervisor you have a major role, perhaps the most important role, in handling complaints and grievances. Indeed, your ability to handle them may determine how effective a supervisor you really are.

Gripes, complaints, and grievances

When we talk about griping we are talking about the kind of complaining people do simply to let off steam. People who gripe usually do not expect a change and may not even want one. It is their way of relieving the strain of living with a situation that they know they cannot change. The man who gripes about the traffic jam on the way to work and the woman who gripes about the food in the cafeteria are using words to help make the best of situations they dislike.

The next level of dissatisfaction—the complaint—is more serious because it does require that a change be made. Complaints frequently involve relatively minor matters at work that can be settled on the spot. If an employee complains, for example, that his equipment still has not been fixed, or that the new employee working with him still does not know how to do his job, a phone call or some reassuring words might well take care of the matter.

Both gripes and complaints can grow and become formal grievances if they are not handled satisfactorily. If a gripe or complaint becomes a formal grievance, there must be a step-by-step process for resolving it. A formal grievance is a written expression of an employee's dissatisfaction with some part of the job or working relations with others on the job that he or she cannot control. Usually, the basis for a formal grievance is clearly stated in the local government's personnel policies, and the grievance is about a local government policy, rule, regulation, or the like.

It is important that every supervisor make sure that the conditions of employment agreed to by the organization are carried out fairly and honestly—that practice coincides with promises and policies. However, it is equally important that management's rights (your rights) not be encroached upon by the employee. Grievances are not allowed on management issues. For example, management has the right to determine the following:

- Organizational structure
- Work to be performed
- How work is to be performed
- Tools, machines, and equipment to be used (except when a safety hazard is involved)
- Money to be spent in performing the work
- Selection of supervisory personnel
- Standard of selection of employees.

Often employees can make constructive suggestions on the above issues and supervisors should always listen attentively, but a grievance cannot be filed on these subjects.

A grievance grows out of an employee's feeling that he or she has been treated harshly or unfairly by the organization, by fellow employees, or by the supervisor. If employees think they have been wronged (even if it is a misunderstanding) they express their frustrations and resentments in the form of grievances.

When employees have actually been wronged by someone or something, there is a real grievance. Such grievances are usually easy to resolve because the facts are clear and an appropriate change or adjustment can usually be made.

Employees can also have imagined grievances, which may grow out of misunderstandings, rumors, or wrong information. In some cases setting the employee straight will take care of the matter. In other cases the supervisor has to deal with a real issue behind the imagined grievance.

An employee may insist, for example, that the computer makes an error on his paycheck every week. If this turns out not to be true, the supervisor may find that the real problem is that the employee is not getting the salary he expected.

The supervisor's first job is to decide whether the employee is merely griping or complaining, or is voicing a legitimate grievance. If it is a grievance, is it real or imagined? Temporary or permanent? Something that can be resolved or something that is an unchangeable part of the job? Is it a problem that the supervisor can solve? Or is it a grievance that should be settled by upper management? Or does it involve an issue where management rights take precedence and a grievance cannot be filed?

The causes of grievances

In some cases grievances voiced on the job may be reactions to something that is happening in the employee's private life. A person who is unhappy at home often finds reasons to complain in the office. But the kind of grievance we are going to discuss here is *a formal complaint that grows out of a situation at work*. Let us look at some of the situations that cause grievances.

Work assignments

Workers are often dissatisfied if they have more ability than their jobs demand, or if they have less ability, time, or training than is needed to do their jobs properly.

Employees who are already working as hard as they can may feel frustrated if they are assigned rush jobs or overtime by a supervisor who has not given any thought to distributing the work load evenly.

Working conditions

Excessive noise or dirt, poor lighting or ventilation, dangerous equipment, and shortages of tools or supplies are examples of poor working conditions that may become sources of grievances. On the other hand, grievances can grow out of relations with people as well as things. Dissatisfaction can grow out of the nature of the job itself, out of problems with co-workers, or out of difficulties with you, the supervisor.

Problems with co-workers

Despite all your efforts to create a cohesive work team, there may be some workers who do not seem to get along with each other. You'll need to be alert to signs of disputes or animosity among your team members. An all-too-frequent cause of problems among co-workers is discriminatory behavior toward workers of another race, ethnic background, or gender.

Sexual harassment is a form of employee misconduct that undermines the integrity of the work place. Generally, sexual harassment refers to behavior that is unwelcome and personally offensive, such as sexually oriented verbal "kidding" or abuse, subtle pressure for sexual activity, or sexual remarks about a person's clothing or body. As a supervisor you will want to create a work environment that is free from any form of harassment. Make sure there is no display of sexually oriented materials (posters, magazines, photographs) in offices or lockers. Make sure your work unit is aware of the seriousness of sexual harassment,

and explain your organization's policy, procedure for handling complaints, and disciplinary actions.

As an effective supervisor you will set a tone of respect and regard for everyone in your unit, regardless of their gender, ethnicity, religion, or race. You will also need to be especially attentive to the treatment of anyone with a disability within your work unit. Many workers can unwittingly make jokes or remarks about a person's disability that are hurtful even if the intent is to be humorous.

Relations with the supervisor

Most employees want to like and to get along with the supervisor. When they do not, the reason can be a misunderstanding, or a personality clash. At other times, however, it is the supervisor's mistakes that lead to complaints and grievances. Workers are often dissatisfied if supervisors have been guilty of the following:

- Failing to set forth clear job policies
- Failing to plan work properly
- Giving too much or too little supervision
- Setting unreasonably high or low work standards
- Failing to listen to employees
- Failing to delegate work authority to employees
- Failing to keep employees informed
- Allowing rumors to go unchecked

- Criticizing an employee in front of others
- Using sarcasm or ridicule instead of constructive and task-oriented criticism
- Being inconsistent or unfair in enforcing rules
- Treating employees unequally on the basis of their gender, age, religion, race, life-style, or physical abilities.

Personal problems

Employees, like supervisors, bring their whole personalities—including their personal problems—to work with them each day. Personal problems stemming from the home environment can emerge in the guise of grievances. It is the supervisor's responsibility to be able to distinguish a problem that began at home from a real work grievance. In the case of the former, the employee may need counseling or other personal help. How to deal with this kind of problem is the subject of Chapter 10.

It is obvious, then, that as a supervisor you have to know your workers as individuals. Call them by name, get to know something about their families and personal interests, and keep an interest in their lives outside of working hours.

Recognizing and preventing grievances

Recognizing a grievance is not difficult. When a problem has reached such proportions the worker with the grievance will probably make the matter obvious. That is the purpose of a grievance—to call attention to what an employee feels is an unfair situation. It is more difficult to recognize a gripe or complaint that could develop into a grievance.

The supervisor who wants to keep trouble from developing should watch for danger signals. Grievances may first show up as a change in employee behavior, especially a change from good to bad habits, attitudes, or work habits.

Happy workers may become moody and gloomy. Sociable people may begin to keep to themselves. Enthusiastic workers may begin coming to work late and may appear to drag through the day. Careful workers may become careless daydreamers.

Sometimes the danger signal is a flare-up. A worker may refuse to follow orders, or may tell you off. In short, you should suspect some dissatisfaction when any of the following danger signals appears:

- Lack of enthusiasm or cheerfulness
- Excessive griping about the local government, the department, or the work group
- Lack of interest in the work
- Excessive tardiness or loafing
- Too many errors
- Reluctance to assume responsibility
- Decline in output
- Excessive short-term sickness.

Through preventive measures an effective supervisor should catch problems when they are small and easier to deal with. And when you correct unsatisfactory conditions before they get out of hand, your workers will feel (and rightly) that you are interested in them.

Some of the important ingredients of a preventive maintenance program are talking frequently with employees, providing an outlet for complaints, observing employees, keeping track of working conditions, showing appreciation, and helping employees get ahead.

Talking frequently with employees

Be approachable. Keep employees posted on what upper management is doing. Do not let them get all their information from the grapevine. When they have the facts they will understand why things are done in a particular way and will be more likely to cooperate with management policies.

WORK ASSIGNMENTS

WORKING CONDITIONS

RELATIONS WITH SUPERVISORS

PERSONAL PROBLEMS BROUGHT TO WORK

MOST GRIEVANCES CAN BE PREVENTED BY:

- TALKING FREQUENTLY WITH EMPLOYEES
- PROVIDING AN OUTLET FOR COMPLAINTS
- OBSERVING EMPLOYEES AND WORKING CONDITIONS
- SHOWING APPRECIATION
- HELPING EMPLOYEES GET AHEAD

The causes and prevention of grievances.

Put all policies and practices in writing so that all employees know what to expect from the organization and what the organization expects from them.

Develop a genuine interest in your workers, their interests, families, and problems away from work. Of course, a balance should be struck between showing interest and concern and what may strike employees as prying. The message to convey is that you are available for advice and referral and that you have a genuine interest in them as individuals. This type of effort certainly pays off in fewer gripes and complaints.

Providing an outlet for complaints

It is important to create an atmosphere in which employees feel they can express their complaints without fear of punishment. Such an atmosphere provides a safety valve for letting off steam. Remember that employees have a *right* to voice grievances, and they should feel free to tell you about their complaints. And it is far better for them to complain to you than to fellow employees, or not to complain at all. The effective supervisor, then, not only provides opportunities for workers to blow off steam but *encourages* them to do so.

These supervisors are aware of something else: by talking with a sympathetic and understanding listener, a person can gain valuable insights into a personal problem. Employees may begin to understand and solve their own problems when they have a chance to tell them to someone.

Failure to consult with employees on matters directly affecting their jobs is a primary cause of grievances.

Effective supervisors also know that grievances are not personal criticisms. They listen carefully and show by their actions that (1) they are concerned about their workers' problems, (2) they will try to do something about the complaints brought to them, and (3) bringing up complaints will never have any bad effect upon an employee's relationship with the supervisor—or with anyone else in the organization.

Observing employees and working conditions

You should be sensitive to changes and danger signals in employees' moods and work habits. Are they getting the work done? Are they working well with others? Do they need more training? Are they interested in what they are doing? If not, what can be done?

An employee cannot put in a good day's work without proper tools, supplies, equipment, protective clothing, and cooperation from other workers. And no one functions well in a work area that is stuffy, dark, or dirty. Do not wait until workers complain about working conditions. Check these conditions continually to see if they can be improved or if any changes need to be made.

Even when a supervisor does not hear any complaints, he or she should not assume that everyone is happy and satisfied. It could be that there is no procedure for handling complaints, the procedure is not working well, or the employees lack confidence in the supervisor. Whatever the reason, it is up to the supervisor to help open up the lines of communication by encouraging the workers to speak out.

Showing appreciation

No one likes to be taken for granted. If an employee does something that deserves recognition, let that employee know you appreciate it. A word of appreciation will do a lot toward building morale and satisfaction with the job.

Helping employees get ahead

If you think employees have the ability to qualify for promotion, tell them how to do it and encourage them to try. This can be one of the best ways of raising morale and increasing job satisfaction. It can also help to eliminate griping.

Systems for handling grievances

Sooner or later the day will come when you are faced with a grievance that you were unable to foresee or prevent. How are such situations handled?

There are many different systems set up to help employees air and settle their grievances. In unionized organizations, formal procedures are usually set up and employees and supervisors are required to follow these procedures step by step, whenever a grievance is filed.

The procedures in nonunionized local governments are sometimes as formal as those in unionized organizations. Whether procedures are formal or informal, the objective of these systems is the same: to make sure that employee grievances are heard, and to make sure employees can seek relief without fear of penalties for expressing their feelings.

Systems for handling grievances should contain the following elements. They should:

- Protect an employee's basic rights as a citizen

- Fit the size, complexity, and operating conditions of the organization

- Be simple and easily understood by employees

- Allow the employee to be accompanied or represented by an individual of the employee's choice

- Be written out and brought to the attention of all employees

- Provide a prompt, satisfactory response

- Be fully understood and supported by all levels of management.

The last point is especially important. Unless all managers above the supervisor believe the grievance system is important and are committed to making it work, the system will fail regardless of how well it is designed.

Most formal grievance systems specify a number of steps an employee can follow. Almost all of them require that the grievance be put in writing and reported to the supervisor first. If at all possible, a grievance should be settled at this point.

Procedure for handling grievances

Once an employee presents you with a grievance, in person or in writing, and you have decided that you are the proper person to hear it, you must decide what to do about it. No matter what the formal procedure is in your organization, you can probably get best results by following these suggestions:

■ Determine responsibility for trying to settle the grievance.

■ Listen attentively as the grievance is presented.

■ Question the employee to gather all the facts.

■ Get additional facts and verify statements made by the employee.

■ Keep adequate records to show that the grievance has been investigated thoroughly.

■ Analyze your alternatives.

■ Decide who has the authority to act.

■ Make your decision promptly.

■ Explain your decision to the employee.

■ Follow up your decision.

Here are some techniques you can use to carry out these recommendations for handling grievances.

EMPLOYEE GRIEVANCE PROCEDURE
☐ Listen – take notes as necessary
☐ Ask questions. get employee's version of events
☐ Get additional facts from other sources. Verify statements
☐ Check records. keep all past records
☐ Analyze alternatives
☐ Decide who has authority to act
☐ Make decision
☐ Explain decision
☐ Follow up on decision

Suggested steps in processing employee grievances.

Accept responsibility

To decide whether you should consider an employee's grievance personally or refer it to someone else, ask yourself the following questions:

- Does the employee work for me or for someone else?

- What is the local government's procedure and policy?

- Am I responsible for correcting the situation?

- What does the union contract specify?

As an employee's immediate supervisor, you have a responsibility to try to resolve the grievance. You are in the best position to get information about the problem and you can act more promptly than anyone else. You should not pass the buck unless the problem is clearly someone else's responsibility. (But keep in mind that if the employee is not satisfied with the solution you propose, he or she may appeal the decision and have it reviewed by managers at higher levels.)

Nor should you ignore a complaint because it seems trivial to you. Remember, many serious grievances had their beginnings as minor complaints.

Listen attentively

How you listen may have a lot to do with how easy it is to settle the grievance. Always bring employees with grievances to your office, if you have one, or some other private place. Put them at ease. Let them know they are welcome and that you are interested in what they have to say.

Demonstrate your interest by listening calmly and carefully to the employee's story from beginning to end. Listen with an open mind and attentive attitude. Do not show emotion—especially disapproval or disbelief. Do not argue or cross-examine. And always keep your temper, even if the employee does not.

Try to see the situation from the employee's point of view. Taking a grievance to a supervisor is often a nerve-racking experience. It means taking the initiative and taking it in a situation that might be very controversial. The employee knows that his or her position represents only one point of view.

Now try to understand that point of view and the reasons behind it. If the grievance turns out to be unfounded, treat it as though it were real because it *is* real in the employee's mind. Calmly ask the employee to repeat the story. It is very important that you understand every word. Also the first telling may not reveal what is really bothering the employee, while the second telling often gets at the underlying causes of the trouble. Take a few notes to help you keep the facts straight and to assure the employee that you are taking the grievance seriously.

Question the employee

Take your time to get all the facts; remember, when an employee submits a grievance to you, you are being asked to correct a situation or an action. You cannot decide whether to do either one unless you have a complete picture of the situation. Use your active listening skills, asking open-ended questions. You will want to determine the exact nature of the grievance—is it related to work procedures, or does it involve discrimination or sexual harassment? Facts will decide the case. And when the employee sees that you will not act before you get all the facts, he or she is less likely to misrepresent them.

At this point you should remember that the employee has given you a set of facts designed to support his or her case and to get a settlement in his or her favor. Ask yourself whether there are any other facts in the situation. Ask yourself particularly whether there are any facts that do not support the employee's case.

To find out you should ask some basic who, what, when, where, why, and how questions about the case. Try to phrase the questions so as to get more than a simple yes or no answer. When these answers are in, state the grievance in your own words and ask the employee whether your statement of the problem is correct. Until you and the employee can agree on a statement of the problem you do not have a common understanding of what the grievance is about.

Then tell the employee you plan to gather more information about the problem from other sources and that you will discuss the matter with him or her again when this has been done.

If possible, give the employee some idea of when you will do this.

Do not, at this point, make any statements at all about the merit of the grievance, especially not statements that would lead the employee to think you have taken sides in the matter.

Get additional facts and verify statements

In any grievance procedure you must base your decision on facts, not personal opinions or statements that have not been checked. It is important that you verify information given to you by the employee and gather more information. Check records and reports; get other people's observations and ideas; and talk to witnesses, others who know about the case, and people who have been through similar experiences. Other critical matters to check are any policies of your local government that may have been violated; any departmental policies and practices that may apply to the case; any previous grievance settlements that may provide a precedent.

Many situations may exist in the local government that you are not familiar with. Consult your supervisor, other supervisors, and staff specialists such as the personnel officer to get advice or to get more information. A technical opinion from an expert is often helpful as well. You might want to ask a mechanic, for example, whether the brakes on a fire truck involved in a grievance were in good working order.

Keep adequate records

You should take notes throughout the grievance procedure. And it is especially important to keep a written record of the employee's statements that you have been able to verify and of the facts that you get from other people. Be especially careful to keep a record of basic facts such as names, dates, and times.

Keep your written records; they will be needed by the next management level if your decision on the grievance is appealed. In fact, do not discard written records of any grievance procedure—even those that were settled to everyone's satisfaction.

Analyze your alternatives

When you have all the information you need in writing, put the facts together in an orderly way and list the decisions that you could reach in the case. Test each alternative by thinking about the impact it might have on the employee, on other employees in your work group, and on the organization as a whole. More specifically, ask yourself these questions about each of your alternatives:

■ Is it fair?

■ Will it solve the underlying problem?

■ Does the solution conform to local government policy, rules, and regulations?

■ Is it consistent with past actions taken?

■ Does it establish a good precedent?

If you answer no to any of these questions, or if you are not sure of the answer, check with your supervisor to get suggestions.

Decide who has the authority to act

Before you choose one of the alternatives for action, be sure that you have the authority to act. Many grievances involve laws, ordinances, budgets, local government policies, or other factors over which you have no control.

You may have to consult with your own supervisor or the personnel office to get the advice or support you need if you have any doubts about your authority to settle a grievance. You should also check to see whether your organization has a formal grievance procedure that tells you what to do if you are unable to settle a grievance yourself.

Grievances involving suspensions, salary reductions, demotions, and dismissals are likely to be difficult to resolve and in many cases will be appealed to your department head, local government manager, personnel board, or local elected council. If you do not have the authority to make a decision (or if the employee decides to appeal), pass all the facts to the next level, which in most cases will be the department head.

Make your decision promptly

Putting off decisions is a human thing to do, but it gives employees with grievances the impression that you are against them, and that the settlement—even if it is a satisfactory one—is made grudgingly. A speedy decision is especially important in settling grievances that involve an employee's health and safety. Such grievances often bring out strong emotions in employees and should be resolved as soon as possible. Be sure to put your decision in writing.

Explain your decision

Explain carefully and calmly what the written decision is, how it was reached, and why it was made that way. Be clear and straightforward. If action is to be taken by the organization explain what will be done and by what date.

If the fault was yours, admit it. Do not put the blame on someone else. Your honesty will encourage employees to admit any mistakes they themselves may have made.

Ask the employee whether the decision is acceptable. If it is not, be sure the employee understands that an appeal may be filed. Review with the employee the procedure for appealing the decision. Let the employee know you are glad he or she came to you with the grievance. Tell the employee that you bear no grudges, and encourage the employee to come back if new facts are found or if he or she wishes to discuss the problem further.

When your talk with the employee is over, write down what was said and what was decided. Keep this written record along with all the other records of the grievance procedure.

Follow up your decision

Be sure to live up to your commitments and check to see that others involved in the decision live up to theirs. If action was referred to someone else, find out whether the matter was actually settled.

Some time after the decision has been explained to the employee get in touch with him or her again to report any new developments, to indicate that you are still interested in the employee, and to find out whether the grievance has actually been resolved from the employee's point of view.

Special considerations in unionized local governments

In unionized local governments, the grievance procedure is one of the most important parts of the year-round administration of the labor contract. You should be familiar with the contract grievance definitions, procedures, and timetable to assure full compliance with the contract. Many supervisors and managers do not understand the importance of careful and consistent handling of grievances. Remember that grievance decisions set precedents and these precedents are as binding as the labor contract. Be sure you know the limits of your authority to settle grievances under the labor contract.

While grievances should be resolved promptly, they should not be handled hastily under pressure from the union or the employee. Also, you should not hesitate to get help from the personnel or labor relations offices about personnel rules or contract provisions.

You should never be casual, humorous, or hostile in conducting grievance proceedings. If an employee or union steward feels a matter is important enough to appeal formally under the contract procedure, your sensitivity to the personal feelings of the employee as well as the legal considerations will help in successfully resolving the matter.

Finally, you should understand that resolving a contract grievance is often not a matter of who is right or wrong but of what works best for both sides. Approaching grievance disputes with rigid attitudes usually works against successful problem solving. Willingness on the part of the supervisor and employee to "mediate" voluntarily can help create a satisfactory result for all. This will require technical knowledge, proper authority, and thought from you to bring about the successful resolution of a grievance. Remember, every settled grievance is a legal precedent and may affect the outcome of the next grievance that comes up.

Union-management relationships are often adversarial because of the we-they approach taken to contract negotiation and work place relationships. Increasingly, this type of relationship is changing as participatory management, including team problem solving and decision making, shapes organizational cultures. As a result of this changing relationship, the mechanism of collective bargaining is also changing. Today, mutual gains bargaining is a form of negotiation that relies on consensus building to settle disputes and negotiate wage and benefit settlements.

As a supervisor, you may be asked to participate in union negotiations, which could provide you with an excellent opportunity to use your team-building skills, including consensus problem solving and decision making. Even if your organization participates in more traditional collective bargaining methods, you can use your skills within your own bargaining team.

Checklist

Know your employees: their work, their problems, and their interests.

Watch for situations that cause grievances.

Correct such situations before a grievance is filed.

Make sure your work place provides a non-discriminatory atmosphere.

Provide training on federal guidelines and rules concerning sexual harassment and rights of disabled individuals.

Know your union contract(s).

Give an employee a good grievance hearing; listen attentively and seriously without interrupting.

When the employee has finished stating his or her case, ask questions, but take no position.

Ask the employee to repeat his or her story, then repeat the essentials in your own words.

Take notes and keep records on the hearing.

Get all the facts available.

Check departmental policy and practices.

Seek advice if necessary.

Check previous grievance settlements for precedents.

Check the experience of others in similar cases.

Make a proper settlement as quickly as possible.

Explain your written position to the employee.

Once a decision is made, stick to it unless new facts come to light.

Pass all the facts to the next level if you do not have the necessary authority to make a decision or if the employee decides to appeal your decision.

Take the corrective action required by your decision.

Follow up to make sure that action has been carried out.

Supervisory situation 14/1

Sharon is a paraplegic who lost the use of her legs in a car accident two-and-a-half years ago. She continued in her job as a licensing clerk in the county's motor vehicle bureau when she returned from an extended leave of absence following the accident.

Marian, her immediate supervisor, had not expected Sharon to return to her job, and was surprised and somewhat disappointed that she did. She felt that the work load would be too much for a disabled person to handle, and it seems as though she was right. Despite a concerted effort on Sharon's part, she found she could no longer handle the long hours at the computer without feeling tired and frustrated, and she complained to Marian about the work load.

Marian told Sharon that everyone in the office was expected to perform all the job duties as required. She was not going to give anyone any special favors. Now the motor vehicle bureau has been cited by the state human rights commission for not providing reasonable accommodation for a disabled person.

1. *If Marian had acted in the spirit of the Americans with Disabilities Act (ADA), how might she have handled Sharon's initial complaint?*

Supervisory situation 14/2

As a supervisor in the water department, Frank has always stressed safety, especially when his crew is working in trenches.

He has counseled Brian on a number of occasions about his unsafe work habits and has provided him with a number of safety training opportunities. However, Brian's accident record continues to be below standard.

Frank recently gave Brian a three-day suspension for digging a trench without properly shoring the sides. Brian was the crew leader for the assignment. Brian has filed a grievance saying he has dug similar size trenches in the past without shoring and was never disciplined.

Frank has looked through both his own files and the records he keeps on each employee. He can find no record of any specific discussion he had with Brian about trenching and shoring requirements. In addition, Frank notices that he does not have any written documentation regarding any training that Brian was provided.

1. *Even though Frank has shown concern about his crew's safety practices, what additional actions could he have taken that would have helped him avoid this grievance?*

WORK PLACE SAFETY AND WELLNESS

*Supervision and safety
go hand in hand.*

National Safety Council

CHAPTER 15

WORK PLACE SAFETY AND WELLNESS

Why is safety important to you and to your employees?

How do accidents happen?

How can you learn from near misses?

Where can you get help?

What are the elements of a safety and wellness plan?

The most valuable resource of any organization is its employees. Helping your employees to work safely and in good health is an effective way to preserve this resource.

We pay a high price when employees are lost to the work force. Whether the loss is due to accident, illness, or absenteeism, everyone pays! Monies spent for liability payments or training new employees are not available for delivering services to citizens, increasing pay for employees, or upgrading facilities and equipment. The price we pay in dollars and in emotional stress is especially unfortunate because it is so unnecessary. In times of tight money when we have to do more with less, loss control is a vital part of every supervisor's job.

What can and should the supervisor do to control losses? Where does the supervisor fit into a comprehensive safety and wellness management program? What are the consequences of an accident or prolonged illness for the supervisor, the employees, and the organization? How can the work place be made more secure? This chapter tries to answer those questions.

Are safety and wellness programs really necessary?

Think about it. What happens if a worker is injured or even killed at work? First, the worker and his or her family suffer physical pain and emotional upset. The worker loses income (workers' compensation insurance provides only partial income). The loss of regular pay strains the family's budget when it may already be struggling with medical bills.

The cost of an accident to the city or county can be very high—even if no one is injured. There may be higher insurance premiums; damage to buildings, equipment, tools, or vehicles; service delays. Perhaps time will be lost as new workers are trained, the work load is rescheduled, the accident is investigated, and reports are completed.

Illness and poor health also take their toll on the work force. Both major and minor health conditions affect the productivity and morale of your work team. When a work team member is absent due to illness, picking up the slack quite naturally puts an additional strain on the rest of the work team.

Many organizations have formalized safety and wellness programs in order to create a safer work place and a healthier work force.

These programs often include safety procedures training, regularly scheduled safety meetings, defensive driving classes, safety "tailgate" sessions for field crews, use of safety/wellness videos, availability of a safety/wellness library, and manuals that include safety regulations (such as mandatory use of protective hardhats for construction jobs). Your organization's wellness program may include regular blood pressure and cholesterol screening, CPR and first-aid certification courses, defensive driving classes, nutrition workshops, health fairs, and exercise equipment available for employee use.

As a supervisor you play an important part in implementing your organization's program. Or, you may want to develop your own program with your work team if your organization does not have one. At the very least you'll want to make sure your work team is both safety and health conscious, obeying standard safety procedures and wellness practices.

What causes accidents?

Although we know that people do not plan or intend to have an accident, accidents are *caused*, they don't just happen! Fortunately the causes can be determined and controlled—and prevented.

It helps to understand what the sources of accidents are, and to think of these specifically in *your* work place. There are four sources, which can interact to cause an accident.

The first source of accidents is *people*—all of the employees in the organization. Training, performance evaluation, and motivation (covered in Chapters 7, 8, and 11) play a big role

in preventing accidents. Employees must have the know-how and the willingness to work safely! *Equipment* is the second source. This includes everything from vehicles to hammers. Using faulty equipment or adapting it to perform tasks for which it isn't designed can lead to accidents. *Materials* that employees use can contribute to accidents. They may be sharp, heavy, hot, or toxic! Finally, there is the *environment*, which includes the buildings employees work in as well as the air they breathe, and how their office space is arranged.

Ergonomics (design of the work environment to meet the health and safety needs of the worker) has an important impact on the health of workers. Improper work stations (for example, a too-high keyboard) can cause back injury and repetitive motion strain. With over 28.5 million workers operating computers, supervisors need to be aware of techniques to help workers avoid office-related injuries.

When there is an accident, the supervisor should consider each of the four sources in determining the cause. An update of H.W. Heinrich's domino explanation of accidents illustrates how accidents happen and shows what supervisors can do to help prevent them.

Lack of control by management

The first domino in the sequence of events that leads to loss is lack of "control" by management. Something you can do as a supervisor to maintain proper control is to make sure there is proper orientation and training, and that

rules are established and followed. Inspecting worksites and equipment, holding safety meetings, and investigating all accidents are also important. Almost without exception, the first domino will fall for the supervisor who does not plan and organize the work, and who doesn't motivate and lead employees to the proper level of performance.

Basic causes

Lack of management control permits underlying or basic causes of accidents to exist. Basic causes can be divided into two groups:

Personal factors that cause poor performance include lack of knowledge or skill, poor motivation, and physical and mental problems. Job factors are inadequate work standards, inadequate maintenance or design of equipment or materials, normal wear and tear, and abnormal usage. If a supervisor fails to recognize and change or correct these basic causes of accidents the second domino falls.

Immediate causes

When the basic causes exist, they set the stage for unsafe practices and conditions.

Unsafe practices include operating without authority, operating at improper speed, using defective equipment, using equipment improperly, failing to use personal safety equipment, horseplay, and drinking and drug abuse.

Unsafe conditions can be inadequate guards or protection, defective tools or equipment, inadequate warning systems, fire and explosive

The employee is not the only loser in an accident.

hazards, substandard housekeeping, hazardous conditions (fumes, noise, etc.), congestion, poorly arranged computer work stations, improperly adjusted office equipment, inadequate office lighting, and overcrowding.

These are only *symptoms* of the basic causes, but failure to remedy them means failing to keep the third domino from falling.

The accident

When unsafe practices or conditions are allowed to exist then an accident or a near accident is usually the result. An employee may trip or fall; be struck by something; be caught between or against or under something; or be electrocuted, burned, or poisoned. The fourth domino has fallen.

The loss

Once the entire sequence has taken place and there is an accident, whether to people or property, the resulting loss is usually determined by chance. It can be a minor, a major, or a catastrophic loss to people or to the city or county government. But long before that last domino falls there are many things a wise supervisor can do.

Supervising with safety and wellness in mind

Accidents are most easily prevented at the point where the work is done—that's why, even if your government has a safety coordinator, you as a supervisor play a key role. But you cannot prevent accidents single-handedly. You will need the help of upper management to provide proper conditions and facilitate proper practices. You will need the help of your employees to design a safety and wellness program and to cooperate to make it successful.

Making employees safety conscious

Helping employees to be safety conscious is a good start in preventing accidents and controlling losses. Safety precautions are often thought of as unnecessary nuisances even when they involve very little effort. (Think of how many thousands of people are killed in car accidents each year because they do not want to take two seconds to snap a seat belt closed.) Successful teaching always involves setting a good example. If the supervisor shows dedication to a safety program by his or her daily actions, employees will tend to follow the lead. Example is more effective than lecturing or scolding.

Discussions are another way of focusing attention on safety. Whether they are with individual employees or groups, formal or informal, the important thing is to encourage employees to do the talking. Help them to think about their own behavior and its effect—about what is safe or dangerous.

Often it is easier for employees to talk about specific incidents or problems than about the large, vague topic of safety. You might ask them questions to get them started: What are they doing that is safe? What are they doing that is dangerous? Why did a certain accident occur?

Discuss details as much as possible. Try to get everyone's ideas on what caused a particular accident. By the end of the discussion everyone should have contributed something and the entire group should agree on how this type of accident can be avoided in the future.

In addition to discussion, you might demonstrate some safety techniques—how to lift heavy objects, for example—and then allow members of the group to practice. But no matter how you focus attention on safety, keep your meetings lively and worthwhile. If they are a routine chore for you they will be dull for those who attend.

Think topics out in advance and be well prepared, so that no one's time will be wasted. Choose topics that are current and timely—how to use a new piece of equipment, or how to behave in a specific emergency. Try using some of the visual aids and other training ideas available from the sources listed later in this chapter.

Above all, remember that people will be committed to working safely only if they have a voice in pinpointing the problems and suggesting the solutions. An effective way to involve employees is to form a safety committee that meets on a regular basis. This committee can be made up of a cross section of employees representing different levels and types of work. The committee can review accidents and determine whether they were preventable or unpreventable; conduct on-site inspections at the work place for hazards; and develop a safety awards program. An awards program can spark interest and awareness among employees. Awards themselves can be anything from recognition and a personal letter to a cash bonus. Several different events throughout the year keep safety and loss control in the minds of employees.

Reporting

One of the most important things you can do is to ensure that *all* accidents are reported. This includes those accidents that don't involve injury. Near misses can be significant!

Keeping records of the type of accidents that occur in your work unit can help you spot trends that demand special attention. Accident reports will help you pinpoint training needs, modify work procedures, and eliminate special hazards on the job. Equally important, the documentation is essential for worker compensation claims.

Learning from near accidents

Often when there is a near accident we breathe a sigh of relief, count our blessings, and go on about business as usual. What we need to do is take advantage of those close calls to look for underlying *causes*. As you can see from the compilation below, made in a study of almost two million accidents, for every accident in which serious injury occurs there are several

When the supervisor is gazing at the horizon; when no one is paying attention to job methods; when one bad habit leads to another; when employees are not working as a team—accidents are bound to happen.

hundred near accidents. If we investigate only serious accidents, we may be missing the boat.

1	serious injury
10	minor injury
30	property damage
600	no visible injury or damage (near accidents)

You have probably read that the Federal Aviation Administration investigates near misses. The lucky pilots are alive and well and can report what *almost* happened. If the FAA waited to investigate only accidents, it would not get many first-hand reports of what *did* happen. Investigating the near miss leads to improved procedures and elimination of particularly dangerous situations or work routines, so that a real accident is prevented.

Being prepared

You can prepare for emergencies. Knowing first aid and CPR, and having a plan for getting prompt emergency care could save an employee's life. It's too important to leave to chance! The National Safety Council and your local Red Cross are sources of training in CPR and first aid for you and members of your work unit.

Be sure all accidents are reported. Serious injuries are only one part of the total loss picture.

Getting help

There are many sources of help available to you in promoting safety. Some of these are listed below:

■ The insurance company or state agency that handles your workers' compensation claims can provide posters, films, and other safety training materials, as well as accident report forms and advice on safety engineering.

■ The department of industrial safety in your state has experts in all fields of engineering—mechanical, electrical, and mining engineering, for example—who can usually help you solve your safety problems.

■ Many private businesses have experts on their payroll who can help you with specific problems.

■ Many local health departments (state and federal agencies, too) have a variety of information available for local government use. Most public health departments will act very quickly if a supervisor reports an occupational health hazard.

■ The National Safety Council has many services for members (your locality might want to join), including bulletins, posters, and safety training aids. The public employee section of the council publishes a newsletter devoted exclusively to safety problems (and solutions) in government operations.

■ Your local chapter of the American Red Cross is a source of safety and wellness programs, including CPR and first-aid instruction.

■ The American Heart Association as well as your local hospitals often has organized wellness programs with information on diet and nutrition. Remember, safety and wellness go hand in hand.

■ Professional and trade associations such as the American Public Works Association and the American Water Works Association can also provide information and assistance in safety matters.

■ Don't overlook the sources in your own organization. Employees who work in fire prevention, in emergency medical services, and in inspection and police investigation all have special skills that can be very helpful.

Avoiding pitfalls

A common error to avoid is leaving the identification and solution of problems to management alone. Employees resent a safety program imposed from above and often resist it. They may disregard the program, report in sick, or do careless work. Whatever form it takes, employee resistance wastes time and money—and does not bring about a safer work environment. Remember to involve your employees in planning and implementing a safety program.

Another common error is looking for physical causes of accidents or other losses while overlooking the attitudes and feelings of workers, which are frequently to blame. For example, some workers who dislike their jobs will work carelessly (without realizing it) as a way of striking back at management. Any resentment or stress in work or personal life can lead to loss or accident on the job.

Some supervisors may consider stress just the price we pay for working in a competitive society. However, it is a high price to pay. Recent studies show that in the U.S. over $120 billion per year is lost in work days due to stress-related injury or illness.

If you don't watch for danger points, you won't find them.

Finally, it is well to be aware that poorly planned safety programs can actually increase accidents by arousing hostility in employees. When workers feel that safety policies are inconvenient, unnecessary, or inappropriate, or that they do not work well, they will not use the safety equipment, will ignore the safety rules, and may express their resentment by doing something careless that causes an accident.

Again, a way of avoiding these mistakes is to use the workers' knowledge of their jobs and their interest in working safely as a team. If employees have a meaningful part in creating the program they will be far more likely to support it.

Security in the work place

Unfortunately, crime statistics are showing a marked increase in work place violence. Disgruntled employees, former employees with grudges, and employees under emotional stress are acting out their grievances in violent ways. It is not uncommon to read a story in the daily newspaper about a dissatisfied employee who arrives at the work place with a gun and shoots his or her supervisor and fellow employees. Citizens are also increasingly expressing their dissatisfaction or complaints by being verbally abusive and sometimes by physically threatening public service workers.

As a supervisor, what can you do to make the work place more secure for yourself and your

All too often, job safety is limited to visual inspection of our immediate surroundings.

work unit? Realistically, there is probably not much you can do if someone is really out to cause harm. However, there are some precautions that can be taken:

■ When you conduct an exit interview when an employee leaves your work unit, be aware of the emotional state of that person. Is he or she angry or verbally abusive? Take note of the employee's state of mind and inform upper management of the situation. It is important to take any threats or emotional outbursts seriously.

■ Notice any changes in an employee's attitude or frame of mind. Severe distress or depression needs to be dealt with immediately. You'll want to counsel a disturbed employee and quite possibly refer him or her to your organization's employee assistance program or another resource.

■ Look for any warning signs of potential violence. For example, watch for an employee who is consistently angry and is known to be a heavy drinker off the job, or an employee who makes "idle threats" of violence.

■ Install an emergency button or alarm system near work stations where employees are in frequent face-to-face contact with the public. And provide training in when and how to use the alarm or call 911.

■ Provide training for your work unit in nonviolent conflict resolution. This type of training builds employees' problem-solving and negotiating skills. It also gives employees practical techniques for diffusing explosive situations.

■ Let your employees know that you care and that you are ready and willing to listen to their concerns. Your receptive attitude can often smooth over hostile or angry feelings.

Checklist

Remember that your attitude toward safety sets an example for all workers.

Be sure that you have the support of upper management in getting the money, worker time, and policy changes needed to provide safe conditions and encourage safe practices.

Remember that safety and wellness planning must be done by and for the workers. You cannot plan a safety and wellness program alone and expect it to work.

Remember that workers must be safety and health conscious if accidents and losses are to be prevented: you will need to stir up and maintain interest in a safety and wellness program.

Remember the domino sequence and *learn* from accidents and near accidents. Don't just *count* them!

Remember that a little prevention may save a lot of pain.

Supervisory situation 15/1

Sylvia is an employee in the purchasing department, responsible for procuring office supplies and materials. Her work requires maintenance of paper files as well as computer files. Sylvia's supervisor, Joan, has noticed that when Sylvia uses the metal cabinet files in the office, she habitually leaves one or two drawers open. When Joan brought this to Sylvia's attention, Sylvia explained that she is constantly in and out of the files. Occasionally she leaves a drawer open when she knows she will be returning to the file in a few minutes.

1. *What measures could Joan take to ensure a safer office environment?*

2. *How can Joan raise Sylvia's safety consciousness?*

Supervisory situation 15/2

In a memo to all departments, the manager announced his intention of putting new life into the city's safety program. His memorandum cited facts and figures on how expensive accidents were and how important it was to reduce these costs. The memo concluded by naming a committee to work with him in developing a new attack on accidents and in reorganizing the entire safety program. The committee consisted of sixteen persons including a representative from each department and major division.

Two names appeared on the committee that surprised some city personnel. One was a lieutenant in the fire department and the other an outspoken firefighter who in the past had actively participated in attempts to organize the firefighters.

At the first meeting of the safety committee the manager appointed his assistant as permanent chairperson and then made this general statement: "I consider this an important committee. I hope that each of you will feel free to speak your mind while you are here. This is a democratic process, so let's take advantage of the talent that is in this room."

The manager left the room. The new chairperson requested that each committee member consider ways in which the existing safety program could be improved.

The firefighter raised his hand. When recognized, he said: "One of the main things we have to do is to make sure the workers don't get ignored in this process. We are the ones who have to make the program work. But if this program is like most, the workers are the last to know anything and the first to be blamed when anything goes wrong."

The lieutenant flushed and almost shouted across the room, "What is that supposed to mean? If that's a slap at me and the chief, I resent it, and you and I will have a talk with the chief as soon as this meeting is over." The room immediately buzzed with conversation.

The chairperson called for order, saying, "Now look, we've got to come up with a plan. Let's try to get through this as quickly and painlessly as possible."

Another representative from the non-supervisory ranks then spoke up. "What about giving an award to the worker who goes six months without an accident. Then give a bigger award if the guy goes a year, then two, etc., etc."

"I suppose the award would be days off with pay, right, Jackson?" asked the chairperson. "Then we would be paying you guys for not hurting yourselves. We already pay you for just showing up."

After a general round of laughter, someone proposed that the group was not getting very far and should adjourn until the following week.

1. What went wrong?

WORKING WITH THE BUDGET

*Where thrift is in its place,
and prudence is in its place...
there the great city stands.*

Walt Whitman

WORKING WITH THE BUDGET

This chapter provides information, guidelines, and strategies to help you, the supervisor, understand your local government's budget, the process used in preparing it, your role and responsibilities, and how you can manage your part of the process better.

Functions of a budget

Your local government, by law, must prepare a budget every year. From start to finish, the process will take three to six months, endless departmental meetings, council work sessions, and public hearings. Yet, in the final analysis, this year's budget may look pretty much like last year's—making you ask yourself, "What's all the fuss over the budget anyway?"

The fuss over the budget, and the reason it takes so long to develop, is that a local government budget is much more than just account codes and dollar figures. The budget serves three very different functions: control, management, and planning. Some people use the budget only for control, and others only for management; still others are interested in all three purposes. Confused? Let's briefly look at each function of the budget.

Control

First and foremost, your local government budget is a legal document. Once it is approved by your elected officials, you and other government officials are bound by law to adhere to it.

Therefore, you should spend only the allocation specified in the budget for your department unless approval to do otherwise is given by elected officials. Your expenditures will be carefully watched to ensure that you spend funds in accordance with the purposes described in the adopted budget. Once your budget is approved, if it calls for you to buy a new police car, you cannot decide to buy new uniforms instead—at least not without a lengthy justification.

You may feel that the control purpose of the budget is somewhat negative, but you should not think of it in this way. Instead, remember that you are spending public tax dollars on programs for the citizens in your community and therefore you should be held accountable for your actions.

Management

As a management tool the budget is a way of stating what your local government plans to accomplish during the coming year. Your responsibility is to make sure you find the most efficient way of providing a service, given the budget you have to work with. For example, you may determine that the least costly way for the parks and recreation department to operate is to maintain large parks with municipal crews and hire private contractors to maintain small traffic medians.

Planning

As a planning tool the budget reflects the major program and policy objectives set by your elected officials for the coming year. Many times elected officials become frustrated when they realize how little of the budget they can control. Salaries, benefits, pension fund obligations, debt payments, street maintenance expenditures, and other fixed costs necessary to maintain your local government leave little room for elected officials to cut taxes, begin new programs, or increase expenditures for pet projects.

The budget shows how your community elects to spend its tax money, a limited resource; some programs receive more money this year while others receive less. For example, your elected officials may decide they want to spend money for a large number of recreation programs to keep adolescents off the streets rather than spend more money to have the police keep them out of trouble. This particular objective or "plan" would be shown in the budget by an increase in the number of dollars spent by the recreation department, and a hold on the dollars for the police department. The council is using the budget for planning and for deciding how money should be spent. As a supervisor, it is your responsibility to carry out these plans.

Who uses the budget?

The budget is not only a local government document, but also a public document. It is used by local government officials and citizens alike. Below is a review of the different people who will use the budget during the year.

Elected officials

As mentioned above, elected officials use the budget for planning, in order to set general policy for the community. The budget reflects their wishes as to what programs and services should be provided and how much money should be spent on these activities. During the course of the year the council may frequently refer to the budget to make sure programs are being carried out according to its directions.

Management

The chief administrator and department heads use the budget to manage and control. They want to make sure that you are doing your job in the most efficient way. They will be checking to see that you stay within the budget approved for your section by the elected officials.

Citizens

First and foremost, citizens are interested in the bottom line of the budget, that is, how the total budget has changed since last year and what effect the change will have on their tax rates. The budget should assure them that their tax dollars are being used wisely.

Citizens look at individual programs and services listed in the budget to find ways to save

tax dollars. For example, they may suggest that the refuse department change from backyard to curbside trash pickup to save money. They may also propose changes to the budget if they want elected officials to increase or decrease the level or quality of a particular service.

Interest groups

These groups may be the "Northwest Neighborhood for Safer Streets," "Mothers for Day Care," or any other group interested in a specific program or activity in the budget. Generally, an interest group will want more money spent on this program or activity. It will usually be the elected officials who have to deal with these groups. Interest groups will also watch you and your department, however, to make sure you are delivering services in the best possible way.

Business groups

Business groups, such as the downtown merchants, take both a broad and a narrow view of the budget. Since they are usually major taxpayers in the community, they want to know how the budget's bottom line will affect tax rates. They will also be interested in specific services, such as road maintenance or police protection, that are important to their businesses.

You, the supervisor

The budget is your authority to operate. It is the most important guideline you have for your operations, and it is used to hold you accountable for the dollars you are allocated. The budget will lay out what services and programs you are responsible for and the dollars you can spend on them. How you actually accomplish these tasks is largely up to you. If you need to spend more than was approved in your budget, it is usually necessary to get approval from management. If the change is significant enough, your elected officials may have to approve it through a budget revision action.

Types of budget

Nearly all local governments have two separate budgets: an operating budget, which includes revenue estimates for the year and planned expenditures for all ongoing government activities, and the capital budget, which includes revenue sources and planned expenditures for all equipment and facilities to be purchased that year. Frequently these two budgets are combined in a single budget document, but they should be considered by you and your elected officials separately. Below is a discussion of each type of budget.

Operating budget

The operating budget is the local government's plan for allocating resources (tax dollars and other revenues) for personnel, supplies, equipment, and the operation of facilities needed to provide services to citizens and run the other activities of the government. There are several kinds of operating budget formats used

The budget lays out the component costs to finish the project and shows you how much money you will have to spend.

by city and county governments. You should check with your department head or budget officer to see what budget format you will be working with as a supervisor. The most usual ones are line-item, program, and performance budgets, and less frequently, the zero-base budget. A brief description of each follows.

The line-item format organizes a budget by categories of expenses for each department, division, or agency within the local government. There are generally two broad expenditure categories in the line-item budget: "Salaries" and "Other expenses." Under "Salaries," department heads and supervisors distinguish between regular salaries, part-time, overtime, and so forth. In the "Other expenses" category, there will be separate amounts for contractual services, materials and supplies (gasoline, pads, pencils, utilities, tools), and equipment (two-way radios, repair parts). Many local governments use a line-item budget because it provides a clear explanation of what will be purchased with tax revenues. It is designed primarily to prevent overspending, and provides strong central control over departmental expenditures and aids elected officials in comparing the new budget with prior ones. The line-item budget is widely used by smaller local governments.

The program format organizes a budget by major activities, such as trash collection, street sweeping, vehicle repair, crime investigation, and summer recreation. Many local governments that budget by program also include some line-item detail in order to iden-

tify and control the cost factors (personnel, supplies) in each program. A program budget is used by many medium-size and large local governments.

The performance format organizes a budget by the work to be accomplished in each program (building inspection, street maintenance, tax collection) and the cost to do it. For example, a performance budget will list the number of miles of streets to be swept in a year and the cost per mile. A performance budget is similar to a program budget in that it organizes the budget by activity. However, the performance budget goes a step further, by also listing and pricing the *amount* of work to be accomplished in each program. Because computers have facilitated the additional record keeping required, more local governments are beginning to use this format.

A zero-base budget (ZBB) is organized like a program budget, but during the budget process elected officials consider a variety of funding levels for each program and then select the level they believe best meets the needs of citizens, given tax dollars available. For example, a public works department may list three levels for street sweeping: low level—sweep each residential street at least once per year; moderate level—sweep each residential street three times per year; high level—sweep each residential street monthly. The advantages, disadvantages, and cost of performing an activity at each level of service are also included. Each level of service for each program is ranked by the department head.

Expenditures are not made at random but rather are planned for specific targets.

Elected officials may then give their own rankings to levels of any service according to their priorities. Resources are given first to those programs that are of highest priority to the local government. While a ZBB calls for the preparation of alternative budgets for all programs in order to determine the advantages and disadvantages for each, only one of the alternatives is chosen to be included in the overall local government budget adopted for the year. ZBB is used by a small number of local governments.

Capital budget

Before reviewing the capital budget we need to briefly discuss a related document, the capital improvement program (CIP). The CIP is a multiyear plan for making major purchases of equipment or facilities, such as a new wing for city hall, a library, a new road, sewers, heavy equipment, or data-processing equipment. It would not include items such as personal computers, supplies, or anything used or "consumed" in the day-to-day operations of the local government. Capital items, therefore, are different from other government purchases in that they are generally more costly and nonrecurring in nature. The CIP also proposes the means for financing capital items.

The capital budget is published with the operating budget and explains the spending plan for the first year of the CIP. Financing for the capital budget may come from local government tax revenues, a state or federal grant, or long-term borrowing. The capital budget is usually not a separate budget as such, but is included as a section of your government's operating budget. It may be shown in different ways. There may be a few pages at the beginning or end of your operating budget summarizing the capital budget expenditures for the year. Or each department's operating budget may include its capital budget request as one of the line-item or program categories. Or capital expenses may be shown both ways. In any case, remember that the operating portion of the budget shows recurring, day-to-day expenses while the capital portion of the budget shows major, usually one-time purchases of equipment or facilities.

While capital improvement programming and budgeting is an important planning device, many small local governments may not have a capital program or a capital budget. Generally these jurisdictions have an item or items in their regular operating budget called "capital outlay," where items of a capital nature are listed.

The advantages of a capital improvement program are:

- It can reduce major fluctuations in tax rates by scheduling and financing the costs of capital facilities over a number of years.

- It encourages the coordination of capital and operating expenditures, so that the impact of capital projects on the operating budget can be anticipated. For example, the building of a new library, a capital expense, will affect the operating budget since the local government will have to staff and maintain the new facility.

- It allows flexibility in scheduling bond issues, which may result in more favorable rates when the local government borrows money.

- It helps coordinate capital projects with state and federal aid programs. Urban renewal grants, for example, require that a municipality have a capital program.

- A capital program is a good public relations tool in that it helps the taxpayer understand the community's long-range needs and what is being done to meet them.

- It can assist in pinpointing the reasons for a tax increase and show whether the increase is related to operating costs, capital costs, or both.

Other local budgets

Some local governments require other budgets in addition to their annual operating and capital budgets. They are almost always for a specific purpose or the operation of a specific facility. Some of these other budgets depend on federal aid programs and therefore are not fully integrated into either the operating or capital budget. Some arise out of special financing arrangements whereby fees or even some taxes are paid directly to municipal agencies and are dedicated to the support of a particular service. Water and sewer systems, electric utilities, and housing programs are often operated in this way. Generally, each separate fund will require a separate budget.

The budget document

After many hours of work by you and your department head, and review by citizens and elected officials, the operating budget is adopted. As a legal public document the budget is available for all to see. Here is what it will include:

The budget message

This is usually submitted by the mayor or chief administrator to communicate to the council, the citizens, and the media the major elements of the budgets, including total projected expenditures for the year, any new taxes or increases in taxes, new programs and activities, and an overall analysis of the local government's financial health.

Revenue estimates

This is a statement of the estimated revenues (and their sources) necessary to fund the operations of the government. Frequently, information from the one or two preceding years will be included so that increases or decreases in revenues can be seen. An explanation of any new revenue sources may also be given.

Program expenditures

This will show where money is being spent and for what purposes. Your activity's budget may or may not be separately shown depending on the type of budget your local government uses (e.g., program, performance, or line-item).

Work statements

These are either general or specific statements of what your local government will accomplish during the coming year. For example, 210 miles of street will be swept monthly (public works); 16 girls' softball teams will be organized (recreation); 160 inquiries at the library will be answered each month (libraries). If your budget includes work statements they will be integrated with the section on program expenditures so that it is apparent how much each particular activity costs.

The budget process and your role in it

In all likelihood you will work closely with your department head in organizing your budget. However, it is important that you learn how to prepare and present a well-thought-out budget request. The better you are able to develop and present your budget to management (and ultimately to elected officials), the more likely it is that your request will be approved. Below are the five primary steps in the budget process and your role in each step.

Step 1: Budget planning

The preparation of a budget begins three to five months prior to the beginning of your local government's fiscal year. During this period the people responsible for the overall budget prepare estimates of revenues for the coming year based on tax projections, anticipated state and federal grants, and estimates of fees and charges and other miscellaneous revenues. If you are responsible for a service for which a fee is charged (e.g., inspections, recreation programs), you may be asked for information to help prepare the revenue estimates.

Step 2: Departmental budget preparation

Usually four months before the new fiscal year, supervisors and their department heads will prepare their individual budgets.

Generally, budget forms, instructions, and work sheets required for preparing the budget will be provided by the budget staff. If you have never used these forms before, you will need to review them carefully so that you understand exactly what is required. Before completing the budget forms, you and your department head will consider the work and activities your unit will be involved in for the coming year.

You may plan to repeat past years' activities or you may propose to add, discontinue, or change some activities. For example, as the supervisor of a recreation center you may feel that you need to offer more programs for senior citizens because the composition of your neighborhood has changed. Or, as the supervisor of a police shift, you may be aware that elected officials want to increase police patrols in the center of town during evening hours. You will have to factor this possible increase in service into your budget request. Each activity of your unit should be translated into work load data (number of new senior citizen programs, frequency of patrols needed). The key to work load data is that it must be credible and understandable. It will be the basis for your budget request.

Once you establish your work load for the year you will calculate the personnel, equipment, material, and other costs needed to complete it. For example, if five major snow storms per year are typical for your area and the council wants all primary streets cleared within twenty-four hours, you should determine the number of miles of road involved and the number of miles each snowplow can clear per hour. You can then calculate and justify the need for specific levels of personnel and equipment. Your department head or the budget staff can assist you in calculating personnel, supply, and equipment costs.

In preparing your budget request there are three guidelines you should remember:

Keep the budget simple. Use simple language and basic terms that can be easily understood and explained. Everyone viewing your budget needs to understand the terms you use. Don't assume that all people understand abbreviations or understand why you need to purchase a certain commodity. Your goal is to promote understanding of your particular budget. Informed decisions by local officials regarding the budget will result in a more cost-efficient government.

Provide enough detail so that citizens and elected officials can understand what is being requested and why. For example, data on the miles of streets to be maintained, the number of inspections, the types of inspections, etc., provide the detail needed. In justifying salaries and wages, show the number of hours worked, hourly rates, and numbers of people occupying part-time and full-time positions. Show the position titles rather than individual names whenever possible. Don't assume this year's budget should be the same budget as last year's, "plus a little more." If a budget request is reduced by elected officials and the proper budget detail has been provided, spending reductions will be related to service reductions, such as reducing the number of inspections or of recreation programs offered.

Separate the capital items from the operating expenses. Capital items are those used for more than one year, usually three or more years. Any capital equipment request should describe which items are replacements and which are new. The age of existing equipment should be shown as well as the original cost. The need for any new equipment should be explained and related to a new or expanded service whenever possible. If a new vehicle is needed, then include a thorough explanation of the need as well as the trade-in value of the old vehicle.

Once the departmental budgets have been prepared, they are organized into the preliminary local government budget by those people who coordinate the overall budget. At this stage in the budget process estimated expenditures usually exceed projected revenues. Since revenues must equal expenditures in a balanced budget, some adjustments will be necessary.

Step 3: Internal budget review

At this step the chief administrator and other key persons will review budget requests with department heads and prepare a balanced budget to send to elected officials. Very likely many changes will be made during this stage. Requests that seem high will be cut back. If your department head cannot explain your budget request, it may be sent back to you for more details. You may be asked whether you can do the same work with less staff, or whether you can find less costly ways of performing a task. At the conclusion of the internal budget review the budget will be very close to being in balance and can then be sent on to elected officials for consideration.

Step 4: External budget review

During this step elected officials will review the budget and hold public hearings so that citizens have an opportunity to comment. Elected officials and the chief administrator will also hold a number of work sessions to reshape the budget according to the needs of citizens. Both sides of the budget, revenue and expenditure, will be reviewed, and either may be changed. If the proposed budget requires increased revenue, and elected officials do not want to raise taxes, both revenue projections and expenditures may be lowered by a similar amount to keep the budget balanced. Elected officials may make these cuts themselves or they may ask the chief administrator and department heads to propose budget reductions.

This process will result in the final local government budget, which, when approved by elected officials, is a legal document.

Step 5: Implementation

Once the budget has been passed it is up to department heads and supervisors to carry out programs and activities within the funding restrictions of the approved budget. As a supervisor you should let your staff know how the new budget will affect them. Will any positions be cut, added, or left unfilled? How will the work change—will employees be doing more of one activity and less of another? Can they expect any new equipment during the year or will they have to make do with what they have? Did elected officials have any specific criticism or praise for the work they have done? It is up to you to see that your employees know and understand the new budget. You may be able to do this yourself or you may need to have your department head do it since he or she will have a broader understanding of the overall budget. In any case, give it to them straight, without judging the rightness or wrongness of the decisions that were made.

During the year you need to make sure you stay within your approved budget. To help you monitor your budget you will likely receive a monthly or quarterly budget report showing how much your unit has spent so far during the year. Chances are that your department head has already reviewed it, but you should probably review the report briefly just in case an error has been made in staff or supplies

"All we need is a basic bridge...but you know what inflation has done to the dollar!"

"I want nothing but the best...but you know we don't have that kind of money!"

charged to your account. If you have been spending funds more rapidly than was expected, your department head will probably want to know why.

Unforeseen circumstances may require that your budget be changed. For example, if a tornado or hurricane strikes your community, the public works department may have to spend many hours of overtime clearing downed trees. Or, if tax receipts are much lower than expected, you may be required to cut your budget by a certain percentage. Your department head will usually work with you if your budget needs to be changed. It will be your responsibility to determine what effect budget changes will have on your activities and staffing levels.

Step 6: Planning for next year

What can you do to make the budget process go more smoothly next year? Here are some tips:

▪ **Prepare early.** During the year keep track of changes you want to make in your activities for the next year. Will these changes have an impact on your budget? Is there a new piece of equipment that will allow you to operate more efficiently? Think about how you will propose desired changes during the next budget process.

▪ **Keep track of changes in your work load.** Are some activities taking more or less time? If so, why? Try to keep track of these changes and let your department head know

about them. This will make it easier to justify changes in your budget and activities next year.

▪ **Identify ways in which your unit can become more efficient.** Listen to your employees. They may be able to suggest new ways of doing things that can save money. If you think of these things during the year it will be much easier to prepare your next budget, especially if you are asked to do the same work with less money.

▪ **Talk with other supervisors.** Have they identified new ways to prepare for the budget process? What techniques are they using to stretch every dollar?

▪ **Practice.** You will be doing a budget every year, so don't fight it. Think about new ways of doing it better. Talk with your department head about your ideas. The budget process is the one time of the year when your activities will be looked at and evaluated very closely. Take advantage of this by presenting yourself, your employees, and your work in the best possible way.

The politics of the budget process (or why your budget was changed)

Once you have completed your portion of the budget, many people will review and change it so that the final version may look quite different from the one you initially recommended to your department head. Your department head may change your budget request before

submitting it to the chief administrator or budget staff; it may be changed by elected officials during budget work sessions; it may be changed based on comments from citizens. The question is, why has your budget been changed? After all, you are closest to the work and know what is needed to accomplish it. Here are some reasons why your budget request may have been changed:

▪ **You asked for more money than was necessary, figuring your budget would be cut anyway.** Your department head realized that your budget was inflated and would never pass the scrutiny of the budget director, city manager, and elected officials. So your department head lowered your budget.

▪ **Your budget requests were not clear.** Someone, the council, the manager, or the citizens, could not understand the justifications for your budget requests. They weren't sure what you planned to do differently this year that required more staff, or extra supplies and equipment. In a nutshell, your budget wasn't defensible. In most cases your department head will be asked to defend your budget to those responsible for the overall budget. If he or she doesn't have the right answers, be prepared to see your budget changed.

▪ **Money is tight.** There is never enough money to do everything that needs to be done. Even if your budget is 100 percent accurate, and justified, it may be reduced along with others to balance the overall budget.

■ Priorities have changed. Last year the elected officials thought it was important to keep streets extra clean so the street-sweeping budget was increased. This year it is more important for the police department to purchase motor scooters to patrol the parks, so the police budget is increased while others are decreased.

■ The process of developing the budget wasn't a good one. When elected officials are overwhelmed by the budget, they sometimes make cuts or changes just to demonstrate that they have had some say in the budget process. Elected officials need to have confidence that the details underlying the budget are based on sound analysis. In order for elected officials to be effective, budget materials must permit them to understand the local government's overall financial condition, revenue potential for the coming year, and options for meeting the service needs of the community. It is up to the senior management officials to see that elected officials feel comfortable with the budget process and the information they receive.

■ Bad luck. You think your street repair crew is one of the best in the city, but council members heard that they finish their work forty-five minutes early every day, so they figure you need fewer people.

■ Good luck. Sometimes your budget will be increased. Usually this occurs when elected officials want to see a new service added or service levels improved. This means that during the coming year you will have to provide the new or improved service level requested, and be able to demonstrate that you have done so.

Remember, the budget is a tool used to control, manage, and plan how tax money should be spent. Elected officials and management depend on you for accurate information to formulate the budget, and they depend on your effective supervision to provide citizens with the highest quality of service possible with the money available.

Checklist

Think of your budget as your operating guide.

Learn how to do your part in your local government's budget process.

Start collecting information for your budget request early in the year.

Remember that your budget request will be looked at by your department head, top management, elected officials, and citizens.

Promote understanding of your budget request by detailing the costs of services provided.

Keep your employees informed about budget decisions.

Supervisory situation 16/1

Rosemary is a supervisor in the county library reference department. It is time for each department to develop its budget requests for the coming fiscal year. Rosemary is anxious about this year's budget because the county budget director has instructed all departments to reduce their total budget by 5 percent from the current allocation.

Rosemary is glad she collected work-load indicators this past year. She feels she will be better able to substantiate her request if she can show the amount and type of work in her department. She has also collected data on the numbers of questions answered by her staff, the number of reference books charged out, the hours of research her staff has conducted, and the number of citizens served.

Rosemary has taken time to show the major activities within her division and the staff that are assigned to those activities. Rosemary plans on showing any major changes in these activities and the cost associated with those changes.

1. *How might Rosemary's approach to the budget process help her make decisions?*

2. *What other information might Rosemary want to prepare in order to justify her budget and avoid budget cuts?*

Supervisory situation 16/2

A recent increase in burglaries in the small city of Ferndale has created a public outcry for increased police patrols. The city manager and the police chief have decided to take immediate measures by increasing police coverage through overtime.

As the police captain in charge of the patrol unit, Christine Colfax has the responsibility of scheduling her unit. While she understands the urgency of providing more police coverage, she is not quite sure if overtime is the best solution. In fact, Captain Colfax has calculated that her annual overtime budget allocation will be exceeded by 25 percent if she schedules two extra officers per shift for the next six months as she has been directed. She is further concerned that her officers will not be willing to work overtime for such an extended period of time.

Captain Colfax feels she is facing two potential problems: (1) her unit's overtime budget will be greatly overextended, and (2) her staff may file grievances if too many overtime hours are required.

At first, Christine thought she would just go along with the directive. However, the more she thought about it the more uneasy she felt. "I am responsible for my budget and also for the morale of my unit," she explained to the chief. "I need to be very frank with you about the impact this overtime requirement will have on my budget and staff."

The chief was surprised at the captain's comments. "If you have a problem with my directive, then what alternatives do you propose?" he asked. Christine was not entirely prepared to respond and asked the chief for another few days to report back to him with an answer.

1. *Was Christine correct in bringing her concerns to the police chief? What additional budget information could she provide that might help the chief respond to the public's demand for more police coverage?*

2. *What are some techniques that Christine could use to let her unit know about the budget problem?*

3. *How might Christine use this situation to help her prepare for next year's budget?*

PROVIDING QUALITY CITIZEN SERVICE

Where council members, the mayor, and the chief administrator are proud of their city, this feeling will spread.

David S. Arnold

CHAPTER 17

PROVIDING QUALITY CITIZEN SERVICE

What is your job in working with the people who live in your community? One way to find out is to ask people what they think about their local government. You might get answers like these:

"I think they do a pretty good job of running this county. Went down to the courthouse the other day to pay my taxes and had no trouble finding the right office or filling out the forms. They've got some real nice, helpful people down there, and everything seems to be organized to make things fast...."

"I don't think they know or care what they do at city hall. The other day they blocked off my street for three hours to fill in potholes and never even let me know. And that was the day I had to park two blocks away and go back and forth to bring six bags of groceries into the house...."

"I don't know about the rest of the city government, but we sure have a good police department. Do you know they came out and patrolled our street the whole time we were on vacation? And they showed us how to keep burglars out before we left. This is a great town to live in."

Is this a fair way to size up a government? Perhaps not, but people do it that way. Their attitudes about government are based on their own experiences with the people they see doing the work of the government—city and county employees. Right or wrong, you and your fellow workers represent your city or county whenever you deal with a citizen or an out-of-town visitor.

People today demand that business, industry, schools, and government have good leadership, good management, and good services. And they will hold all of these institutions accountable. People today will not support or cooperate with a government agency that fails to deliver services promptly, efficiently, and courteously.

Delivering quality service

As a supervisor one of your major responsibilities is to provide quality service. The citizens (customers) to whom you deliver services judge the quality of those services by two basic criteria: (1) How well you deliver what you promise; and (2) How you handle their problems and expectations.

Customers are people who pay to receive goods or services. Citizens are therefore considered local government "customers" since they receive services that their government delivers (such as street sweeping, fire protection, refuse collection) and pay for those services through their taxes. Government departments also provide services to each other and as internal customers might receive such services as building maintenance and payroll.

Quality customer service is actually defined by your customers, whether they are citizens or internal departments. It quite simply comes down to the difference between what the customers receive and what they expect to receive. For example, your citizen customers may expect their refuse to be picked up regularly on a certain day of the week. They may also expect their refuse containers to be returned to the curb in front of their residence with the lids put back on top of the containers.

If the refuse is not picked up on schedule, or containers are not returned to the front of residences, or the lids are not put back on, then your customers are not going to be happy. They will not perceive refuse collection as a quality service.

Service standards, on the other hand, reflect how local government units define customer service. In order to help ensure quality customer service it is necessary to reconcile service standards with customer satisfaction. Supervisors need to continually monitor and analyze current service standards to ensure that the standards that are developed do, in fact, meet customer expectations and result in customer satisfaction.

As a supervisor you should continuously improve how you do your work in order to provide quality service that meets your customers'

needs. In other words, you need to be process-oriented and to continuously look for ways to deliver services that will please your customers.

You and public relations

You and your employees are doing things every hour of the working day that affect the way people feel about your city or county government. Your job is to see that the impressions made are good impressions—the kind that win friends and create public support for what you and your government are trying to accomplish. This is a major part of what many people call public relations.

A good public opinion of you, your fellow workers, and your local government has to be *earned*. Do not confuse it with publicity, which means tooting your own horn—*telling* other people what a good job you are doing.

Public relations starts with providing good service. Your department should always be looking for better and less expensive ways of getting the job done. It should also be trying to prevent problems if at all possible.

For example, the fire department helps people learn how to prevent fires and to recognize fire hazards. The building inspector's office advises people on how to construct a safe, strong home or office building. The recreation department encourages physical fitness. The police department gives tips on ways to prevent burglaries. Is there a preventive or educational service *your*

department can provide to reduce its work load and improve the health, safety, or well-being of the people in your city or county?

Public relations is a job for everybody—the mayor, the switchboard operator, the maintenance worker, the fire chief, the secretary. It is not something you can delegate to a public relations director or public information officer. Every city or county employee represents the local government to the people. This is true both on the job and off. Many people in your community may never meet the mayor or the major department heads, but their impression of local government will be created by you and other employees—the traffic officer who investigates their fender-bender, the refuse collector who empties their garbage cans, or the receptionist who directs them to the right office.

Think of the citizens you serve as your customers, all of whom wear several different hats and belong to several different groups. When you try to determine what your citizen customers think of the quality of service you deliver—and you should be doing this on a regular basis—it may be easier to find ways to get this kind of information if you examine your relationship with these groups.

The following list of groups is by no means complete, but it should help you get started in making a list of your own:

- Taxpayers: homeowners, business operators

- Visitors: from other cities and states

■ Public officials: city officials, county officials, state and federal officials

■ Students and teachers: elementary schools, high schools, colleges

■ Community organizations: chamber of commerce, civic associations, service clubs, lodges, veterans groups, neighborhood associations

■ Churches: all faiths and denominations

■ Communications media: local and area newspapers, radio, television, specialized magazines

■ Demographic groups: disabled persons, elderly citizens, young people, ethnic groups, minorities.

It is a common mistake on the part of government officials to assume that newspaper coverage, because it is extensive and informative, will reach all segments of the community. A similar mistake is to assume that a diversified governmental reporting program—an annual report, tax leaflets, informational fliers, and frequent newspaper announcements—will reach all segments of the community.

Some people can't read; some people won't read. You and others in your local government can best reach these hard-to-reach people by serving them well. Let people you serve know that they are important to you. Think about their personal convenience (as well as yours) when you plan your work schedule. When you and your associates serve all people well, you

Every employee represents the local government; to some people, he or she is the local government.

will be sending a positive message to all people in your community.

Practice timing and courtesy by letting people know when work must be done and by being courteous at all times with all people:

- Building inspectors should not expect a friendly welcome if they knock on a door unannounced. Owners of homes or businesses should be notified a few days in advance and given a choice of dates and times if they are to be visited by fire or building code inspectors.

- When a water main must be repaired or extended, citizens should be told when and for how long the water will be cut off.

- Announcements in newspapers and on the radio should warn motorists about streets that will be closed for repairs. In addition, prominent signs should be posted on and near the streets that will be closed.

- If a branch library must be closed for renovation, post notices in all libraries and use newspaper and radio announcements.

A direct way to find out the level of citizen satisfaction with the services you deliver is to conduct a comprehensive citizen satisfaction survey. Chances are you will need the cooperation of your department or your entire organization in order to accomplish this task. You'll need some expert help in designing a meaningful survey and determining the right size of sample for statistically valid results. Your local community college or university can probably provide assistance in developing a citizen survey. There are a number of professional consultants who will also assist you.

Another method of capturing how citizens feel about the quality of service your work unit provides is to create a short questionnaire. These forms are often in a checklist format that can be easily distributed or made available at your work site, such as on a counter-top where citizens conduct their business with you.

This type of form provides you with instant and direct feedback that can yield excellent results. Citizens will perceive that you really do care about what they think, and you will receive some helpful feedback on the level of quality you provide. This kind of information can prove invaluable for budget preparation and for developing short- and long-range work schedules and plans.

Know your government

Your local government is the sum of many parts: paid employees, local taxes, streets and parks, libraries and other buildings, trucks and police cars, and state laws and local ordinances that make it possible for you and others to get your work done. The "identity" of the local government will come from the way its employees think and feel about it. The neighborhood refuse collector, the police officer directing traffic in the rain, the inspector of weights and measures in a grocery store or supermarket, the ticket collector at the zoo, the secretary behind the desk, the technician in the public health laboratory, the supervisor at a playground all give the government they represent an identity.

To help make sure your government has a positive identity, you as a supervisor should have some knowledge and understanding of your government's services, taxes, and officials. Remember that most citizens do not go to the mayor, the city or county manager, or a government department head to have their questions answered. If you are a neighbor, they probably will ask you why the water rate went up or when the recreation department's baseball league starts. If you (or your employees) can give a complete and accurate answer, you will have done your part for public relations.

Do you and your employees know enough about your government? Ask yourself these questions:

- How much do I know about departments and divisions other than my own?

- How many officials do I know by name?

- When was the last time I attended a council or board meeting? (Was that the time salaries for my department were being reviewed?)

- Do I read the bulletins and announcements distributed to supervisors and employees?

- Do I discuss bulletins, announcements, and other kinds of information with employees in my work group?

You and your workers can keep informed about your government by reading the employee newsletter, bulletin board notices, memos, the annual report, and whatever other sources of information your government publishes.

Services

In a general way you should know what programs and services are provided by your city or county government. Nobody expects you to be an expert in immunology, library classification, or cost accounting, but you should know generally what your city or county does and where to go for further information. If your local government issues an annual report, this is an excellent place to get an overview of the services your local government provides.

Taxes

In these days of tax and expenditure limitations, almost everybody is concerned about who pays for what. It is a good idea to learn something about your city or county taxes, especially the property tax. In many parts of the country, the taxes for public schools make up one-half to two-thirds of the total property tax bill—a fact that many people don't know. The annual report for your local government and various tax leaflets and fliers will provide most of the information you need. When you don't have the answer, you can refer people to the finance department.

City council or county board

Be sure you know the names of the members of the city council or county board or at least, in a larger city or county, the name of the

It is good public relations to let people know in advance when public improvements and repairs are scheduled.

council or board member from your ward or district. People may ask you questions on primary and general elections, the composition of the city council or county board, and the kinds of powers they have. In most parts of the country the city council or the county board can adopt local ordinances and local taxes but not state laws or state taxes. This may seem obvious to you, but many people are not aware that state and local governments have different zones of authority.

Know yourself

You probably find that you can communicate better with your spouse, your children, close friends, and a few people at work than you can with people you know only casually. One of the reasons is that you know your family and friends well and you trust them. You have a lot in common with them, and you have, therefore, developed interpersonal communication that works well for both senders and receivers.

You can use interpersonal communication to develop better working relations with employees and others whom you do not know as well. It is important to remember that everything about you communicates. Your ability as a supervisor often is measured by what and how well you communicate. Let's look again at some of the elements of communication mentioned in Chapter 9.

Personal appearance

Appearances do matter. How a person looks is important to other people. The public will judge the attitude and abilities of local government employees by the way they look. An office full of people with messy hair, dirty fingernails, and rumpled clothing conveys a message of indifference or dislike. Dirty uniforms on a work crew say that these employees do not care—either about themselves or about others.

Surroundings are important, too. Furniture, machines, and equipment should be well lighted, clean, and well maintained. An automotive repair garage can be just as neat and well organized as an office. Street construction and repair work should include good lighting, signs, and barricades to convey a message of concern for the safety and convenience of the public.

The way you talk

Whether you talk with a regional accent or with the neutrality of radio and television announcers, the way your words are expressed as well as their content carries a message. Sometimes it is helpful to speak slowly and distinctly to give a citizen or a co-worker time to absorb information. Often the person you are talking to (the receiver) must tune in before he or she can begin to follow what you are saying.

The same care is needed when you are listening. If you do not pay attention, the person will be talking at you and you will not understand completely the message coming to you. Sometimes this works both ways. When you are talking the other person doesn't listen, and when the other person is talking you are not listening. If you are not sure you understand, it helps to repeat information to make sure that you and the other person are talking about the same thing.

Personal behavior

Your surroundings, your appearance, and the way you talk come together in your personal behavior, which either helps or hinders in getting messages across. Here are some suggestions that may be helpful:

▪ Stay away from words that put your audience on the defensive. Judgmental words, such as "stupid," "incompetent," and "ignorant" are high-risk words. They are likely to irritate and anger people. When someone is talking, do not interrupt to finish his or her message. Give that person a chance to say what he or she is saying. Do not use humor that may offend, such as jokes that are sexist, racist, or off-color.

▪ Take your time. Listen carefully. When you are asked a question, phrase your reply to make it as clear as possible.

▪ Be careful that you do not overagree or nod too much while the other person is talking. You may think your behavior conveys understanding, but the sender of the message may think that you are not listening.

▪ Don't fidget, doodle, look out the window, or otherwise fail to concentrate when someone is talking to you. If you do not have time to talk, say so, but then be sure to give the person a chance to talk to you later.

Questions and complaints

Answering questions and dealing with complaints from homeowners, business operators, public officials, and other citizens is part of a day's work. Questions and complaints usually come in three forms: in person, on the phone, or through the mail. All require prompt, courteous, and accurate replies.

Complaints are especially important because they are danger signals that something is wrong. If complaints are given prompt, careful attention, your city or county can improve its services as well as its public relations.

Your employees should know that complaints must be investigated and corrected promptly. Once the source of the problem has been found, the citizen should be told what will (or will not) be done and why. It is important to find out also whether the problem has been corrected and to ask the person who complained whether there is anything else you and other employees can do to help straighten matters out.

Questions and complaints should be considered together because a question that is poorly handled will often lead to a complaint.

Face to face

The best way to handle either a question or a complaint is face to face, especially if the problem is technical. It is easier because both you and the citizen can observe each other, listen to each other, ask questions to clarify other questions, and agree on the facts.

It is important not only to be pleasant and polite but also to be convincing. Could you look a citizen straight in the eye and say: "My name is Jessica Jones. I work for your city government, and I am here for the sole purpose of serving you"? Perhaps you would be embarrassed at this grand language, but you should not be embarrassed to put it this way: "My name is Jessica Jones, and as an employee of this city, I'm here to help you out."

Take a look at these specific suggestions and see how many you can apply:

■ When someone approaches you, always acknowledge that person's presence either by speaking or by nodding if you are engaged in some other important task and cannot talk to the person immediately. Remember, nobody likes to be ignored.

■ Do not blame the person who brings a question. Instead, look at the question as a chance to provide information and possibly to correct some aspect of the program in your local government that is deficient.

■ Pay attention and show interest. Sometimes a helpful way to do this is to ask questions yourself to be sure that both you and the citizen are talking about the same thing.

■ Provide as much information as you can, factually and promptly. Do not make excuses.

■ Do not argue.

■ Whether it is a question or a complaint, help the person to find the information if you don't have it. If necessary, refer the person to the right office or agency either in your government or elsewhere. If you don't know where to send the person for further information, help him or her by looking it up.

■ Give the person the benefit of the doubt. If your city or county is wrong, say so. Admission that your local government can be wrong helps to humanize that government in the eyes of the citizens who are served.

Telephone

The telephone is a popular way to handle questions and complaints. It is quick, easy, and inexpensive. Think about how you may sound on the phone. You may think your phone voice is businesslike and efficient, but the person on the other end of the line may think it is brusque or cold. To make the best use of the telephone, the following guidelines should be observed:

■ Answer the phone promptly (at least by the third ring).

■ Identify yourself and your department.

■ Speak clearly, naturally, and distinctly.

■ Keep a pencil and paper next to the phone to note important information and messages.

■ If the caller is upset, remain calm, listen carefully, and do not argue. Get the facts.

■ If a call must be transferred, relay all pertinent information to the person to whom the call is transferred, so that the caller does not have to repeat the question or complaint from the beginning.

- Do not keep the caller waiting while you are looking up information. If necessary, tell the person that you need time to look up the information and that you will call back as soon as possible.

- Be careful with the "hold" button! If you put someone on hold, make it short—twenty to thirty seconds at the most.

- Deliver all phone messages promptly to prevent delays in returning calls or embarrassment to the person for whom the call was intended.

- End a telephone call as courteously as it began; a good final impression is important.

Letters and memoranda

Writing is difficult for many people. And in many governments, it is overdone. Therefore, before you begin to write a letter, ask yourself whether a phone call or a face-to-face conversation would get the job done better and easier.

If you decide that a letter is necessary, give some thought to its form and content. You might ask yourself what the purpose of the letter is. What do you expect the letter to achieve? Making a simple outline first can help you write a good letter. Make clear in your conclusion what you expect the receiver of the letter to do. Just as in speaking, the language in the letter should be simple, clear, and direct. After you have drafted the letter, you may want to read it again to see whether a call or a face-to-face conversation might be better after all.

In some government offices, memoranda are used to excess. Therefore, before you write a memorandum, ask yourself: "Is this memo necessary?" Often a phone call is better. Look for shortcuts. If you get a lengthy memorandum about a staff meeting, it may be enough to put your name in the upper right-hand corner, write "I will be there," and return the memo to the sender.

How to say no

No matter how polite you are, no matter how carefully you speak and listen, no matter how conscientiously you put information together, the time inevitably comes when you have to say "no." Most of us would rather say yes, but this is not always possible. It is, therefore, important to learn to say no in a way that people understand and accept.

Suppose, for example, a resident wants permission to build within five yards of the property line and you know the minimum zoning setback is ten yards. You could say, "No, you can't do it." But a better way of saying no might be: "Five yards from your property line? Let's take a look at the code, Mrs. Humphrey, and see whether we can find a way for you to do that."

At this point, you and Mrs. Humphrey look at the housing and zoning code regulations together. "Here it is. It says, 'side yard setback must be ten yards.' I am afraid it can't be done in this case. I'm sorry, but the code won't allow you to build within five yards of your property line."

Going through this procedure helps the citizen understand why the request cannot be granted. Besides, she realizes you have done all you can. It is not you or the "government" but the code that is preventing her from doing what she wants to do.

When you have to say no, you should break the news as gently and courteously as possible. At the same time you must make it clear that you *are* saying "no." Do not use evasive or ambiguous words that might lead the person to think that you have said "maybe." If it is possible to refer the person somewhere else for more information or help, then do so and avoid at all costs the attitude of a judge pronouncing sentence on a culprit.

The media

The news media—newspapers, radio, and television—consider government news coverage one of their most important jobs. Since most people are intensely interested in local government developments, it is helpful for you to be familiar with what news means and how the media work.

News is the reporting of an event by words, sound, or pictures, with timely information for the general public. News is gathered, evaluated, and written up by trained reporters who often have a particular interest in major decisions that affect individual lives—increases or decreases in property taxes, approvals or disapprovals for the location of shopping centers, adoption of

Two ways to say "no."

bond issues, and location of streets and highways. Newspapers (more than radio and television) often are interested in reporting not only the event but some of the circumstances behind the event. For example, a newspaper account may describe a major downtown development project and also provide information on the financing, programs, and other conditions that made the project possible.

News reporters are likely to talk first to the mayor, the city or county manager, members of the city council or county board, and department heads. They know that these are the sources for the most complete information on events, particularly policy and management decisions. If your city or county has a public information officer, news reporters will turn to that person to get information. The public information officer generally has experience that helps him or her spot the news taking place and can provide fast and competent help for reporters. It is his or her job to establish good working relations with media representatives.

If a reporter should phone you or stop by your work station for information, three general guidelines may be helpful:

Recognize that any conscientious reporter wants to be accurate in gathering and reporting the news but that the limitations imposed by deadlines and work load may prevent absolute accuracy in every detail reported. This leads to the second point.

Try to give reporters as complete and accurate information as possible, within your area of experience. No reporter will expect you to have information on every aspect of your local government. This leads to the third point.

Encourage the reporter to talk to the mayor, the city or county manager, members of the city council or county board, and department heads. These are the people who can round out the information the reporter needs.

Take pride in your government

Good local government does not just happen. It is created by an informed citizenry, conscientious elected officials and public managers, and dedicated employees working together. You can take pride in being a part of the effort to provide police protection, guard against fire, assess taxes, supply water, maintain streets, educate consumers, care for the elderly, find housing for citizens, and provide many other services to the community.

If you take pride in your government you will want to tell citizens what a good job it is doing. Praise coming directly from an employee can be more effective than a publicity release. It is important that you and your employees be well informed about all aspects of your government and that your facts be correct. After all, the people you talk to will assume you are the expert. And useful information about your government shared with others benefits everyone—the government as well as individual citizens.

Checklist

Provide the best service possible; set an example for your work group.

Be sure your employees know how to do their jobs.

Stay posted on the use of new equipment and new methods for carrying out the work of your unit.

Practice courtesy by letting people know in advance whether service is to be interrupted or delayed.

Keep posted on the work of your city or county government so that you can share this information with others.

Know yourself—your appearance, the way you talk, and your behavior.

Keep buildings, grounds, and equipment in good condition.

Avoid taking authorized work breaks in public areas.

Answer questions from the public promptly, courteously, clearly, and accurately.

Review the way you and your employees handle questions and complaints.

Meet with your employees to discuss how to say no in a clear and courteous manner.

Learn the ground rules that news reporters use in gathering and reporting the news.

Take pride in your government! Tell people what you and your fellow workers are doing.

Supervisory situation 17/1

Anne is the supervisor of the municipal parking commission. She oversees the operations of the three city-owned parking garages in the central business district. Anne is concerned about the number of customer complaints that she has received in the past three months. The complaints seem to be centered on problems at the ticket booths. Apparently, long lines form at peak periods of the day, which have frustrated customers. In addition, several of the ticket collectors have been rude to customers.

Anne has considered disciplining the ticket collectors but she isn't sure that will solve the problem. She is also concerned about how to handle the large volumes of vehicles at rush hour and other peak periods.

1. *Is Anne overly concerned about this situation? If not, then why not?*

2. *What steps would you advise Anne to follow to analyze the situation?*

3. *How might Anne improve the customer service skills of her ticket collectors?*

Supervisory situation 17/2

As the supervisor of the water billing division of the county water department, Dave is constantly in contact with citizen customers. His staff of three billing clerks—Peter, Shulamith, and Latoya—also have frequent customer contact, either on the telephone or with walk-in customers. All too frequently, Dave's staff must deal with angry or frustrated customers who are upset about their water bill. Dave knows that the stress of the job can take its toll on his staff. At the same time he firmly stands by the principle that the customer is always right. Dave has noticed that his staff do not always practice this principle in the way they handle some customer complaints.

For example, last week a citizen entered the billing division office about twenty minutes before closing and was visibly upset while waiting in line. Finally, when it was her turn, the customer fumed at Peter: "My name is Roseanne Smith, and I do not understand why my bill has doubled for this billing period. You have obviously made a stupid mistake. Somebody better have a good answer for this." Peter looked first at the clock, and then replied, "Well, madam, if it's such a big problem, why did you wait until so late in the day to come in? I'll take a look at your bill, but I can't promise I can resolve the problem today. We close in five minutes."

The customer looked at her watch and snapped, "I've been waiting in line for over fifteen minutes. Can I help it if you people are so slow? I want an answer, today. I don't have the time to come back because of your mistake."

"OK," said Peter. "Let me take a look." Peter quickly reviewed Ms. Smith's bill, added some figures on his calculator, and replied, "Looks like you've got a real problem controlling how much water you use. This bill adds up OK to me." At that point, Ms. Smith grabbed the bill from Peter and quickly turned to walk out. "I've had enough of this—I'll be back tomorrow to talk to your manager," she called over her shoulder as she headed for the door.

Peter shrugged his shoulders. "It takes all kinds—what a day this has been."

1. *What are some methods Dave can suggest to his staff to help them deal effectively with difficult customers such as Ms. Smith?*

2. *How do you think Dave could get his staff to more readily accept his principle that the customer is always right?*

3. *What are some methods Dave can suggest to his staff to relieve the stress of dealing with customers all day long?*

SELECTED BIBLIOGRAPHY

Adler, Richard B., and Neil Towne. *Looking Out, Looking In: Interpersonal Communication*. New York: Holt, Rinehart and Winston, 1990.

Berkman, Robert I. *Find It Online*. New York: Windcrest/McGraw-Hill, 1994.

Blanchard, Ken. *The One Minute Manager/ Builds High Performing Teams*. New York: Morrow, 1991.

Covey, Stephen R. *The Seven Habits of Highly Effective People*. Taft, TX: S&S Trade, 1989.

Drucker, Peter. *Innovation and Entrepreneurship: Practice and Principles*. New York: Harper Business, 1993.

Gardner, Howard. *Frames of Mind: The Theory of Multiple Intelligences*. New York: Basic Books, 1993.

Hammer, Michael, and James Champy. *Reengineering the Corporation*. New York: Harper Business, 1993.

Juran, Joseph. *Quality Planning and Analysis*. 3d ed. New York: McGraw-Hill, 1993.

Kline, Peter. *The Everyday Genius*. Arlington, VA: Great Ocean, 1988.

McGregor, Douglas. *The Human Side of Enterprise*. New York: Van Nostrand Reinhold, 1968.

Maslow, Abraham. *Motivation and Personality*. 2d ed. New York: Harper & Row, 1970.

Nilles, Jack M. *Making Telecommuting Happen: A Guide for Telemanagers and Telecommuters*. New York: Van Nostrand Reinhold, 1994.

Osborne, David, and Ted Gaebler. *Reinventing Government*. Reading, MA: Addison-Wesley, 1992.

Peters, Thomas. *Liberation Management: Necessary Disorganization for the Nanosecond Nineties*. New York: Knopf, 1992.

Schein, Edgar H. *Organizational Psychology*. 3d ed. Englewood Cliffs, NJ: Prentice-Hall, 1980.

Scholtes, Peter R. *The Team Handbook*. Madison, WI: Joiner Associates, 1988.

Tannen, Deborah. *You Just Don't Understand*. New York: Ballantine, 1991.

Thomas, R. Roosevelt, Jr. *Beyond Race and Gender: Unleashing the Power of Your Total Workforce by Managing Diversity*. New York: AMACOM, 1991.

Tuckman, B. W. "Developmental Sequences in Small Groups." *Psychological Bulletin* 63 (June 1965).

ACKNOWLEDGMENTS

Chapter 2 (p. 23). Excerpt from *Reinventing Government*, pp. 19-20. Copyright by David Osborne and Ted Gaebler. Reprinted by permission of Addison-Wesley Publishing Company.

Chapter 9 (p. 116). Excerpt from *You Just Don't Understand: Men and Women in Conversation*, by Deborah Tannen, Ph.D. Copyright 1990 by Deborah Tannen. Reprinted by permission of William Morrow, Inc.

Effective Supervisory Practices
Third Edition

Text type
Century Expanded
Helvetica

Printer
Edwards Brothers, Inc.
Ann Arbor, Michigan